THE ENGLISH CIVIL WAR
1642–1651

THE ENGLISH CIVIL WAR 1642–1651

AN ILLUSTRATED MILITARY HISTORY

PHILIP J HAYTHORNTHWAITE
Colour illustrations by Jeffrey Burn

O Lord! Thou knowest how busy I must be this day.
If I forget thee, do not Thou forget me
PRAYER OF SIR JACOB ASTLEY, EDGEHILL

BROCKHAMPTON PRESS
LONDON

First published in the UK 1983 by Blandford Press
This printing Arms and Armour Press
An imprint of the Cassell Group
Wellington House,
125 Strand, London WC2R 0BB

Reprinted 1984, 1985

This edition published 1998 by Brockhampton Press.
    an imprint of the Caxton Publishing Gorup

Reprint 2002

ISBN 1 86019 8600

British Library Cataloguing-in-Publication Data
A catalogue entry for this title is available from the British
Library

Frontispiece
The image of monarchy: King Charles I in cuirassier armour.
Portrait by Sir Anthony Van Dyck, c. 1637–38. (Reproduced
by courtesy of the Trustees, The National Gallery, London)

Printed at Oriental Press, Dubai, U.A.E.

CONTENTS

Colour
Illustrations

Acknowledge-ments

Sincere thanks are due to the staffs of the many libraries, museums and galleries which rendered assistance during the preparation of this book. Among the many, the following should be mentioned in particular: the National Army Museum, London; the Trustees of the National Gallery, London; the National Portrait Gallery, London; Roy Butler of Wallis & Wallis, Lewes; Jonathan Cooter of Hereford City Museums, for his photographs of Birch's mortar, 'Roaring Meg'; Barry Gregory, for his editorial assistance; Richard Green of the City of York Art Gallery; and H.V. Radcliffe of Newark District Council Museum.

Especial thanks to Jeffrey Burn, for interpreting so superbly the mass of contemporary material and sketches with which I supplied him for the colour plates; and to H.V. Wilkinson for his help in tracing many rare, contemporary sources.

Finally, I owe an especial debt to Mrs Irene Mulholland, in whose school and at an early age I first learned the fascination of the era of the English Civil Wars.

P.J.H.

PREFACE

A purely 'military' history of the English Civil Wars is scarcely possible, for the military manoeuvres studied in isolation present a picture totally distorted by the omission of political, religious and social affairs which, it will be seen, had perhaps more influence upon military events than in any war involving British participation before or since. The following text, whilst concentrating upon the military events of the Civil Wars, the armies, their composition, equipment and life, includes as much of the 'general' history of the Civil Wars as is necessary to illuminate the causes and influences upon the military aspects. The published literature concerning the wars is vast, and aided by the notes and bibliography the reader will be able to pursue in greater depth those topics which are, of necessity, only sketched here.

Notes are provided in the conventional manner, with one exception; references to Clarendon's *History of the Rebellion* refer to book and paragraph number, as is the usual practice, instead of to volume and page number. In all cases the 1888 Oxford edition has been used.

In an age when any degree of literacy was exceptional, seventeenth-century spelling was arbitrary; as Ben Jonson remarked, it was a dull man who could spell a word only one way. In many cases contemporary spelling has been retained, but in others some modernization has been necessary, especially with proper names; it would only serve to cause confusion to retain, for example, the spelling 'Lashley' for Leslie or 'Worley' for Wardlawe. Similarly, designations which strictly are incorrect have been retained for the sake of convenience; thus, for example, 'Civil War' should be taken as referring to the three wars which occurred between 1642 and 1651, and the term 'New Model' as concerning not only the Parliamentary army which bore that name between 1645 and 1647, but also to the Standing Army which replaced it. In any case, 'New Model' was never a universal term, 'the Army under Sir Thomas Fairfax' being the most common contemporary designation. Throughout the text, the contemporary terms 'horse' and 'foot' have been used instead of the modern 'cavalry' and 'infantry', and dates are expressed in the old style, except that the modern practice of beginning a year on 1 January (rather than 25 March) has been followed.

The terms 'Roundhead' and 'Cavalier' were not at the time used as frequently as modern practice might suggest; Clarendon states that they came to be used in 1641, the former deriving from the short haircuts favoured by Puritans, and the latter describing the King's party, from the French and Italian words signifying a horseman (or, to Parliament, those 'without having respect to the laws of the land, or any fear either of God or man ... ready to commit all manner of outrage and violence ...[1]). In any case, though the Roundheads of 1642 may have had cropped hair, 'two or three years after, any stranger that had seen them, would have inquired the reason of that name'[2].

Whilst contemporary sources form the foundations of historical research, many Civil War sources are influenced by political or religious bias; and, as one Royalist commented, 'the next man can hardly make a true relation of the actions of him that is next to him; for in such a hurry and smoke as in a set field a man takes note of nothing but what relates to his own safety'.

1 THE ROAD TO CIVIL WAR

On 22 August 1642 the royal standard of King Charles I was raised in Nottingham, formally beginning the first civil war in England since the crown of Richard III was recovered from under a bush at Bosworth Field 157 years before. But the war opened by the raising of the standard, which was to cause fundamental changes in English life, might reasonably be said to have begun in earnest in the midsummer of 1642, when the governor of Hull at first refused his sovereign admission and, in July, successfully withstood an incompetent siege. But the origins of the Civil Wars go back much further; indeed, one modern historian has taken the date 1603 as a convenient embarkation on the subject[1]. Its roots may be traced even further.

The English Civil Wars have engendered perhaps more misapprehensions than any other. Just as many believe the war to have been fought between long-haired cavaliers and crop-headed Puritans, its long-term and immediate causes have been seen in simplistic terms and occasionally with almost as much political colouring as some of the news-sheets of the 1640s. Whilst there is little space for even a cursory assessment of the roots of conflict in the present work, when numerous volumes have been devoted exclusively to the subject, a brief explanation is necessary to put into perspective the military affairs of the nine years' violence which afflicted the country after the raising of the standard at Nottingham.

In one sense, economic difficulties were a contributory factor to the outbreak of war; not on the part of the population or landowners (whose improving prosperity made those in the House of Commons conscious of a right to increased political power), but in the lack of funds of the central government itself and the King's inability to undertake the Scottish expeditions of 1639–40 without recalling Parliament (after 11 years' break) to render financial assistance. During this parliamentary hiatus revenue had been garnered by a number of increasingly unpopular taxes, levied without parliamentary sanction: tonnage and poundage (duties on imports and exports), the reviving of feudal rights (such as fining all gentlemen with land worth £40 per annum if they refused a knighthood!), the granting of 'patents' and, above all, the infamous 'ship money'. Originally a tax levied on coastal counties to pay for the Royal Navy, in 1638 it was extended to inland counties and aroused intense opposition. A Buckinghamshire squire, John

John Hampden (engraving by Houbraken)

Hampden, actually brought a test case over it, but the judges upheld the King's right to collect it, and that he was the only authority capable of assessing the necessity for such collection.

The intensity of opposition over the imposition of taxes was matched by the animosity of the Puritans towards the leaders of the Church of England. Though the religious element in the causes of the Civil Wars has been over-emphasized in the past, there is no doubt that the Puritans played a leading rôle. Believing that the individual could establish direct contact with the Almighty without intercession of Church or minister, the Puritans considered preaching more important than established prayers, that in some cases predestination (the belief that salvation was preordained, irrespective of conduct on earth) was fact, and that resemblances to

Roman Catholic ritual should be eliminated from services. Church courts and tithes (in effect paying for the upkeep of ministers whom they did not support) were further grievances, which Puritan ministers aired when the opportunity arose, criticizing the Church heirarchy and, by implication, its head, the King. Charles I, who favoured order in all things, disliked the iconoclast Puritans and probably regarded them as political subversives, as did the Church heirarchy, and appointed William Laud as Archbishop of Canterbury in 1633 to attempt the elimination of Puritanism. By then, however, the Puritans had too strong a hold, and their attempts to overthrow the Church establishment spilled over into the political sphere as Parliamentarians opposed to government policy, though basically not Puritan themselves, took them as allies.

The theory that the Civil Wars were wars of class still finds favour, sometimes at the expense of the religious causes. Broad assertions that the nobility and gentry were Royalist and the merchants and yeomanry Parliamentarian seem to be incorrect, as support for one side or the other seems to have depended as much, if not more, upon geography rather than matters of birth or finance. Whilst few areas were wholly loyal to one side or the other, distinct territorial patterns were seen, with the gentry of the poorer areas and pastoral shires like Lancashire and Cheshire, much of Wales and the southwest being staunchly Royalist, whereas the more prosperous farming counties like Kent and East Anglia were the cornerstones of Parliamentary support. Even the large trading centres such as London, Bristol and Newcastle, controlled by the merchant class and usually regarded as wholly Parliamentarian, contained numbers of committed Royalists. As in all things, shades of grey are more accurate than black and white.

The long-term causes of the Civil Wars – grievances over taxation and Church organization and demands for an increasing rôle for Parliament – whilst instigating criticism of the King, never envisaged his deposition. The early Parliamentarian aims were to 'recover the King out of the hands of a Popish Malignant Company, that have seduced His Majesty with their wicked Counsels, and have withdrawne him from his Parliament ... To rescue the King out of his and the Kingdomes enemies; and to maintain his Honour and just Prerogatives'[2]; their cry was 'King and Parliament', not just 'Parliament'. The more immediate causes of the war, however, perhaps provided more justice for criticism of the King's government.

King Charles I was a serious, even solemn, character, 'the most worthy of the title of an honest man'[3], possessing many virtues but lacking self-confidence and a real sense of humour: '... an excellent understanding, but was not confident enough of it; which made him oftentimes change his own opinion for a worse, and follow the advice of a man that did not judge so well as himself'[4]. He inherited such a man in his father's favourite, the

Archbishop Laud (engraving by R. Taylor)

Duke of Buckingham, when he acceeded to the throne in 1625. Buckingham's arrogance and mishandling probably originated the swell of criticism which came to be levelled at his royal master. Through the late 1620s King and Parliament battled over the finance needed to fight wars against Spain and France, into which the country had been drawn by Buckingham's foreign policy, and eventually unpopular taxation was levied without Parliamentary authority. Criticism of the King increased over his religious policy, the Commons condemning a supposed 'growth of popery' and the Arminian sect which held that all men were free to gain salvation. Predominantly Calvinist for over half a century, the Church of England's official acceptance of predestination was under serious challenge by the King's reissue in 1628 of the Thirty-Nine Articles, which was regarded by the House of Commons as a rejection of predestination and thus the first influence of Rome; for were not Roman Catholics gaining influence at court, and was not the King's French wife also of that persuasion? In March 1629, with the Speaker forcibly held in his chair as he tried to adjourn, the Commons passed three resolutions: a condemnation of religious innovation, of tonnage and poundage levied without Parliamentary authority, and that any merchant who paid 'illegal' taxes betrayed the liberty of England as much as the authority which levied them. Then the House of Commons broke up and did not reconvene for 11 years.

During this period opposition to the King's policies (directed towards the King himself since Buckingham's murder in 1628) was expressed best in the local government of the counties. The gentry was antagonized by government mishandling; the yeomanry and tradesmen resented the arbitrary taxes and the impressment and quartering of soldiers. Even a staunch Royalist like Sir Ralph Hopton, who became one of the King's most capable generals, was a Puritan suspicious of popery and critical of forced loans and ship money; and the M.P.s of Cornwall, later the most Royalist of all counties, opposed the King's taxes. No organized opposition to the King's religious policy existed, for the Presbyterians (who wished to abolish bishops and replace them with a government like that of the Scottish Kirk) were few in number; and the Puritans formed an integral part of the Church of England, seeking to change it from within, most believing that the King was attempting with the aid of Roman Catholic ministers and wife to turn the Church towards Rome.

The King cannot have been unaware of the rising tide of opposition, but in the words of his declaration to the people after the dissolution of Parliament in 1629, he believed that 'princes are not bound to give account of their actions but to God alone'; yet this same document attempted to show that *he*, the King, was the conservative force in the country by quoting precedents for the levying of taxes without Parliamentary sanction, and by resisting any innovation in the Church. The day after Parliament adjourned in 1629 the King arrested nine members of the Commons on charges of sedition, consigning three to an unspecified term of imprisonment, which only exacerbated the feelings of the anti-Buckingham lobby, for one of the victims was Sir John Eliot, whose speeches the King considered responsible for his minister's assassination. Eliot's death in the Tower three years later only made feelings run higher.

By 'illegal' taxes and the conclusion of hostilities, the King was able to make his income suffice without the help of Parliament, but few measures (though all made with the highest of motives) mollified the opposition to the King; indeed, they made it worse. Even Laud's insistence that clergy should wear a surplice and that congregations should bow towards the altar increased the belief in a Romish takeover. Nevertheless, government ran reasonably smoothly until 1638, when two events changed everything. Firstly, as only seven out of twelve judges in the Hampden case supported the King's right to levy ship money, most of the King's opposition became focussed upon the hated tax and the judgement was taken as an excuse to avoid paying it; confiscation of property of those unwilling to pay aroused even more indignation.

The second dramatic event was the King's decision to compel the Scottish Kirk to accept a new prayer book, which resulted in riots and the formulation of a National Covenant protesting the Lowlanders' solidarity against religious interference from England. Charles' actions, hopelessly misguided, were occasioned simply, as Gardiner wrote, by his love of order and sheer ignorance of mankind. Charles was told that the imposition of the *Book of Common Prayer* upon the Calvinist-influenced Kirk would require the support of 40,000 men, but not having sufficient funds or matériel he played for time, calling a General Assembly of the Kirk. The defiance of this body was such that it even abolished the bishops forced upon them by Charles' father. The war which followed was not fought over the original question; it promoted a Scottish national movement led by the Presbyterian ministers in general opposition to the King, and provided itself with an army which encompassed the Lowlands, trained by professional officers returned from the Thirty Years' War, and which was far too good for the impoverished militia which Charles could field. (The Highland chiefs, mostly Roman Catholics, took no part in the war, save for the saturnine Archibald Campbell, Marquis of Argyll, whose clan was the only one to oppose the King.)

Abandoning an unsuccessful invasion of Scotland, Charles' advisors persuaded him to conclude peace by the Pacification of Berwick (1639), but the King remained determined to crush his rebellious northern subjects and sent for his Lord Deputy in Ireland, Viscount Strafford, to advise him. Though opposed to the Scottish war, Strafford (and Archbishop Laud) persuaded the King to recall Parliament to provide funds for a proper prosecution of the campaign. In return for his advice, promise of troops from Ireland and a presumed manipulation of the Commons, Strafford received an earldom and the post of Lord-Lieutenant of Ireland; but when Parliament assembled its reaction was very different from that anticipated by the royal councillors. Airing 11 years and more of grievances, John Pym, long one of the King's leading critics, demanded that the liberties of Parliament be examined and the ship-money verdict be discussed. Charles offered to abandon the latter tax – in fact it was now largely uncollectable, such was popular opposition – if the Commons would provide enough cash to reopen hostilities. Their refusal resulted in the dissolution of this so-called 'Short Parliament' and Charles attempted to prosecute the Scottish war without Parliamentary aid. The result was a fiasco; Strafford, so ill that he had to travel by litter, was pessimistic when appointed commander-in-chief, and a brisk invasion by the Scottish over the Tyne routed the opposition. Charles was forced to accept the humiliating Treaty of Ripon (21 October 1640), by which Scottish forces were allowed to stay in Durham and Northumberland until a final settlement was concluded; but more importantly, as it transpired, the so-called 'Long Parliament' had to be convened in November.

John Pym (engraving after Houbraken)

the civil unrest already caused by the King's hesitation. On 20 May 1641 Strafford was beheaded.

The mobs which had intimidated the King and members of the House of Lords into abandoning Strafford to his unjust fate seem to have been orchestrated by members of the anti-Royal faction. Pym seems genuinely to have supported the existing establishment and been loyal to the monarchy, but his aims were more than simply to remove the King from the influence of evil counsels, but apparently to increase the power of Parliament at the expense of the King's. Throughout the summer of 1641 it appeared as if this revolutionary process was beginning, as the King made concessions to the will of Parliament, including the Triennial Act which allowed Parliament to be summoned without royal command, and the declaration that ship money was illegal. As power continued to tilt towards the hands of Parliament, many of the King's former critics began to believe that reform had gone far enough; but an outbreak of revolt in Ireland caused Parliament to pass propositions that the King's advisers and ministers be approved by Parliament, and that Parliament, not the King, should be responsible for the Kingdom's defence. The publication by Pym of a 'Grand Remonstrance' which catalogued all the grievances against the government since the reign began, coupled with further civil unrest following Charles' upholding of the *Book of Common Prayer* and his appointment of new bishops, together with increasing divisions within the Commons, persuaded the King to act.

On 4 January 1642 Charles arrived in person at the House of Commons to arrest five M.P.s for treason, including Pym and Hampden. All five slipped away and went into hiding, and the King removed his court from Whitehall to Hampton Court; his next return to London was to stand trial for his life. Although both factions began to prepare for war (the Queen going abroad to pawn the crown jewels to buy arms), negotiations continued until March when the break was finally made over the Militia Ordinance, whereby control of the militia – virtually the only armed body in the country – was to be taken from the King and passed to Parliament. By May, Charles had established his headquarters in York and in the following month commissioners from Westminster brought him their terms of peace, the 'Nineteen Propositions' which in effect would have given Parliament full sovereignty and left the monarch as a figurehead. The King and his supporters bargained for a partnership rather than seeking a reversion to absolute power, but any quests for peace were in vain; in July Parliament commanded the Earl of Warwick to take command of the navy, which was almost entirely Parliamentary in sympathy, and for the Earl of Essex to command a Parliamentary army. Charles called upon his loyal subjects for assistance in crushing the rebellion, and raised the royal standard formerly on 22 August 1642, officially opening the Civil War.

Pym's House of Commons (for he was leader against the King's policies) was virtually united in its opposition. Future Royalists and even Royal appointees such as Sir Edmund Verney, the Knight Marshal of the Household who died defending the King's banner at Edgehill, steadily voted in opposition, an opposition built not only on the mismanagement of government and the assault on Parliamentary rights, but aggravated by the 11 years' Parliamentary hiatus and the presence of a Covenanting army on English soil. The strength of feeling was such that Pym was able to obtain the support of members whose opinions were so divergent as to ultimately cause civil war. Deflecting more radical bills (such as one requiring the abolition of bishops, supported by the Cambridge M.P., Oliver Cromwell), Pym's first objectives were an act to compel Parliament to meet once every five years, and the impeachment of Strafford, who was used by both sides as a scapegoat. Though (unfairly) blaming Strafford for the disaster in the north, the King tried to save his loyal servant, even attempting his rescue from the Tower of London, which failed when the Lieutenant of the Tower refused to admit Charles' troops. Strafford himself begged the King to give royal assent to the Bill of Attainder condemning him to death as a traitor for attempting to divide King and Parliament, to prevent an increase in

Prince Rupert (engraving after portrait by Van Dyck)

2 THE ARMIES

Before the events of the Civil Wars can be considered, it is important to cover some details of how both sides were able to assemble the necessary matériel to conduct a war – men, equipment and finance. The support for each faction, however, was by no means as clear cut as is often presumed. Peers supported both King and Parliament, though the nobility in general naturally sympathized with the King, but the gentry were divided evenly, to such an extent that the 'civil' war might be regarded as much a 'family' war; brother fought brother, friend opposed friend, thus increasing the tragedy which accompanies any conflict. Even at the highest level families were split; the republican Sir Henry Vane had a Royalist brother; Sir Richard Feilding, Royalist defender of Reading, had a brother fighting for Parliament; Ralph Verney, brother of the King's Knight Marshal, was against the King and thus was told by brother Edmund that he was now an enemy; the son of the regicide Sir Thomas Mauleverer fought (and was imprisoned) for the King; Denzil Holles, one of the King's most vehement critics, had three Royalist cousins; the Earls of Denbigh and Dover, serving as troopers in the King's Lifeguard at Edgehill, both had sons in the opposing army, Lords Feilding and Rochford; at least six members of the Cromwell family bore arms for the King. As two close friends, the Royalist leader Sir Ralph Hopton and the Parliamentary general Sir William Waller, succinctly termed the war, it was one 'without an enemy'.

If factions were formed more by geography than class, then economics also influenced the support for one side or the other, though even so the geography of support is best expressed in shades of grey. If most Royalists were to be found in the poorer regions and if the country could be divided into pro- and anti-Royalist areas (the west, west Midlands, east Yorkshire and the far north for the King, the Home Counties, east and south-east for Parliament), there were no lasting, clear divisions; areas might be Royalist one year and Parliamentary the next, depending upon a number of factors, not least the proximity of an army belonging to one side or the other. Similarly, the composition of battlelines was influenced by old or family rivalries, an often-neglected factor in later assessments of loyalties during the wars. Even the merchant class was ambivalent in its support, some trading centres supporting the King and others Parliament, often from personal motives rather than political or religious convictions. Thus the City of London financiers who backed Parliament in 1642 were probably influenced most by the levying of customs and duties by the King without Parliamentary approval, only to discover that the taxes introduced by 'King Pym' to finance Parliament's war effort were more severe than anything levied by the crown.

But if the political and religious conviction of many participants could and did give rise to the most fanatical actions, it is quite incorrect to regard the Civil Wars as involving everyone by reason of conviction. Although the most bitter fighting sometimes occurred in areas away from the main spheres of campaigning – largely a never-ending succession of skirmishes aggravated by long-held feuds and rivalries – a large proportion of the gentry and probably a majority of the artisan classes, especially in rural areas, wished only to be left alone. The 'neutralist' movements and the sentiments which caused them probably explain why, in most areas, the existing structure of local government and administration was able to keep running with remarkably few interruptions, save where economy and life were disrupted by the passage of an army or the raising of supplies for one. It appears that neutralist movements existed in at least 22 counties[1], including a number of demilitarization pacts between those ostensibly fighting the war, such as the Royal Commissioners of Array and the Parliamentary Militia Commissioners, both responsible for the formation of armies and prosecution of hostilities. Examples include the pact agreed in Cheshire in December 1642, and that between Lord Fairfax and other Yorkshire Parliamentarians and their Royalist neighbours, the latter earning a stiff rebuke from Parliament which considered a demilitarized Yorkshire to be in the Royalist interest. Attempts to save their own counties from strife resulted in some neutralist gentry endeavouring to forswear support for either side, attempting to ignore the whole business except for measures to protect their own property; in Lincolnshire, for example, some gentlemen proposed to raise a troop of horse to protect themselves from whichever side should try to molest them!

Such neutralist movements adumbrated the 'club-men' of the mid 1640s, which will be mentioned later. But amidst all the vehemence of political and religious doctrine which afflicted both sides, such as the Parliamentary statement that 'We are not now to look at our enemies as Country-men, or Kinsmen ... but as the enemies of God and our Religion, and siders with Antichrist; so our eye is not to pitie them, nor our sword to spare them ...'[2], there were contemporary statements which illuminated the opinions of those who simply wanted to mind their own business, who cared 'not what government they live under so as they may plough and go to market', of country people who loved 'their pudding at home better than a musket and pike abroad, and if they could have peace, care not what side had the better'[3], or as Dr Plumtre of Nottingham remarked, 'what is the cause to me if my goods be lost?'[4]. Others, sadly, cared little 'for either of the causes but they would have taken any side for pay and plunder'.

The latter motives might be presumed the explanation for the many changes of side which occurred throughout the wars (though Sir John Urry's triple defection is exceptional); but whilst true in some cases, a greater cause of changing allegiance was alteration of circumstances around an unchanging personal belief; as Sir William Waller wrote, explaining his transfer of support between the Independent and Presbyterian parties, 'the change was not in me but in others ... I changed my company but not my mind'[5].

And if the officers shared similar social backgrounds, it was probably even more true of the men. Given that there *were* 'rakehells' in the Royal armies and religious fanatics in those of Parliament (or as one Royalist said, 'in our army we have the sins of men (drinking and wenching) but in yours you have those of devils, spiritual pride and rebellion'[6]), the majority of the rank and file on both sides were reasonable, ordinary people with traditional loyalties towards monarch, Church and seigneur, and with no great vehemence of feeling one way or another until compelled.

Three factors were necessary to put an army into the field: finance, men, and equipment. The first could be levied in taxation, provided by patriotic gifts, or to a certain extent dispensed with by the invidious system of 'free quarter' and plunder of provisions and matériel, which will be noted in greater detail. The extent to which private individuals became financially committed was exemplified by the Marquises of Newcastle and Worcester, who each spent nearly one million pounds on the Royal cause. The less affluent sold their plate, jewellery and other possessions, whilst merchants also expended considerable sums, though many of the latter who supported Parliament eventually made a profit on their patriotism! In raising the troops, however, there were always difficulties, for no 'standing army' existed; indeed, the very concept of such was to remain anathema to many for a considerable time after the Civil Wars, a view no doubt strengthened by the army's eventual assumption of power (one writer began his treatise by stating that 'If any Man doubts whether a Standing Army is Slavery, Popery, Mahometism, Atheism, or any thing which they please...'[7]).

Armies were formed of regiments of foot and horse, raised for a specific task or campaign and disbanded at the conclusion of hostilities; there was thus no 'regimental' continuity as came to be understood in the following three centuries, and forces suffered in terms of discipline and experience as a result. At least until the formation of the New Model, regiments in both

Officers with 'leading staff' and partizan, from 17th century engravings (from Goold-Walker's *Honourable Artillery Company*)

Ensign and sergeant, from 17th-century engravings (from Goold-Walker's *Honourable Artillery Company*)

armies were transient entities and their personnel ever-changing. There was, however, one body always in existence in some manner, the militia or 'trained bands'[8]. There is insufficient space to describe in detail their formation and equipping, but in brief this part-time 'home guard' was levied, in both recruits and arms, from people of sufficient affluence, graded according to their possessions. The old system, which Charles I attempted to remedy, for example specified that (in 1621) a man with land worth £10 per annum was to provide a whole 'foot armour' and half the cost of him that wore it; if £40 per annum, two foot armours; if £80 per annum, a light horse and foot armour, etc. The assessment of such 'taxes' was a contributory grievance to the outbreak of war. An outstanding source for the militia's history up to the Civil Wars is *The Elizabethan Militia* by L. Boynton, (Newton Abbot, 1971).

It has been common to accept the contemporary view that the trained bands were neither trained nor disciplined, as Dryden succinctly wrote:

The country rings around with loud alarms,
And raw in fields the rude militia swarms;
Mouths without hands; maintain'd at vast expense,
In peace a charge, in war a weak defence;
Stout once a month they march, a blustering band,
And ever, but in times of need, at hand.[9]

Some of these criticisms were justified, in some counties the trained bands being in such disrepair that they might as well not have existed. In Northumberland in the 1630s, for example, preparedness was so wretched that the trained band officials did not even answer correspondence, and numerous other cases of inefficiency are recorded; the Essex trained bands once took about six days and the Suffolk five days to become even partly operational. One contemporary critic claimed that even the monthly training sessions were not taken seriously: 'by the time the arms be all viewed ... it draws toward dinner time, and indeed officers love their bellies so well that they are loth to take too much pains ...',[10] and Venn claimed they worshipped not Mars but Bacchus! Another wrote that they were 'effeminate in courage and incapable of discipline, because their whole course of life alienated from warlike employment'[11]. This lack of training manifested itself in the worst ways; at Basing House, for example, one regiment (apparently the Westminster Auxiliaries) forgot their drill to such an extent that the rear rank shot down their own front ranks!

One exception to this state of decay were the trained bands of London, which originated with the corps of citizens raised in the Middle Ages. Formed into four regiments in 1616, in 1642 the Common Council increased their number to 40 companies of 200 men each, organized in six regiments named from the colouring

of their flags: Red, White, Yellow, Blue, Green and Orange Regiments; Southwark, Westminster and Tower Hamlets each raised a regiment, and in addition the city formed six weaker and probably less-efficient auxiliary regiments. Many of these men (especially apprentices) held strong political and religious convictions, which combined with good officers and adequate training turned the London regiments into the most professional corps in the early stages of the war. Experienced officers were loaned from the best professional military body in the realm, the Company of the

'An Officer of Pikemen' (engraving by N.C. Goodnight)

Artillery Garden, existing as the 'Fraternitie or Guylde of St George' in 1537 if not before, and still surviving as the Honourable Artillery Company. Though the Company did not serve as a unit in the Civil War, the influence of its members, not least William Bariffe whose drill book was a standard work, was considerable. The officer corps of the London regiments seems to have represented the expected merchant class; in September 1643 the White Regiment totalled 600 musketeers and 520 pikemen, with at least six of the seven company commanders members of the Artillery Company, including two merchants, a hosier, the Clerk of Leathersellers Hall and a 'slopmaker for Seamen'; and at the same time the Yellow Regiment's six company commanders comprised four drapers, a haberdasher and a grocer. These unlikely soldiers saved Parliament at Turnham Green.

Not all provincial trained bands were as decayed as many have claimed; a number seem to have been well trained and equipped and of genuine value to the community. The Yarmouth Artillery Company, for example, even hired permanently a mercenary from Europe, Captain de Eugaine, to train their men and arrange the most elaborate sham fights; after one such field day in 1638 the Company was reported so proficient that 'God be gloried, there was not either man, woman or child had the least hurt done at all … although I have seen good service in the Netherlands and other places, yet never saw a better thing …'[12]. This corps held Great Yarmouth for Parliament throughout the war. Similarly, other local bands were not a negligible force; in 1643 and 1644 the Mayor of Colchester begged for the return of their contingent as their absence rendered the town open to 'our unruly multitude whoe are ready upon all occasions to worke mischeife'[13], whilst the Totnes Band, which had trained for years prior to the war with shooting competitions, was the subject of a petition that they might not be sent out of the locality and thus leave the town 'so naked and indefensible'[14]. And even when they did not muster for service in units, there is evidence that members were filtered into other regiments to provide a 'stiffening' of trained weapon handlers; for example, it appears that such men served in Northampton's and Pennyman's Regiments at Edgehill.

Despite good service, even the best trained bands had imperfections. When London's Yellow Auxiliaries were ordered to muster on 16 October 1643 they arrived so piecemeal that their colonel decided that they should all go home and try again the next day! And when trained band units decided that their term of enlistment had expired, they raised what Waller called their 'old song' of 'Home! Home!' Having won a victory at Alton, the London trained bands 'loaned' to Waller reminded him that they wanted to be home for Christmas, and left. The same commander's plans were disrupted in 1644 when his London brigade flatly refused to march, not

having been paid; and though the Cornish bands resolutely defended their own county they refused to move into Devon, causing the Royalist command to form a new, largely untrained army for that purpose, which duly met with disaster. As late as 1645–6 Hopton's army included Cornish trained band men 'full of complaints and all sorts of distempers'. A further complication was the process of muster; the trained bands could only be mobilized by orders from the King or Lord-Lieutenant, which caused notable confusion in

Musketeer with matchlock musket; clothing predates Civil War (engraving after de Gheyn)

April 1642, when Charles I was refused admission to Hull and denied access to its armouries by Sir John Hotham, who on Parliament's order had mobilized 800 men. As the Lord-Lieutenancy was vacant (since the execution of the last, Strafford) this act was, in the King's eyes, illegal, and *he* called out the other Yorkshire trained bands to suppress those of Hull!

To raise a Royal army, a 'Commission of Array' would be issued to the Lord-Lieutenant or Sheriff of the county, by which they were empowered to 'Array and

Harquebusier in full equipment; few Civil War troopers can have been equipped so completely, the open-faced helmet and gorget being replaced by the 'pot' helmet with face-bars (engraving after Cruso's *Militarie Instructions*)

PLATE 1

1 Gentleman in everyday dress 1640s
2 Pikeman 1640s
3 Musketeer 1640s

Plate 1 illustrates costume typical just before the Civil War. Although a number of old-fashioned styles were in use throughout (depending upon the taste or wealth of the individual), figure 1 shows a gentleman of some quality wearing a rather stylish costume of 'slashed' doublet and matching trousers, the 'slashing' on the sleeves and breast allowing the shirt or (in this case) the contrasting suit lining to show through. The suit illustrates the decline of padding and starching to produce the softer lines of the mid seventeenth century, exemplified by the soft lace collar in place of the starched ruff; lace was the prerogative of the wealthy, most others favouring plain linen. The doublet with panelled skirts was already declining in use by the 1640s, but was still worn by many; decoration was determined by the wearer's affluence or choice, plain clothing being the preference of the sober-minded. The old-fashioned *Pluderhosen* or 'cloak-bag' breeches, baggy in the extreme, gave way to more close-fitting, almost tubular patterns by the late 1640s, often not gathered but open-ended and loose around the knee; as these became more voluminous the term 'petticoat breeches' was coined. Boots were worn on many occasions, not just when mounted; soft leather boots with wide 'bucket' tops, large 'butterfly' spur leathers and ornate spurs were fashionable. The fine linen hose covering the lower leg were usually protected by a second pair of 'boot-hose', sometimes with lace tops turned down over the upper edge of the boot. Red hat feathers, red boot heels and sole edges were again the mark of fashion. The short cloak, worn Spanish style from the left shoulder, had declined in use with the development of the longer cloak or sleeved cassock.

The pikeman illustrated wears a full corselet of breastplate, backplate and tassets (thigh protectors), and a comparatively modern helmet. Certain of the better-equipped trained bands and associations like the Honourable Artillery Company (which went under various titles such as the 'Voluntary Company of the Artillery Garden' or the 'Military Company of the City of London') would include members whose personal affluence allowed them to dress well, even though serving as ordinary soldiers; some even wore the totally impractical spurred boots. Some of these companies had distinctive uniform, for example the two trained band companies of Beverley, Yorkshire, for which in 1640 'everie common soldier for this town shall have a grey coat for the value of eight shillings or thereabouts'[1]. Older styles, the doublet, breeches and buff-coat as illustrated, were no doubt seen throughout the war.

NOTES
1 Norfolk, R.W.S. *Militia, Yeomanry and Volunteer Forces of the East Riding 1689–1908* (York, 1965) p. 4

PLATE 1

1 Gentleman 1640s

2 Pikeman 1640s

3 Musketeer 1640s

train all the inhabitants in your County . . . which are of body able, and estate competent to beare armes . . . and to . . . finde armes for other men in a proportion sutable to their estates . . .'[15]; but, in effect, a regiment was raised by the issue of a commission to its colonel or proprietor, a process more modern than medieval. Such regiments (other than trained bands, to whom the Commissions of Array principally referred) were then raised 'by beat of drum', securing either volunteers or the tenants and servants of the officers. These regiments often had a territorial origin; thus some were primarily Lancastrian, Northumbrian, etc., whilst others recruited from several areas, for example Byron's Foot in the Marston Moor campaign which drew its recruits from Denbighshire, Cheshire, Shropshire and Flint. Parliamentary regiments were formed in a similar manner, the Militia Ordinance (over which the final schism had occurred) giving Parliament the legal right to muster its own forces under its own commanders. Voluntary enlistment did not always result in the rank and file being drawn from the labouring classes, for if the King's Lifeguard, in which peers of the realm served as troopers, was exceptional, other corps (particularly horse) included a high proportion of gentlemen; in Oxford in 1643, for example, two auxiliary regiments were comprised exclusively of gentlemen and their servants and scholars of the University. But voluntary enlistment depended to a degree upon the popularity of the colonel (known landowners in provincial areas or popular Parliamentarians like Sir Arthur Haselrig

Musketeers backed by stand of pikes; the figure in left foreground, bearing a partizan, appears to wear a 'montero' cap (engraving by Jacques Callot from *Misères et Malheures de Guerre* (1633))

Buff-coat: rear
(National Army Museum, London)

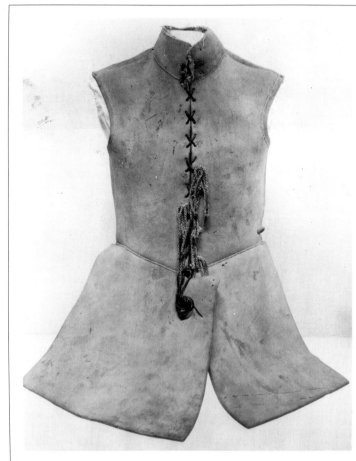

Buff-coat: front
(National Army Museum, London)

in London, for example), and could never fill the army completely, so other forms of recruiting became necessary.

Impressment (or conscription) was understandably unpopular and difficult to organize, for desertion was rife among impressed men and the standard of recruit was often poor as the local officials responsible for finding them usually impressed the worst or least useful members of the community; as a Norfolk high constable advised, 'have an especiall care to take idle servingmen and such other able persons as live dissolutely or idly without any imployment' [16]. The problem was exascerbated by the fact that trained men, such as trained band members, were exempt from impressment. Desertion was such that, for example, when the Essex levies were marched out in September 1643 (albeit unarmed) the local bands and troops of horse were mobilized to prevent them rioting; about half deserted. Reaction to impressment was intense: 'Prince Rupert marches up and down ... but can raise noe force ... The Countrey people tell him that he shall rather cutt theire throates

at home than carry them abroad to be slaine, as their Countrey men have beene ...' [17]. The standard of recruit was often miserable, and the committees appointed to find them were driven to distraction: 'wee are to finde men well affected ... but where wee shall finde them god in heaven knowes, for wee doe not ...' [18]; when these Essex men *were* found, they were 'so mutinous, that I may justly fear they would cut my throat', wrote Cromwell [19]. Equally wretched was the impressment of prisoners of war, never a satisfactory method of obtaining useful mouths.

Trained officers were equally hard to find. Parliament appears to have made great efforts in early 1642 to guarantee the services of trained but unemployed officers or 'reformadoes' (i.e. those officers often holding a commission but with no regiment) by paying them ostensibly for an expedition to Ireland. Wharton's regiment of 1642, for example, seems largely to have been recruited for Ireland and then diverted into Parliament's army, perhaps leading to dissatisfaction and resulting in their flight at Edgehill; Ballard's greycoats, also raised for

Ireland, performed rather better. The best source of experienced officers was Europe, where the Thirty Years' War was still raging. Large numbers of British officers had seen service as mercenaries or adventurers in Europe, and more returned home when the Civil War began. Officers with service in German, French, Dutch, Danish and Swedish armies were legion, and included some of the leading commanders; for example, Essex had served in the Netherlands, Lord Forth for the King of Sweden (and was ennobled as Earl of Kirchberg by Gustavus Adolphus), William Waller as a mercenary for Venice and the King of Bohemia, and his friend Ralph Hopton with Bohemia and in Mansfeldt's mercenary army. The influence of returned Scottish mercenaries was such that, for example, in Leslie's army of the Solemn League and Covenant in 1644, only two general officers (the Treasurer and Commissary-General, both administrators) had not served abroad, and 53 out of 87 regimental field officers had served with Scandinavian or other European armies.

In addition, foreign mercenaries were recruited in surprising numbers. Some were simply avaricious rogues, like the Croatian captain Carlo Fantom recorded by Aubrey, a 'great Ravisher' who deserted Parliament for the Royalists (who ultimately hanged him): 'Sd. he, I care not for your Cause: I come to fight for your halfe-crowne, and your handsome woemen ... I have fought for the Christians against the Turkes; and for the Turkes against the Christians'[20]. (An incidental but interesting comment upon seventeenth-century superstition was the belief that Fantom was a 'hard man', an enchanted man who could only be harmed by a silver bullet or a club!) Not all foreign mercenaries were unprincipled, however; the German engineer Colonel John Rosworm was hired by the town of Manchester as resident military expert for £60 per annum, yet rejected a royalist gift of £150 to tempt him to defect, 'valuing honesty more than gold'[21]. Indeed, some of the returned British officers were worse than the foreign mercenaries, like the infamous Colonel Hide, a typical desperado who 'brought into England the worst features of Continental military licence ... became terrors, not only to the garrisons to which they belonged, but also to the country'[22], and were justly unpopular, like Lieutenant-Colonel Henry Billingsley who was described by a subordinate as 'a Godamme blade, and doubtlesse hatche in hell, and we all desire that either the Parliament would depose him, or God convert him, or the Devill fetch him away quick'[23].

Not all the foreigners held high office, for many junior officers and even rank and file fell into this category: the Queen's Horse in 1644, for example, was described as 'most Frenche'[24] (perhaps an exaggeration), with two French troop commanders, and led by Raoul Fleury at Cheriton. Even the New Model contained its proportion of foreign officers; Rainborow's Regiment, for example, had a high proportion of New Englanders,

PLATE 2
4 King Charles I
5 Sir Edward Walker, Secretary-at-War
6 Charles, Prince of Wales

The figures illustrated are taken from an anonymous portrait of the King and his Secretary-at-War, Sir Edward Walker, and a portrait by William Dobson of the young Prince of Wales. These show not the conventional full armour beloved of regal portraitists but what was probably the usual dress of senior officers, gold-laced buff-coats and conventional suits with a minimum of defensive armour. The Prince of Wales wears only the back and breast of a magnificent black and gilt armour still extant. Interesting features include the King's wearing of a riband of the Order of the Garter, with one boot top pushed low to reveal a Garter-blue ribbon tied around the leg. The bâtons carried by the King and Prince of Wales were the traditional insignia of command, surviving into the present century in the form of bâtons presented symbolically to field marshals. Many early bâtons were more decorative than the plain wooden type with gilded ends illustrated; long white sticks were common, whilst the captains of the Great Yarmouth trained band in 1638 carried 'truncheons', painted and 'waved' in their own colours, three feet (91 centimetres) long[1].

Several uniforms worn by staff officers are recorded; the King wore full cuirassier armour at times, probably only for ceremonial occasions, as noted at Leicester, 'on horseback, in bright armour'[2], but his more usual dress was probably that worn at Edgehill, a black velvet coat lined with ermine and a steel cap covered with velvet. Just before the siege of Hull, the Prince of Wales was described at York as commanding 'as brave a Troop as ever came into the field', wearing 'a very curious guilt armour' and riding a white horse caparisoned with velvet 'all studded with burning waves of gold'[3].

NOTES
1 Roberts, J. *Great Yarmouth Exercise*; see Castle, M.A. *History of the Yarmouth Battery* (Norwich, 1927) p. 9
2 Quoted Sherwood, R.E. *Civil Strife in the Midlands 1642–51* (Chichester, 1974)
3 Reckitt, B.N. *Charles the First and Hull* (London, 1952) p. 57

while a French colonel, Mazères, was apparently cashiered for his love of drink, gaming and women. Frequent references may be found to foreigners in positions of responsibility, often in technical rôles like the engineer Rosworm or Monsieur de la Roche in charge of the Royalist mortar at Cirencester in February 1643. These returned, experienced officers and foreign mercenaries, together with those rank and file with experience of campaigning in Ireland or against the Scots, enabled what might have been an untrained rabble to take the field in a cohesive body. By 1643–4 all armies had achieved their own experience by the melancholy business of fighting over their own homeland.

PLATE 2

4 King Charles I   5 Sir Edward Walker   6 Charles, Prince of Wales

3 ORGANIZATION, EQUIPMENT AND TACTICS

FOOT

Organization, weaponry and tactics of the Civil Wars were interrelated, and although numerous specific examples are quoted below it should be noted that the following general statements were not universally true and that exceptions existed. Each of the 'arms' of an army will be covered in order, beginning with the foot or infantry.

Although hand-to-hand combat was still a feature of seventeenth-century warfare, the 'missile' element of infantry fighting was increasing steadily, the longbow having been replaced by increasingly efficient firearms, for, as Daniel Lupton wrote, pikemen could 'only receive the messengers of death but Musquetiers can send them'[1]. But as musketeers could not adequately defend themselves against a cavalry charge, men armed with

Regiment of foot arrayed for battle: Rainborough's Regiment (from Sprigge's plan of Naseby)

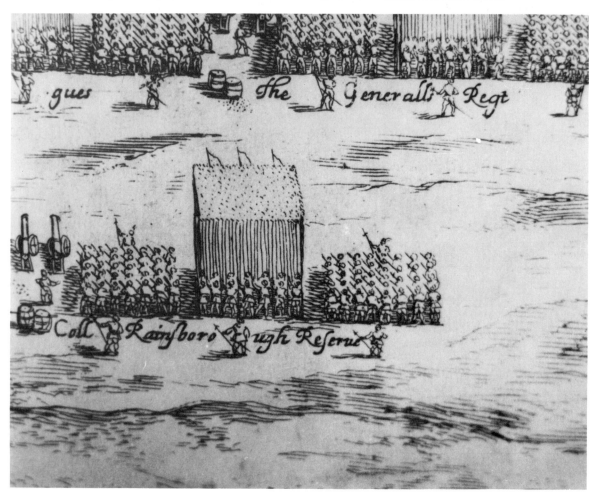

Pikeman's helmet and corselet, the latter bearing armourers' marks of James I (Wallis & Wallis)

collar), though the two latter items declined in use during the Civil Wars as being too cumbersome for their worth; possibly only the London trained bands wore complete 'corselets' or pike armour in any quantity. Markham described the complete ensemble:

... pikemen shall have good combe-caps for their heads, well lined with quilted caps, curaces [2] for their bodies of nimble and good mould, being high pike proof; large and well compact gordgetts for their neckes, fayre and close joyned taches, to arm to the mid-thigh; as for the pouldron or the vantbrace, they may be spared, because they are but cumbersome. All this armour is to be russet, sanguine, or blacke colour, than white or milled, for it will keepe the longer from rust. [3]

Under the corselet could be worn the ubiquitous 'buff-coat', originally a thick jacket of buffalo hide worn for riding and war which became almost *de rigueur* for gentlemen in their everyday wear and a universal protection for soldiers, the hide sufficiently thick to turn a sword blow. The total cost of a pikeman's corselet, excluding buff-coat, was established by Charles I in 1632:[4]

	£	s.	d.
The breast		v	vi
The backe		iiii	vi
The tassets		v	o
The comb'd headpeece lyned		iiii	vi
The gorgett lyned		ii	vi
The totall of the footman's armour	i	ii	o
If the breast, back, and tassets, be lyned with red leather, the price will be	i	iiii	o

(This was for 'russetted' armour, treated to prevent rusting).

The declining use of armour is exemplified in the Honourable Artillery Company's standing orders, which in 1638 referred to men 'compleatly armed in white Corselets', but in 1658–9 only to gorget and pike[5],

pikes remained a necessity for action in the open field, though the proportion of musketeers to pikemen was increasing steadily, until some regiments were fielded without any pikemen, though these were very much the exception.

The pikeman *par excellence* was equipped with a considerable weight of armour to protect himself, including a helmet, breast- and backplates, tassets (thigh guards suspended from the breastplate) and a gorget (an iron

PLATE 3

7 Oliver Cromwell, Lieutenant-General of Horse
8 General officer, Parliamentary staff

Cromwell is shown in the blackened armour of his portrait by R. Walker, *c.* 1649, with tassets instead of complete leg armour, and a 'lobster-tailed' helmet instead of the cuirassier-style close helmet.

The general officer wears a fashionably-laced suit beneath his buff-coat, and carries a hanger instead of a rapier or broadsword, the hilt of which (made of dull iron with polished highlights) resembles that of the contemporary hunting sword.

PLATE 3

7 Oliver Cromwell, Lieutenant-General of Horse   8 General officer, Parliamentary staff

PLATE 4

10 Cuirassier in close helmet

9 Cuirassier in lobster-tail helmet

PLATE 4

9 Cuirassier in lobster-tail helmet
10 Cuirassier in close helmet

Although the armoured cuirassier never enjoyed such prominence in the Civil War as in the Thirty Years' War, at least two units and many wealthy individuals were so equipped; in 1629 'the price of the whole cuirassiers armour amounteth unto' £4 10s., a considerable expense[1], and the refurbishing of old suits (which must have been common in 1642), 'unstriking, new fyling, russetting, new nayling, leathering and lyning'[2] cost £1 3s. The whole ensemble was described by Cruso: '... a close casque or head-piece, gorget, breast, pistoll proof (as all the cuirasse in every piece of it) and calliver proof (by addition of the placcate) the back, poldrons, vanbraces, 2 gauntlets, tassets, cuissets, culets, or guard-de-rein; all fitting to his bodie: A good sword (which was to be very stiff, cutting and sharp pointed) with girdle and hangers ...'[3]. Markham described the 'case of long pistols, firelocks (if it may be), but snaphaunces where they are wanting; the barrels of the pistols should be twenty-six inches [66 centimetres] long, and the bore of thirty-six bullets in the pound [79 per kilogramme], flask, priming box, key and moulders ...'[4]. The whole ensemble, even discounting the lance which was rarely if ever used in England, was so ponderous that it may have been the cause of the defeat of Haselrig's regiment at Roundway Down, so encumbering it as to have rendered it unable to face a flank attack (or perhaps it forced the regiment to stand to receive a charge instead of moving to meet it). Nevertheless, Haselrig's men, 'called by the other side the *regiment of lobsters*, because of their bright iron shells ... the first seen so armed on either side', were 'the first that made any impression upon the King's horse, who, being unarmed, were not able to bear a shock with them; besides that they were secure from hurts of the sword ...'[5].

The figures illustrated show two varieties of cuirassier equipment, the European version with vizored close helmet, and the style with barred 'lobster-tail' helmet favoured in England, one suit being of 'bright' armour and one enamelled black; the mounted cuirassier carries the key of his wheel lock pistol slung across the body. Two patterns of saddle were probably used by cuirassiers, the 'Great Saddle', for use with the 'Great Horse', weighing up to 60 pounds (27 kilogrammes) and with 'an ample stuffed seat, with the pommel rising well in front ... a high well-padded cantle extending round the sides to support the thighs like the body of a well-padded library chair'[6], which seems to have been restricted to cuirassiers alone and is still mentioned as late as 1661; and the 'Morocco' or (to use Markham's term) 'Perfite' saddle, a lighter version, reduced in height but still supporting the back, thighs and knees, with much more room in the seat; this type would also have been used by lighter cavalry. Though the heavy saddle could be decorated with brocaded fabric and metallic lace, their main function was 'to be handsome, made with advantage, fit for the rider, to keep him firm against the violence of a shock'[7], hence the reason for the supporting 'arms' which held the legs firmly.

NOTES

1 Quoted Grose, F. *Military Antiquities, respecting a History of the English Army, with A Treatise on Ancient Armour and Weapons* (London, 1801) vol. II, p. 335
2 Quoted *ibid.*, p. 336
3 Cruso, J. *Militarie Instructions for the Cavallrie* (Cambridge, 1632) pp. 28–9
4 Markham, *Souldiers Accidence*; see Grose, vol. I, pp. 108 ff.
5 Clarendon VII, 105
6 Duke of Newcastle, *Horsemanship*, pub. in French 1658, English translation 1667; see Tylden, Maj. G. *Horses and Saddlery* (London, 1965) pp. 117–20
7 Cruso, pp. 28–9

and in 1670 Sir James Turner bemoaned that 'we see them every where naked'[6] and advocated a return not only to classic pike armour but even to iron arm guards (the pauldrons and vambraces mentioned by Markham), for even if the armour were not proof against pistol balls, 'yet it encourages them who wear it ...'[7]. General Monck, whose *Observations* refer to the Civil War era, recommended that a pikeman wear a buff glove on the left hand and a buff-leather girdle, eight inches (20 centimetres) wide, hooked to the coat and protecting the lower body, which 'I am well assured ... will be much safer, and much more serviceable, and easier for a Pikeman to wear than Taces' (tassets)[8], though it is uncertain whether buff girdles ever existed or whether they were only Monck's idea. The pikeman's arms comprised 'a good stiff Tuck [sword] not very long, with a Belt ... if you arm your men with Swords, half the Swords you have in your Army amongst the common men, will upon the first March you make be broken with the cutting of Boughs'[9]. ('Swords' above presumably

refers to long-bladed rapiers, the 'Tuck' being a shorter-bladed, more robust weapon.) The pike itself was an iron-headed spear mounted upon an ash shaft between 15 and 18 feet (4.6 to 5.5 metres) long, 'strong, straight, yet nimble'[10] which in 1632 cost[11]:

	s.	d.
The staffe	ii	vi
The head	i	viii
Socket and colouring	o	iiii
Summe	iiii	vi

The New Model in 1645 paid between 3s. 10d. and 4s. 2d. each for 16-foot (4.9-metre) pikes. Even within the same regiment pike lengths might differ, Turner noting that 'few exceed fifteen [feet] ... many base Soldiers will cut some off the length of that'[12]. Orrery's *Treatise on the Art of War* recommends $16\frac{1}{2}$-foot (five-metre) pikes with seasoned ash shafts, lozenge heads and iron cheek-pieces four feet (1.2 metres) long, to prevent the heads from being lopped off. Edward Davis added that pikes should have fabric 'grips' and 'at the point and middest trimmed with handsome tassels … to defend the souldiers body from water, which in raine doth runne down alongst the wood'[13]. These trimmings were common; in 1587–8, for example, Norwich bought five yards (4.6 metres) of 'mockadoe' (an inferior wool) to trim their town pikes, and spent a further £3 on long blue and white fringes. Daggers were recommended in the early years of the century (for such obscure reasons as executing prisoners and digging latrine holes!)[14] but were not popular; neither were the small, round shields or 'targets,' despite the attempt by Prince Maurice of Orange to reintroduce them[15], though 'Targettiers' are mentioned in the Artillery Company in 1638[16] and one is shown in a statuette on the staircase at Cromwell House, Highgate, perhaps dating from 1646. If used at all, targets were probably limited to the bodyguards of senior officers and perhaps colour bearers. Other pole arms included the medieval 'brownbill', which even in the 1590s was advocated for use together with pikemen[17], but which was only issued when other weapons were unavailable, though it was mentioned as late as 1681 in use with the Tangier garrison[18]. Light bills might also have been carried by officers as 'leading staffs,' which were more usually partizan-type staff weapons carried as much as a badge of office as a weapon.

The pikeman had to learn a complex exercise to enable formed bodies to act in unison, as a mishandled 16-foot pike could threaten friends as well as enemies. Many drill books appeared before and during the Civil Wars, but must have been followed closely only by those units with sufficient time to learn and practice ceremonial drill. Quite apart from manoeuvring – marching, countermarching and assembling in various formations – there might be more than 20 different 'postures' or basic movements to be learned in handling the pike, expressed as obliquely as:

Your Picke being ordoured at close ordour the but-end of it must bee betwixt your feete, holding the same with your left hand, being ready to present to charge horse, and your right hand to draw your sword, setting forward your left fotte laying your Picke, and left hand upon your left knee the butt being close at the right fotte and your sword in your right hand.[19]

This complexity, and the difficulty in action of making audible such commands as, 'Bringer up stand, the rest pass through to the left and place yourself behind your bringer up', leads to the belief that in practice the complex drill was reduced to a few basic postures and commands; as Essex wrote, 'not to busy them in practising the ceremonious forms of military discipline', but 'be well instructed in the necessary rudiments of war, that they may know to fall on with discretion and retreat with care'[20]. The long practice necessary to achieve textbook precision might lead to confusion and the men becoming 'very untractable & undocile in their postures'[21]. When reduced to basics, pike drill would include: 'Stand to your Arms' (pike held upright in right hand, left hand on hip); 'Advance your Pikes' (pike supported upright on right shoulder); 'Charge your Pike' (pike held horizontally at shoulder level, used for advancing upon an enemy); and 'Charge to horse' (pikeman crouching, pike butt resting on right instep and pike angled upwards to meet enemy at horse-breast height). For marching, the pike would be 'shouldered' or 'trailed', the latter being used mainly at night and for funerals, in which the file leader held his pike horizontally by the head, the man behind held its butt, and so on, so that the column held each other's pikes and prevented anyone from becoming lost. In action, 'at push of pike', the opposing blocks of pikemen would push at one another with pikes 'charged' until one side gave way, though as the use of the pike declined pikemen were used more for protecting the musketeers than for settling the affair themselves. A regiment arrayed eight deep (the Dutch practice which Essex employed) would present a formidable obstacle when pikes were 'charged' and, given steady troops, could only be broken by missile fire.

Though on the field 'the Gentlemen of the Pike craveth the precedence'[22], musketeers increasingly held the key to seventeenth-century warfare. Two basic patterns of musket were in use: the ordinary musket with a

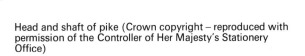

Head and shaft of pike (Crown copyright – reproduced with permission of the Controller of Her Majesty's Stationery Office)

barrel length of 4½ feet (1.4 metres), and the lighter 'caliver' with a 3½-foot (1.1-metre) barrel. The caliver was virtually synonymous with the earlier term 'harquebus', its name probably deriving from a batch of guns described as 'harquebus du calibre de Monsieur le Prince', i.e. expressing a particular calibre, but turned into 'caliver' by 'some man not understanding French'[23]. Muskets were principally of the matchlock pattern, in which ignition of the powder charge was achieved by plunging a burning length of 'match' (combustible cord) into the priming pan, the match held in a spring-loaded metal jaw attached internally to the trigger. To prevent the musket becoming useless by the extinction of its match, it was usual to keep both ends alight, one in the jaws of the 'lock' and one in the musketeer's hand, with a spare length of match wrapped around his waist or hung on his bandolier. *In extremis*, match could be improvised; before Roundway Down, Hopton made his from all the bed cords in Devizes!

Loading the heavy musket via the muzzle with powder, ball and 'wadding' (to prevent the ball rolling out) was a slow but uncomplicated manoeuvre, but musket drill involved up to four dozen 'postures'. Again, these were of use principally for ceremonial occasions; a musketeer of any competency would know, without having to be ordered, how to prepare his weapon for firing, to load and prime it, to blow on the match until it glowed red, to aim and fire, so that instructions in action would be reduced to 'Make ready' (adjust and blow upon match), 'Present' (aim), and 'Give fire'. Because of the weight of the musket it was usual to employ a 'rest', a spike-ended pole with a U-shaped end which would be tied to the musketeer's wrist and used to support the barrel when planted vertically in the ground, with the musket resting in the U. Throughout the Civil Wars, use of the rest declined as muskets became progressively more manageable. Designs of stock varied from the early, curved-butted variety, which would be fired with the butt 'just before above his left pappe'[24], to the modern, straight-butted type, positioned with the butt on the right shoulder. The cost of a new musket with fittings was set in 1632 at 15s. 6d., and 10d. for the rest, though in 1645 the New Model was buying muskets at 10s. each. There was no standardization of bore, despite attempts like that of 1639 when the ordnance officers recommended lighter muskets (3½-foot (1.1-metre) barrel, 10¼ to 11 pounds (4.6 to 5 kilogrammes) in weight, with reduced charges to lessen recoil), to which the Council of War responded by ordering 5,000 muskets with 4½-foot (1.4-metre) barrels at 14 pounds (6.4 kilogrammes) and 10,000 with 3½-foot (1.1-metre) barrels at 12 pounds (5.4 kilogrammes); and in 1643 the King commanded that 'the Musquets be all of a Bore, the Pikes of a length', but as matériel was scarce these orders were only to come into effect when 'the Arms shall be decayed, and must be renewed'[25]. Nevertheless, the heavy lead ball (10 to the

PLATE 5

11 Officer, Royalist horse
12 Trooper, King's Lifeguard 1642

The costume of the officer is based, in part, upon a portrait of Sir John Byron by William Dobson, except that the man illustrated wears double-thickness upper sleeves to his buff-coat, and a triple-barred helmet. The enormous sash knot is a feature shown in a number of contemporary portraits.

The trooper belongs to the King's Lifeguard, which apparently wore a costume sufficiently uniform to be nicknamed (much to their disgust) 'the Troop of Shew'. In January 1643 their equipment comprised a breastplate, backplate, 'head-peece' and 'gorgett', the whole termed 'an horse armour' or 'one Corslett'[1]. Possibly some of this unit wore cuirassier armour, as it was composed exclusively of nobles, gentry and their retainers; at Edgehill the two troops of Lifeguard, about 300 strong, formed a squadron the estates of whose members were reckoned to be worth £100,000 per annum. Amongst the troopers at Edgehill were included the Earls of Denbigh and Dover, Lord Capel and the M.P. Sir Philip Warwick. The Lifeguard served throughout the war and was particularly distinguished at Cropredy Bridge, where it numbered about 100. The trooper illustrated wears the usual 'breast-and-back' with the addition of gorget and tassets, a 'Dutch pot' helmet with fixed peak and single (sliding) nasal bar, and included amongst his horse furniture is a rolled cloak strapped to the rear of the saddle, and 'in his oat sack three or four baits of oats or bread for his horse, and provision for himself'[2].

NOTES

1 See Young, Brig. P. *Edgehill, 1642* (Kineton, 1967) p. 28
2 Sir John Conyers to Capt. John Mennes of Wilmot's Horse, August 1641; *Calendar of State Papers 1641–43*, p. 72, and see Young, *Edgehill*, p. 170

pound tight-fitting or 12 to the pound 'rowling') could inflict the most terrible injuries.

Increasingly in use were firearms with more modern methods of ignition. Some wheel lock muskets (even rifled ones) may have been used by officers, but were expensive and difficult to maintain, having a complex mechanism in which the gun was 'cocked' ready for firing by means of a spanner used to turn the wheel mechanism which ignited the charge by producing a spark when the serrated wheel revolved against a piece of pyrites. The wheel lock was prone to jamming or breaking if left cocked (or 'spanned') for any length of time, 'too curious and too soone distempered with an ignorant hand'[26]. More popular was the 'snaphance' mechanism, an early flintlock, in which a spark was struck to ignite the charge when a piece of flint, held in the jaws of the 'cock', crashed down upon a 'steel'. The name snaphance reputedly came from the Dutch *snaphaan* or 'snapping hen', which the cock resembled, but more common names included 'dog lock', named from the 'dog' or safety-catch which prevented the cock

PLATE 5

11 Officer, Royalist horse   12 Trooper, King's Lifeguard 1642

A

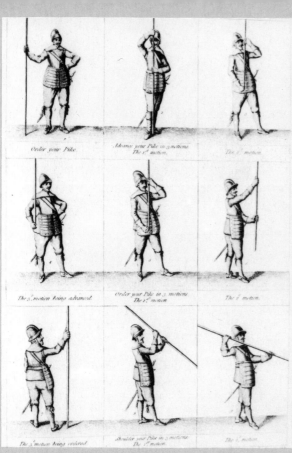

C

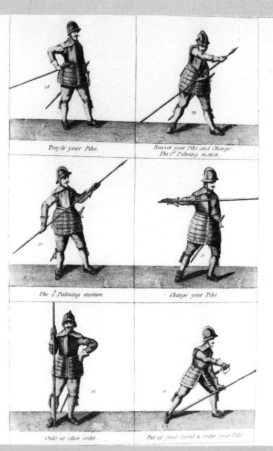

Wheel lock musket, mid 17th century (Wallis & Wallis)

from moving accidentally, or 'English lock', named because it was so popular in this country, incorporating a combined 'steel' and pan cover. These muskets, or 'firelocks', were more expensive than the matchlock (the New Model paid up to 15s. 6d. each in 1645) but infinitely better, preventing the stray sparks which always blew from lighted matches (thus troops guarding munitions and artillery trains were armed, whenever possible, with firelocks), easier to use, more waterproof, invisible at night when lighted matches might 'bewray Enterprizes'[27] and, in Orrery's words, with a firelock 'you have only to cock and are prepared to shoot'. Other firearms were in limited use; a few 'birding pieces' were used by snipers (500 fowling pieces with five-foot (1.5-metre) barrels were ordered for service in Scotland in 1652), mostly privately-owned items in the hands of ex-gamekeepers and chosen marksmen. At Lathom House and Sherborne Castle, for example, the defenders sniped enemy officers and gunners very successfully, but one supposed example, the killing of Lord Brooke at Lichfield in 1643, shot through his open window, was apparently achieved by a deaf-mute (Sir Richard Dyott's son) or 'a common soldier with a musket'[28] rather than by a trained sniper. Monck considered that each company should include six men armed with 'Fouling-pieces' to act upon the flanks and pick off enemy officers[29]. Some fowling pieces had rifled barrels, which had been produced for over a century, but these and such curiosities like breechloaders and even repeaters were rare. Differing calibres led to problems with ammunition, musketeers having to use 'pruning-irons' or even chew their musket balls to make them fit, but in extremis, as at Goodrich Castle, even stones could be fired.

Due to the lack of accurate statistics, it is difficult to assess the effectiveness of musketry. Muskets were wildly inaccurate but when firing at a target several times bigger than the proverbial barn door, a volley at close range could do appalling damage; witness the shattering of Pappenheim's cavalry at Breitenfeld (1631) by Swedish musketry. As late as the Napoleonic Wars the 'common musket' had a maximum effective range of between 200 and 300 yards (183 and 274 metres), whilst Roquerol's *L'artillerie au début des guerres de la Revolution* estimates that only 0.2 to 0.5 per cent of bullets

Musketeer with matchlock musket, with match detached and showing use of forked rest. Style of clothing predates Civil War (engraving after de Gheyn)

Pike exercise: A, part 1; B, part 2; C, part 3; D, part 4 (engravings by N.C. Goodnight after Hexham's *Principles of the Art Militarie* (1637))

fired hit their target. In the seventeenth century various methods of 'giving fire' were employed, including those in which each rear rank of musketeers would move between the forward ranks and fire, so attempting to maintain more or less continuous fusillade, two shots per minute being about the average; when advancing, this tactic was known as 'Fire by Introduction', and when retiring, 'by Extraduction'. Other methods included formation three-deep (as employed by the Irish Brigade at Tippermuir, to make possible one massive volley), or even one volley fired from six- or eight-deep ranks, to 'pour as much Lead in your enemies bosom at one time ... do them more mischief, you quail, daunt, and astonish them ... one long and continuated crack of Thunder is more terrible and dreadful to mortals then ten interrupted and several ones ...'[30].

The musketeer's equipment usually included a buff-leather bandolier from which hung a number of wooden or leather tubes, each containing a measured amount of powder sufficient for one shot, which the musketeer could pour directly into the muzzle of his musket. These tubes, known from their usual number as the 'Twelve Apostles', were a constant hazard; when moving or in a strong wind a regiment's tubes would rattle together so much as to announce the presence of the corps and even drown shouted orders; worse still, they could accidentally take fire, damaging the wearer and all around him and causing (in Gwyn's words) 'an incredible confusion'[31]. On the bandolier went one or two powder flasks (one to use when the 'Twelve Apostles' ran out and one to take finely-ground priming powder), a bullet bag, priming wire to clean the touchhole of the musket, and often a small oil bottle; total cost of this assemblage in 1629 was set at 2s. 6d., but the New Model bought many in 1645 at half that price. More efficient methods of carrying ammunition were coming into use; for example, after listing the defects of the 'Twelve Apostles' Lord Orrery recommends the use of prepared cartridges

Matchlock mechanism, the smouldering match poised above powder in pan

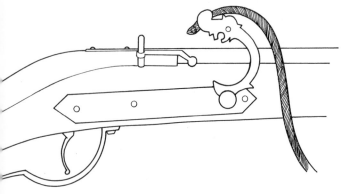

PLATE 6

13 Colonel Alexander Popham
14 Trooper, Popham's Horse

Preserved at Littlecote House in Wiltshire is a remarkable collection of buff-coats and weaponry, the equipment of the troop of horse and regiment of foot formed by Colonel Alexander Popham, who features in this plate, taken from a contemporary portrait. Despite the artistic convention which often demanded that commanders be depicted in armour, the harness illustrated includes a number of singular features which suggest that it was actually worn. Note the matching horse furniture and sword belt, the latter supporting a broad-bladed sabre or hanger, a weapon which probably saw considerable service in the Civil War. The black-enamelled armour includes defences for the lower leg and foot instead of the usual boots, though only the left gauntlet is armoured. Popham carries the usual bâton of office, and visible on the original portrait is a crescent-shaped silver plate on the horse's head strap.

The trooper wears classic 'harquebusier' equipment, though it is likely that few troops were accoutred so well as Popham's; as described by Monck, it comprised: 'A Carbine, or a Musquet-barrel of the length of a Carbine-barrel, well stockt with a Snapance: the which I hold to be much better than a Carbine for Service. Also a case of Pistols, and a good stiff long Tuck, and a belt ... An Head-Piece with three small iron Bars to defend the Face, Back, and Breast; all three Pistol proof: a Gauntlet for his left hand, and a good long Buff Glove ...'[1]. Cruso's description of the harquebusier is similar, with 'the harquebuse of two foot and a half [76 centimetres] long (the bore of 17 bullets in the pound [37 per kilogramme] rowling in) hanging on a belt by a swivell ... His horse ... should be not under 15 hand high, being swift and well managed'[2], and he notes the 'carabinier' in the same mould, save that the carbine or 'petronell' should have 24 bullets in the pound (53 per kilogramme). In 1629 regulated prices stood at £3 for a pair of firelock pistols and all equipment, £2 for a pair of snaphance pistols, £1 16s. for a firelock harquebus, belt and equipment, and £1 for a snaphance carbine[3]. The contract books of the New Model Army give other details: three-barred English helmets 8s. each, 'backs brests and potts' at 20s. a 'suite'[4], pistols and holsters at 18 to 26s. a pair, 'snaphaunce pistolls full bore & [pro]ofe with holsters of Calveskins inside & outside well sewed & liquored at xx[s] iiii[d] a payre'[5], carbines 12s. 9d. each, swords and belts 4s. 8d. each, and carbine belts 'of good leather & strong buckles'[6], 8d. each.

NOTES
1 Monck, General G. (1st Duke of Albemarle) *Observations upon Military and Political Affairs* (London, 1671) p. 24
2 Cruso, pp. 30–31
3 Grose, vol. II, p. 336
4 New Model Army Contract Books; *Journal of the Arms and Armour Society*, VI (1968) 103–4
5 *Ibid.*, pp. 196–7
6 *Ibid.*, p. 91

PLATE 6

13 Col. Alexander Popham   **14 Trooper, Popham's Horse**

(paper tubes each containing enough powder for one shot), in which 'by biting off the bottom of the cartridge, you charge your musket with one ramming'[32], and, by loading the paper as well, prevent the ball from rolling out of the barrel; musketeers using the older system, claimed Orrery, seldom added any 'wadding' to hold the ball in place, for ''tis to that I attribute the little execution I have seen musketeers do in time of fight'[33]. The cartridges were carried in boxes, usually on a waistbelt, often under the coat to keep out rain, for which reason Orrery recommended tin boxes instead of wood. Grose calculated that the use of cartridges could treble the rate of fire. Monck noted that if bandoliers were unavailable, musketeers should have 'twelve Carthrages ... in their right-hand pockets, and twelve Bullets apiece in their pockets besides'[34], though Davies condemned the English practice of carrying loose ammunition in the pockets, the cartridges 'doth shed and loose his powder ... or else is cloddered and rammed together'[35]; he also recommended waterproof match pipes, said to have been invented by Prince Maurice of Orange, to ensure that 'the coale by wet or water go not out'[36]. Turner remarked that the use of waterproof bags to hold 'Patrons' (cartridges) was limited largely to Germany. The quantity of ammunition carried varied with supply, but in November 1642 the Earl of Northampton's regiment was issued with 'Ech man his bandiliers full'[37], amounting to 90 pounds (41 kilogrammes) of powder and 180 pounds (82 kilogrammes) of ball for 180 men; in addition, each company had powder bags upon which its men could draw, 'two great bougets made of dry neats leather, which will hold a hundred weight of powder apeece'[38].

Musketeers' helmets were redundant before the Civil War, though some may have been used in the early stages; they were, said Davies, 'a burthen, more beautiful than beneficiall, and of greater charge than commoditie', making the wearers 'more apt to rest, than

Powder flask of engraved cow horn (Wallis & Wallis)

ready to fight'[39]; in any case, Monck said that a musketeer's best defence was 'a good Courage'. The musketeer's sword, 'a good stiff Tuck not very long'[40] was considered 'despicable'[41] by Turner, who recommended instead that they used the musket butt as a club, which seems to have been an acknowledged British tactic, Louis de Gaya's *Traité des Armes* (1678) saying of them, *Les Fantassins ne se servent presque pas d'Epees, et quand ils ont fair la décharge du Mousquet, ils se battent à coups de Crosse*[42]. With bayonets not yet invented, attempts were made to turn the musket rest into a weapon by incorporating a spike or even a hidden blade, but these proved 'extremely troublesome to themselves, *dangerous* to their *followers*'[43], a statement echoed by Turner who thought rests in general 'more troublesome than helpful'[44]; even worse were attempts to give musketeers a half-pike instead of a rest, but 'one of them was *enough* to trouble a whole *file*'[45]. A compromise was to equip the musketeer with a 'swine-feather' or 'Swedish feather', a five- or six-foot (1.5- or 1.8-metre) stake with a pike head on each end, that was planted like a palisade or even used as a short pike; it was recommended by Monck and Turner (who thought a regiment thus equipped made 'a delightful show, representing a Wood, the Pikes resembling the tall trees, and the Stakes the shrubs'[46]) but was never popular as the musketeer had enough to carry without the extra burden.

Continental matchlock musket with rifled barrel, dated 1619, with forked rest which includes match holder, presumably to allow it to double as linstock (Wallis & Wallis)

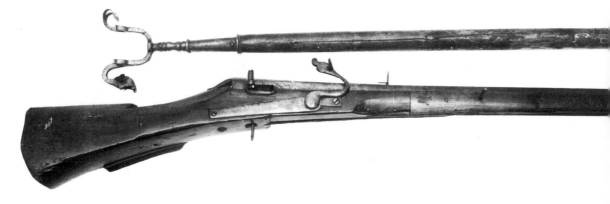

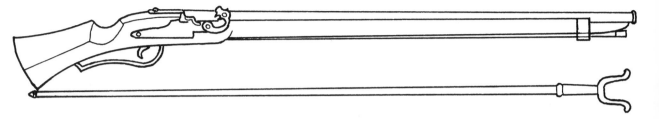

Matchlock musket with rest

Initially, equipment was gathered from the local trained band armouries and from the private collections of adherents to either side. Later in the war, arms were imported or made to order (in 1645, for example, the New Model ordered at least 15,950 matchlocks, 2,300 firelocks, 8,800 pikes, 25,200 bandoliers, 12,400 swords and 1,100 corselets and helmets), but (particularly in the Royalist forces, ill-supplied throughout) equipment in the early stages was sometimes rudimentary and, when drawn from Parish armouries, often antique. Some trained bands (those of London and provincial corps like Great Yarmouth) maintained their equipment well, but elsewhere it was outdated and in poor repair. Totnes' store in 1626 included 33 corselets, 97 muskets, 13 'callyvers' and 95 halberds[47], and many examples of wretched equipment can be quoted: armour worn thin by years of cleaning, 'only fitt to hang over the skreene in a halle the whole age of a man ere yt be taken downe'[48], 'very rawlie furnished, some whereof lacketh a headpiece, somme a sworde, somme one thing or other that is evill, unfitt, or unbeseeminge about him'[49]. The mediocre state of such armouries gave great advantage to whichever side could secure the great state armouries such as that of the Tower (which gave Parliament an early advantage) and Hull, the arsenal for the Scottish war and the object of much manoeuvring to appoint a friendly governor. Strafford, as Lord-Lieutenant, engineered the appointment of Sir Thomas Glemham in September 1640, but he was removed by Parliament in the following July and replaced by Sir John Hotham, whose refusal to admit the King in April 1642 denied the Royalists the use of the Hull arsenal. Private armouries yielded many weapons to the King, but these were often of poor quality; the armoury surveyed at Tutbury Castle in 1608, for example, was composed largely of items 'cancered, rotten, and not worth anie thing saveing the heades of bills, pikes, and some few callivers, but all eaten with cancer'[50]. Other gifts and levies were better; the father of Anthony Wood at Oxford supplied 'the armour or furniture on one man, viz.: a helmet, a back and breast-piece, a pyke, and musket, and other appurtenances, and the eldest of his man-servants ... did appear in those armes, and much ado there was to keep Thomas the eldest son ... from putting on the said

armour ...'[51], and at the start of the war a Captain Robert Millington alone presented the King with 80 muskets.

Despite Charles' earlier attempts to keep Royal munitions in good repair, preventing them from being tampered with by 'cutlers, smyths, tynkers, and other botchers of armes'[52] so that 'wee may not be inforced in tyme of warre to seeke for armes, armours, gunnes, pikes, and bandaliers, in forraine parts'[53], importation was employed by both factions, though with limited

PLATE 7

15 Edward Massey, officer, Parliamentary horse
16 Nathaniel Fiennes, officer, Parliamentary horse
17 Officer, Parliamentary horse

The left-hand figure is based in some respects upon Lely's portrait of Edward Massey (1619?–74?), the capable and energetic Parliamentary governor of Gloucester and a Royalist leader in 1651. His breast- and backplates are supplemented by a close helmet, similar to that shown by Lely but with a face bar attached; whilst the lobster-tail helmet was most common, numbers of close helmets with semi-open faces were also used. Unlike the plain basket-hilted sword shown by Lely, this illustration shows a Venetian-style 'schiavona' with a decorative hilt.

The centre figure is taken from a portrait of Nathaniel Fiennes by Mirevelt. He wears a set of matching, blackened armour with gilt rivets, comprising lobster-tail helmet (the peak and face bar pushed back, as usual when not engaged in combat), back- and breastplates with attached tassets (so short to enable wear on horseback), and an elbow-gauntlet to protect the bridle hand. The buff-coat has double-thickness sleeves, the thicker outer sleeve being cut off at the left elbow to accomodate the gauntlet, with a cut-out portion inside the right elbow to facilitate bending the arm. The knotted neck-cloth affords extra protection, and the officer bears a bâton of office and wears the orange-tawny sash of Essex's army. The dent in the breastplate is an armourer's proof-mark, certifying it able to turn a musket ball.

The right-hand figure wears a sleeved buff-coat with narrow loops of metallic lace on the arms, a popular style which has given rise to the misconception that striped uniforms were worn! The coat is fastened by metal clasps on the breast. He is shown 'spanning' (cocking) his wheel lock pistol, the spanner being slung around the body on a coloured cord.

PLATE 7

15 Edward Massey   16 Nathaniel Fiennes   17 Officer, Parliamentary horse

PLATE 8

18 19 20 Troopers of horse

PLATE 8

18, 19, 20 Troopers of horse

One of the men illustrated (18) wears civilian dress, the cos-tume of a gentleman's outdoor servants, with only his hat ribbon proclaiming his allegiance. The back view shows the flexible lobster-tail of a typical cavalry helmet. Two men (19 and 20) wear the ubiquitous buff-coat, one with sleeves of thinner (and thus more supple) leather, fastened tightly at the wrist; both coats have flared skirts to ensure that the legs would remain covered when sitting astride a saddle. A typical buff-coat with detachable sleeves is described in the Verney Papers[1]:

16 Mar. 1638.	
For Collr & belypeeces & hookes & eyes to a buffe coate	00:02:06
For makeing ye buff coate with 2 paire of sleeues & hose last all ouer	01:15:00
More for 2 shambo skins to make a par sleeues	00:12:00
For buckrum to ym	00:02:00
For gould & silluer Butts to yr 2 paire of sleeue hands & ye hose befor	00:03:00

Cavalry boots were at first of buff or light brown supple leather, but were later blackened and stiffened into the jack-boot or 'gambado' with wide, rigid tops to prevent the knees being crushed in action. The trooper on the right carries a mass-produced and crudely-finished broadsword with a sim-ple iron hilt.

NOTES

1 Quoted in Waugh, N. *The Cut of Men's Clothes* (London, 1964) pp. 44–5

success by the Royalists due to Parliament's control of the navy. Nevertheless, the King did obtain foreign matériel; in February 1643, for example, the Queen arrived at Bridlington with arms for 10,000 men and 32 cannon from Holland, and in 1645 a cargo of Flemish goods landed at Falmouth included 6,040 muskets, 2,000 brace of pistols, 1,200 carbines, 150 swords and great quantities of match and brimstone. Other cargoes were intercepted by Parliament, such as one from Denmark in 1643 which included 2,977 muskets, 493 pistols, 3,040 swords, 3,000 helmets, 1,500 pikes, 3,000 musket rests, 476 barrels of gunpowder, 990 bundles of match and a firkin of pistol keys. Parliament also imported munitions, either centrally or by local orga-nizations, such as the £8,000-worth bought from the Netherlands by the Eastern Association in 1644. All this foreign weaponry prevented any standardization of calibre or pattern and resulted in such inconveniences as French pistols proving too long for English holsters! Weapons could also be salvaged from battlefields, such as the 4,500 muskets and 800 pikes gained by the Eastern Association after Marston Moor.

Fig. A
Musket exercise, part 1 (engraving by N.C. Goodnight after Hexham's *Principles of the Art Militarie* (1637))

Fig. B
Musket exercise, part 2 (engraving by N.C. Goodnight after Hexham's *Principles of the Art Militarie* (1637))

Fig. C
Musket exercise, part 3 (engraving by N.C. Goodnight after Hexham's *Principles of the Art Militarie* (1637))

Fig. D
Musket exercise, part 4 (engraving by N.C. Goodnight after Hexham's *Principles of the Art Militarie* (1637))

Fig. E
Musket exercise, part 5 (engraving by N.C. Goodnight after Hexham's *Principles of the Art Militarie* (1637))

A

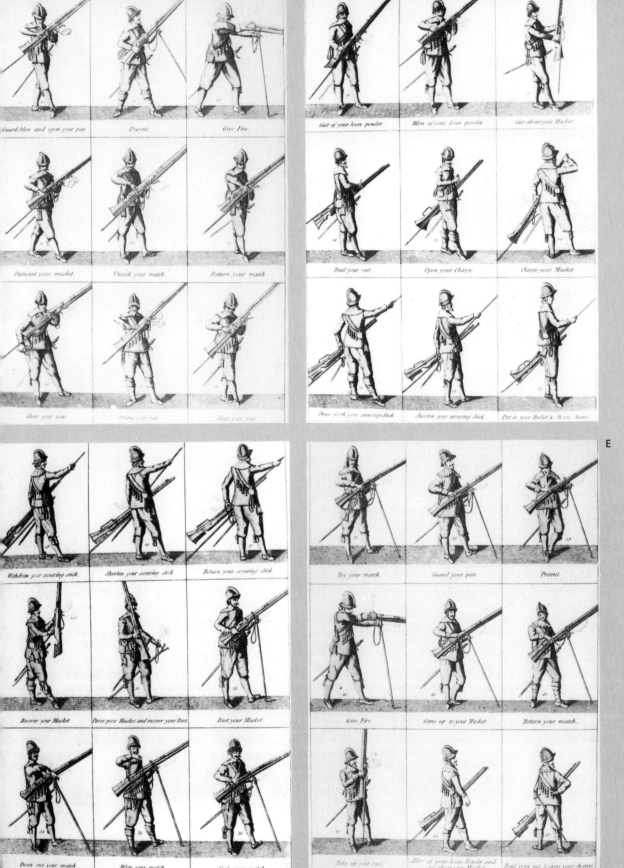

PLATE 9

21 Trumpeter, Lord Hopton's Lifeguard 1644
22 Cornet, Royalist horse

The trumpeter was a relic of the medieval herald; in theory his function was still pacific, as an envoy, messenger and scrutineer of the chivalry of war. As Markham wrote: 'The trumpet is not bound to any armes at all, more than his sword, which in former times was not allowed, but with the point broken: he shall have a faire trumpet, with cordens suitable to his captaine's colours, and to his trumpet shall be made fast a faire banner, containing his captaine's full coat armour; he may weare a scarfe and feather, and all other ordinary accoutrements of a horseman; and for his horse, it shall be a good hackney, with gentleman-like furniture'[1]. A trumpeter 'must also be discreet and judicious; not only to be fit to deliver embassies and messages as they ought, but (at his return) to report what he hath observed concerning the enemies works … he must be wittie and subtile …'[2] and 'must drink but little'[3]! The old courtesies of chivalric war had all but disappeared, however; when the King's herald (Sir William Le Neve, Clarencieux King-at-Arms) was sent to the Parliamentary commanders at Edgehill with the offer of a free pardon, he was manhandled and ridiculed for his insistence upon the knightly virtues of the 'laws' of war. The trumpeters' rôle changed accordingly, but their costume retained the grandeur of the medieval herald, a coat with unfastened, hanging sleeves so becoming their hallmark that by the eighteenth century it was usual for musicians to have imitation sleeves sewn to the shoulders of their coat. Another distinctive insignia may be recorded in the York Chamberlains' Rolls in 1644: 'For redeeming Ed. Trumpeters badge per order of Court 10s'[4]. The trumpeter illustrated wears a rich uniform and fine sword; Lord Hopton's Lifeguard (when he was General of the Ordnance in 1644) had a red standard bearing a gold firing cannon, with the motto *Et Sacris Compescuit Ignibus Ignes*, and it is likely that the troop's trumpet banner would bear the same device, though Hopton's own standard bore the motto 'I will strive to serve my soveraigne King'.

The Cornet bears his troop standard upon a lance, fluted for part of its length and with a handgrip; in Continental fashion, his stirrup has a 'bucket' for the lance butt, but in England it was probably more usual to bear the lance with the butt resting upon the saddle or the rider's thigh. A D-shaped bracket attaches the lance to the standard belt's spring clip. The standard is a recorded example, captured at Marston Moor, of an unidentified troop.

There was no standard pattern of horse furniture, though in 1628 Charles I had required saddlers to submit to the Council of War saddles made to a design of Lord Wimbledon; but during the Civil War any were pressed into service. The use of the 'Great Saddle' being restricted, lighter patterns were more common, the 'Hackney' with an iron tree, the 'French pad' with a down-stuffed seat, and the 'lightest and nimblest' similar to a modern hunting saddle. Monck recommended 'a good pad saddle … three good Girts, a pair of good Stirrups, and Stirrup-leathers; with a crupper, and a Fore-Pattern: also a good bitt, Rains, and Head-stall, with a good leathern halter'[5]; such a saddle is shown in the monument to Sir Jacob Astley, with a square saddle-cloth underneath, the most common type in use. Saddles ordered by the New Model Army included types described as 'Padsaddles with two Loopes behind and noe great Buckles for the Crupper'[6], 'Padsaddles with good iron plates and stran bitts'[7], 'furnished wᵗʰ strand bitts large trees, well plated wᵗʰ iron, & 3 girses'[8], ranging in price from 16s. 6d. to 18s.; dragoons' saddles, like their horses, were much cheaper and inferior, being 7s. 6d. each. In 1627 Charles I forbade the snaffle bridle except for sport, the curb bits used at other times ensuring that the horsemen of England were used to exerting the utmost control over their mounts and thus fit for war.

NOTES

1 See Grose, vol. I, p. 267
2 Cruso, p. 14
3 Turner, p. 235
4 Wenham, P. *The Great and Close Siege of York, 1644* (Kineton, 1970) p. 176.
5 See Tylden, pp. 117–20
6 New Model Army Contract Books, 10 April 1645, *Journal of the Arms and Armour Society* VI (1968) 112
7 *Ibid.*, p. 113 (3 April 1645)
8 *Ibid.*, p. 114 (3 April 1645)

Nevertheless, the condition of some regiments, particularly Royalist ones, was wretched. In the early stages Clarendon records that even after the appropriation of private armouries (usually 'very mean'[54]), borrowing from trained bands 'with so much wariness and caution'[55] and the purchase from Holland of 800 muskets, 1,000 pistols and 200 swords, many of the King's foot carried no other weapon than a cudgel; the rest were 'with muskets and bags for the powder and pikes; but in the whole body there was not one pikemen had a corselet, and very few musketeers who had swords'[56], and others had 'no Arms but Pitchforks, and such like Tools'[57]. Prince Rupert's Foot in 1644 were 'very poor and ragged, very many no arms but swords'[58].

When even antiquated staff weapons like 'brownbills' were unavailable, 'clubs' might be issued, a term probably indicating the old quarterstaff, which had its champions as late as 1803 ('train yourselves to wield a Pitchfork, or a Hedge-stake … practice the old English cudgel-play and quarter staff …'[59]); the King's army in 1643 included 2,000 Welsh clubmen who were to be armed from the Bristol arsenal. Agricultural weapons like pitchforks, scythes and flails were used (as later at Sedgemoor) by such corps as the Parliamentary 'Moorland Dragoons', who formed on their own initiative in the Leek area and were armed with birding guns, clubs and pieces of scythes. Halberds were carried by sergeants as rank distinctions, and small hatchets (Monck

PLATE 9

QUARTA PERENNIS ERIT

22 Cornet, Royalist horse

21 Trumpeter, Lord Hopton's Lifeguard 1644

recommended one between two men) were used for wood cutting to prevent damaging the swords. Explosive hand grenades (recommended by Monck for use on the flanks of each pike division, 'a great advantage, if they were boldly and well thrown'[60]) saw limited use and were employed mostly for clearing buildings as at Bristol in 1643 when Westbury Church was taken by grenading out the defenders. (The use of the term 'granadoes' in the Civil War era was also applied to mortar bombs.) The traditional longbow was still used in some areas, notably Scotland and Ireland, but was hardly a practicable alternative to the musket due to the great length of time needed to train an archer. In 1625 William Nead published *The Double Armed Man*, proposing to equip soldiers with a bow and a pike, but complained that the only encouragement he received for this project was from God! Ward's *Animadversions of Warre* gave qualified support for the continued use of archery (particularly as bowmen could shoot in wet weather, when often musketeers could not), and in the late 1620s Suffolk and Norfolk urged that trained bands revive archery to 'amaze and trouble' any invader. In November 1643 Essex considered raising a company of archers, and in 1642 a company of archers and pikemen was formed in Hereford. Otherwise, bows were used mainly for firing messages into beleaguered towns or to burn them down, though fire arrows could be launched from muskets. Archery was used in combat (an arrow landed between Sir Jacob Astley's feet at Devizes), but a petition to Charles I from bowyers and fletchers urging the King to fight the war with archery to revive their declining business was unsuccessful!

Organization of units of foot varied between regiments, there being little standardization in armies which comprised both formed regiments and semi-independent companies which could be 'regimented' or detached when the occasion demanded; in many cases soldiers probably regarded themselves as members of Captain X's company first and Colonel Y's regiment second. Several rules were observed generally, including that 'the tallest, biggest and strongest should be order'd to carry Pikes, that they may the better endure the weight of their defensive Arms ... I have known Muskets given to those of the biggest stature, and Pikes to the unworthiest and silliest of the Company, as if he who is not worthy to carry a Musket were sufficient to carry a Pike ...'[61]. Markham's *Souldiers Grammar* (1626) and Bariffe's *Military Discipline* (1639) state that the number of pikemen and musketeers in each company should be equal, but when Edward Harley was commissioned to raise a regiment for Parliament in 1643, two-thirds were to be musketeers, a proportion adopted by the New Model. Monck believed that equal numbers were necessary for action in the open field (two-thirds musketeers for siege warfare), as pikemen could only protect musketeers properly if equal in numbers, and it is possible that the Royalists adopted these

proportions more readily than Parliament due to shortages of firearms. Some regiments eventually dispensed with pikemen altogether, such as Montrose's Irish Brigade and Sir Thomas Fairfax's Lifeguard, and in September 1643 the Yellow Auxiliaries had at least two companies composed of 112 musketeers to only 20 pikemen. Ideally, a regiment comprised 10 companies, though eight was probably as common and perhaps easier to control in the field, but circumstances reduced or increased this number; for example, in the Marston Moor campaign the Earl of Manchester's army included one regiment (Manchester's own) with 19 companies, four with ten, one with nine and one with eight, and whilst Leven's Scots probably had 10-company regiments, one had only five (the Minister's Regiment).

Companies were commanded by a field officer or captain, with an ideal strength of a captain, a lieutenant, an ensign (who carried the company colour), a 'gentleman-of-the-arms' (responsible for maintenance of the weaponry, an appointment perhaps peculiar to the Royalists), two sergeants, three corporals and two drummers; the colonel's company would contain 200 men, the lieutenant-colonel's 160, the major's 140 and each captain's 100. Total strength thus numbered just over 1,300. Regimental staff of Parliamentary regiments included quartermaster, chaplain, provost marshal, 'chirurgion' and mate, carriage master and drum major; most companies of the Eastern Association acquired in addition a clerk and two or three 'lanspassadoes', perhaps originally gentlemen-volunteers acting as supernumerary N.C.O.s. Royalist regiments usually had a quartermaster. These strengths were rarely attained in the field, though some regiments were even stronger: in August 1642 Essex's numbered 1,500, and in September 1643 the Red Regiment of London trained bands mustered 1,084 musketeers, 854 pikemen and 80 officers, and the Green Auxiliaries 1,200. The strongest Royal regiment in 1642 was apparently the 'twelve hundred poor Welsh vermin, the offscourings of this nation'[62], and towards the end of that year Royalist regiments varied between Salisbury's 910 and Sir John Beaumont's 320, with an average around 590 men. The regimentation of semi-independent companies appears to have precluded amalgamations of under-strength companies; in March 1644 two of Waller's regiments appeared to exemplify this point, Waller's own regiment having companies ranging from 93 to 41 strong, and Weldon's from 92 to 49 per company. The Eastern Association, for example, usually formed new companies instead of reinforcing existing ones; thus in September 1644 Montagu's regiment had six companies with full complements of officers and N.C.O.s but less than 30 men each, two with only 11! Strengths of the Association's regiments in 1644–5 varied between Manchester's (1,628 in May 1644) to Pickering's 243 in January 1645. Declining company strength is shown by Captain Harvey's company of Hobart's Regiment, which was

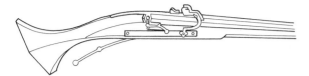

Matchlock musket of old style, with a 'sear' bar trigger

107 strong in March 1644 and was reinforced by 25 men in May and 55 in October; by January 1645 only 27 of the originals, two of the May and 17 of the October reinforcements, were still serving. Prince Rupert's Bluecoats, about 500 in number, was one of the *strongest* Royal regiments at Naseby. Such decline in numbers could result in the combination of two or more regiments to form a single unit, for example Millward's 'division' at Marston Moor (probably an *ad hoc* assembly of companies from Millward's, Frescheville's and Eyre's Derbyshire regiments), and Smith's 'Shrewsbury Foot' at Naseby, formed from the remnants of Tillier's, Broughton's, Warren's and Erneley's regiments.

In the field, regiments would be drawn up six- or eight-deep, the actual formation depending upon whether the commanding officer preferred Swedish or Dutch theories. In general, a regiment would form with its 'stand' of pikes in the centre and two equal bodies of musketeers on either flank; the distance between files would vary from 'Closest Order' (six inches (15 centimetres) apart) to 'Twice Double Distance' (24 feet (7.3 metres) apart), but 'Order' was usual, with files three feet (91 centimetres) apart and sufficient space for the men to use their weapons with ease. A regiment could be split into two or three 'divisions', each commanded by a field officer and each with pikes in the centre and muskets on the flanks, with skirmishing parties or 'forlorn hopes' of musketeers ahead of the main body, and other parties of musketeers withdrawn to protect the regimental baggage. Such regimental divisions might be arrayed in Swedish fashion, with one division withdrawn some distance to cover the gap between the first two, thus presenting a chequerboard appearance. For tactical purposes, regiments of foot could be 'brigaded' into three groups normally termed 'tertias' (or what we would call divisions), and the regiments within each tertia formed into groups of three, or 'brigades'.

HORSE

If Parliament enjoyed a superiority in foot, then (at least in the earlier part of the war) the best horse (cavalry) was that of the Royalists, drawn from country gentry and their servants who could turn out at short notice with little formal training necessary to produce adequate horse; for example, Richard Shuckburgh of

Shuckburgh was hunting on the day before Edgehill when the King asked for his help, whereupon he gathered his tenants immediately and joined the Royal army.

Arms and equipment consisted of the ubiquitous buff-coat (worn for hunting as well as fighting) with a breast- and backplate and often a helmet; Clarendon remarked that in 1642 'officers had their full desire if they were able to procure old backs and breasts and pots, with pistols or carbines for their two or three first ranks, and swords for the rest; themselves ... having gotten, besides their pistols and swords, a short pole-axe'[63]. The heavier armour was bulletproof, for if not 'either the Bullet pierceth through, or beats the Iron into the Horsemans body, which is equally dangerous; but if it be proof, it is exceeding troublesome to both man and horse'[64]. Many breastplates bore a deliberate dent, inflicted by a ball fired by the maker to prove their efficacy. Troops equipped with breast, back and helmet (and sometimes a metal gauntlet on the left forearm to protect the bridle hand) were often said to wear 'harquebusier' equipment, even though they no longer carried that firearm. Some thought the harquebusier should wear only a helmet, but in the Netherlands each man was ordered to have a breast- and backplate as well, which 'condemneth the late practice of our trained Harquebusiers to be erroneous, which have wholly left off their arms, and think themselves safe enough in a calfs skin coat'[65]. In 1629 harquebusier equipment was priced at:[66]

	s.	d.
A breast of pistoll proofe	ix	o
A backe	vii	o
A gorgett	iii	o
A Headpeece with great cheeks, and a barr before the face	xi	o

This equipment was never universal; some Parliamentary horse routed at Huntingdon in August 1645 was singled out because of wearing 'all of them back and breast, headpeice, brace of pistol, officers more'[67], whilst in 1642 Clarendon describes the King's 800 horse as 'few better armed than with swords'[68]. Markham's *Souldiers Accidence* states that harquebusiers should be 'the best of the first inferior degree ... best yeomen or serving men ...'[69].

Horse equipped in harquebusier style were generally regarded as the lighter cavalry (though some disagreed about what was 'light' or 'heavy'); if so, then 'heavy' cavalry was seen on few occasions, for their equipment was a direct descendent of the plate-armoured medieval knight. Styled 'cuirassiers' in the seventeenth century, they were completely encased in armour with the exception of the lower leg (usually covered by a long boot) and the rear of the thigh. It is uncertain how common cuirassier armour was, as artistic convention dictated that generals should be portrayed in full armour, a fashion which persisted until the nineteenth century and can

PLATE 10

23 Dragoon, New Model Army 1645
24 Cornet, Wardlawe's Dragoons 1643
25 Cornet, Essex's Horse 1643

The cornet of Essex's Horse wears a russeted breast- and backplate over a buff-coat, Essex's orange-tawny sash, and a hat with a white handkerchief around it as a field sign. His riding coat is worn over the armour, apparently a common practice; Sir John Smith (of Standard-rescue fame) was once assailed by a pitchfork-wielding peasant who did him no harm 'by reason of his armes under a loose coate'[1], and Atkyns records a skirmish in which 'the enemy were upon me, cutting my coat upon my armour in several places ...'[2]. The cornet's standard bears the popular device of an armoured, sword-bearing arm issuing from a cloud, with the motto *Cave Adsum*, literally meaning 'watch out, we're here', all upon Essex's orange-tawny field.

Dragoons were neither infantry nor cavalry proper; Turner reckoned them no more than infantry who rode into action, then dismounted to fight, and their status in the Eastern Association seems to have been that of foot, recruited partly by impressment. Examples exist of dragoons reverting to foot, but also of conversion to horse, whilst foot could be made into dragoons with apparently little difficulty, quite apart from the use of mounting foot on horseback to expedite their movement. Cruso described dragoons armed with pikes and matchlocks (though the former are not recorded as used in Britain and the latter doubtless replaced by firelocks whenever possible), with a horse 'of the least price, the use thereof being but to expedite his march, allighting to do his service'[3]. Markham's dragoon has a buff-coat and helmet, making him a cavalryman, though another writer remarks that 'dragooniers ... are to be as lightly armed as may be, and therefore they are onlie to have as followeth, calivers and powder flaskes'[4], yet encumbers him with two 56-inch (142-centimetre) swine-feathers with six-inch (15-centimetre) heads. Turner claims that the term 'dragoon' is derived from 'dragon', burning matches making a horseman appear thus, and that when fighting dismounted every tenth man acted as a horse holder. Most dragoon troopers probably wore uniforms like those of the foot, and though cavalry boots might be expected, infantry legwear may have been equally common. The New Model dragoon illustrated wears an infantry coat and bandolier (with the blue-painted cartridge tubes specified in the contract books), a scrap of paper as a field sign in his hat, and carries an English-lock musket and the 'good long tuck' recommended by Monck, who also believed they should carry swine-feathers and be equipped with a belt from which to hang the musket whilst mounted.

Extant records of dragoon costume include a description of John Lilburne (1648) wearing a 'short red coat'[5], whilst Lieutenant-Colonel James Carr, captured at Cirencester in February 1643, lost his personal belongings including a carbine, three pairs of pistols, 'one sute of Spanish Cloth layd with silver lace £7, A long Riding Coate of the same £2, A doublet of Buck Leather and breaches £3, A dutch Coat lyned with Foxes £4, A scarlett mantire [steel skull-cap] layd with silver lace 30s.'[6] The officer illustrated wears a gorget over his buff-coat, and a cloth cap (montero?) with furred flaps which could be let down in bad weather, probably with a steel cap or 'secrete' underneath; coloured caps were presumably not unknown, for the troop of 160 dragoons raised for the 1639 Scottish expedition were known as the 'Yorkshire Redcaps'. Dragoons carried small, double-ended guidons as illustrated, originating (according to Markham) as three-feet (0.9-metre) deep, six-feet (1.8-metre) long pennants, the ends of which could be cut off to form an oblong standard upon the owner's first act of valour, and reduced to a square upon the next occasion, a practice long redundant by the time of the Civil War as Markham notes with regret that its neglect caused Virtue to 'sit mourning at the ladder foot, because shee hath not one true round left to mount by'[7]. The plain guidon illustrated was the personal flag of Colonel Wardlawe (sometimes called 'Worley'), whose corps was largely Scottish. The other guidons of the unit bore the St George canton and a motto; for the lieutenant-colonel, for example, it was *Bella Beatorum Bellum*[8].

NOTES
1 Edward Walsingham, from *Brittannicae Virtutis Imago* (Oxford, 1644) quoted in Young, *Edgehill*, p. 296
2 Atkyns, R. *The Vindication of Richard Atkyns* (1669); see Atkyns, R. & Gwyn, J. *The English Civil War* ed. Young, P. & Tucker, N. (London, 1967) p. 9
3 Cruso, p. 31
4 *A Brief Treatise of War ... in the year of our redemption 1649*, MSS by 'W.T.', quoted by Grose
5 Quoted Young, *Edgehill*, p. 29
6 Quoted Adair, J. *Cheriton, 1644* (Kineton, 1973) p. 191
7 See Grose, vol. I, p. 268
8 See Milne, S.M. *Standards and Colours of the Army 1661–1881*

be misleading. For example, it appears that two portraits of Monck by Michael Wright, two of Charles II by Samuel Cooper, and one of the Earl of Manchester, probably all depict the same, very distinctive, armour, which was perhaps an artistic 'prop'. Probably the most common use of cuirassier armour was in detaching the breast- and backplates for use with a buff-coat and light helmet, which may explain why some extant suits lack these pieces; most who wore such armour were officers or gentlemen-troopers.

Cuirassier armour was extremely heavy; as James I remarked, armour was an excellent invention for it saved the life of the wearer and prevented him hurting anyone else! The weight probably contributed to the defeat at Roundway Down of one of the two units known to have worn it, Haselrig's 'lobsters', who could not face an incoming attack in time due to their cumbersome equipage. Edmund Ludlow of Essex's Lifeguard, the other cuirassier unit, noted that when unhorsed 'I could not without great difficulty recover on horse-back

PLATE 10

The flag shows the text: CAVE ADSVM

23 Dragoon, New Model Army 1645   24 Cornet, Wardlawe's Dragoons 1643   25 Cornet, Essex's Horse 1643

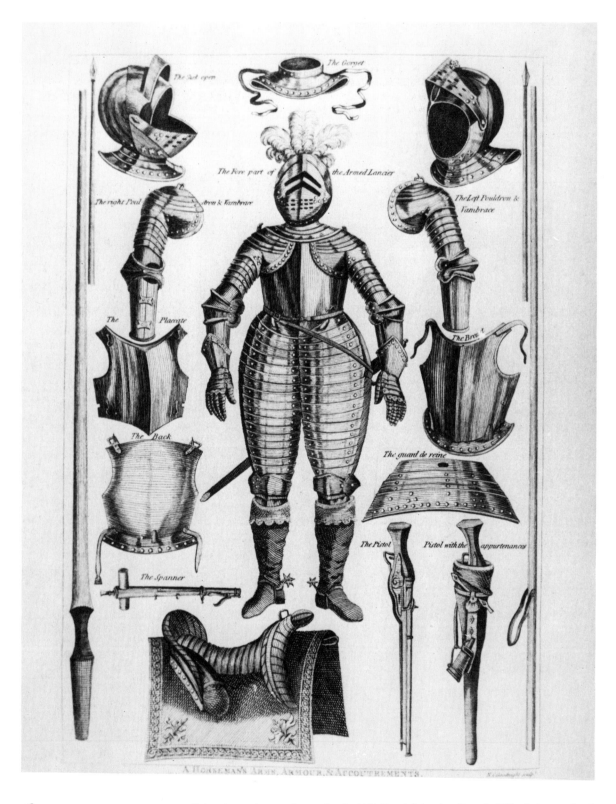

Cuirassier equipment (engraving by N.C. Goodnight after Cruso's *Militarie Instructions*)

again, being loaded with cuirassier's arms'[70]. When in 1639 Sir Edmund Verney was expected to take the field in cuirassier armour he refused, 'for it will kill a man to serve in a whole Curass. I am resolved to use nothing but back, brest and gauntlet; if I had a Pott for the Head that were Pistoll proofe it maye bee I would use it if it were light'[71]. Ironically, Verney seems to have had a premonition of death before Edgehill and was killed wearing neither armour nor buff-coat; Sir George Lisle at Second Newbury shed *his* armour and charged in his shirt for a different reason, to hearten his men. Because of the expense of cuirassier equipment (£4 10s. in 1629), 'these men ought to be of the best degree, because, the meanest in one of those troops, is ever by his place a gentleman'[72], but its efficacy is proven by Richard Atkyns' description of his fight at Roundway Down with Sir Arthur Haselrig himself. Haselrig, wearing armour like his 'regiment of Lobsters', resisted every shot and blow aimed at him: three point-blank pistol shots 'but a flea-biting to him', and numerous sword cuts. After his horse was killed, Haselrig tried to surrender, delaying whilst he attempted to free the sword tied to his wrist, but whilst 'fumbling a great deal' with the knot, he was rescued. The story was related to Charles I, who made a rare joke out of it, saying, 'Had he been victualled as well as fortified, he might have endured a siege of seven years'![73]. The Earl of Northampton when slain at Hopton Heath (1643) was so armoured that his enemies had to remove his helmet to kill him. The armoured cuirassier was sufficiently rare, however, for Monck to ignore them altogether, 'because there are not many Countries that do afford Horses fit for the Service of Cuirassiers'[74].

The cuirassier in Europe was armed with a lance, but this weapon was almost redundant long before the Civil Wars, largely because of the difficulties of finding suitable horses and of using the lance, 'a thing of much labour and industry to learn'[75]. The only lances known to have been used in the Civil Wars were in the hands of Scottish light cavalry, who employed them with some skill. The universal weapon was the sword, usually a heavy-bladed 'broadsword' with a semi-basket hilt, or a 'stiff Tuck' with a strong but lighter blade; the traditional 'gentleman's' weapon, the rapier, Turner says, 'In the time of the late Troubles in *England* ... were used for a while, and then laid aside'[76]. The poleaxe (or polehammer) noted by Clarendon does not seem to have been used extensively, but was the symbol of the Royal bodyguard of Gentlemen-Pensioners which served as a unit apparently only at Edgehill; Gentleman-Pensioner Mathews used his to despatch a Parliamentary cuirassier who had attempted to attack the Prince of Wales, but whose armour was impervious to sword blows.

The firearms used by horse consisted of pistols, carbines, and harquebuses; the two latter may be considered together, both having 2½-foot (76-centimetre) barrels and being suspended from a shoulder belt by

English close helmet with open face and fixed nasal bar (Wallis & Wallis)

means of a swivel, the former having bullets of 24 to the pound (53 per kilogramme) and the harquebus 17 per pound (37 per kilogramme), according to Cruso[77], though Markham classes them together as having 39-inch (99-centimetre) barrels and 20 balls to the pound (44 per kilogramme). The numbers of troops thus armed is unknown, but was certainly a minority of horse; in 1645, for example, the New Model bought only 1,502 carbines to 7,650 pairs of pistols. Both wheel and firelock mechanisms were used for cavalry firearms (the matchlock being largely unmanageable on horseback), with the firelock the most popular due to its simple mechanism and cheap cost. Many pistols were of the wheel lock type, either small 'dags' which 'sparked fire much like a match lighted with gunpowder'[78] as the wheel sparked against the pyrites, or longer, with barrels 'two foot for the longest, sixteen inches for the shortest'[79]; Cruso recommended 18-inch (46-centimetre) barrels with bullets 20 to the pound (44 per kilogramme), whilst Markham preferred 26-inch (66-

49

'Ancient Dragoon'; in actual fact, a trooper of horse with harquebusier equipment (engraving by N.C. Goodnight)

centimetre) barrels and 36 bullets to the pound (79 per kilogramme), and both state that although a horseman should be able to load his firearms from his flask, at least six prepared cartridges should be carried for convenience. The complexity of the wheel lock is reflected by the cost: in 1631 a pair of wheel locks cost £3, against £2 for snaphances or firelocks, but even the latter could be broken easily, the Scottish army for example requesting in May 1644 1,000 pairs, 'because our horsemen's armes do daylie become unuseful or are lost'[80]. Other horse firearms included those of a troop of Walloons in Essex in 1648, 'armed with Blunderbasse Pistols, each of which could carry seven Bullets'[81].

In the early stages, equipment was usually provided by the individual or troop commander; Richard Atkyns' troop, 60 strong in January 1643, for example, were 'almost all of them well armed, Master Dutton giving me 30 steel backs, breasts and head pieces, and two men and horses completely armed'[82]. In July 1642 the Committee of Lords and Commons for the Safety of the Kingdom ordered that each troop commander should receive £280 for the provision of horses, arms and equipment. Many Royalist troops were equipped at their commanders' expense; for example, in October 1642 Prince Rupert ordered '30 tie: paire of your best holster and as many of your best spanners and as many of your best flasks as also one hundred weight of pistoll shot ... for ye arming of mine owne Troop'[83].

The ideal cavalry horse was 'of sufficient stature and strength, nimble of joynts, and sure of foot ... to pace, trot, gallop, or runne in full careere'[84], but was not always to be found. The 'Great Horse' or 'Black Horse', the massive mount of armoured knights which was well over 16 hands, is shown in Civil War portraits but was probably very rare and costly, explaining in part the decline of the cuirassier; Cromwell offered '60 pieces' for 'A Black won in battle' (as against 20 pieces for a dragoon cob)[85]. Most cavalry was mounted upon lighter horses of 'tall stature and lean proportions' according to Markham, though the Scots in particular were always deficient in good horses, as Lord Saye noted, 'light but weak nags ... never able to stand a charge or endure the shock of the enemy's horse'[86]. A man enlisting might have provided his own horse, or a man might have provided either a horse and rider or just a horse, for which he received (from Parliament, which favoured this system) 2s. 6d. or 1s. 4d. per diem respectively. The value of the horse was assessed and regarded as a loan, repayment being promised at eight per cent; the system developed into a forced loan, districts being assessed to provide the requisite quantity of mounts. By 1645, however, the majority of horses were bought outright (remounts £7 10s. each and dragoon mounts £4), other methods having broken down. The Royalists used purchase and impressment, the latter a confiscation by one faction of horses belonging to the other; in 1643, for example, the commander of the Parliamentary horse at Leek was ordered 'to take so many horses of the papists, delinquents, or malignants, as to horse the said troopers'[87]. When troop commanders came from the landed classes, they frequently mounted their men at their own expense.

Theoretically a regiment of horse would comprise 500 men, but was seldom at full strength except when a popular leader was the commander. Normally a regiment comprised six troops, which often fought in three squadrons or 'divisions', and though most had their full complement of officers, were often very weak in troopers, partly due to desertion and casualties but also because many troop commanders found it beyond their means to arm and mount the correct number. Not all the 'other ranks' of a troop might be troopers, especially in the Royal forces; when Atkyns raised his troop, for example, he had 60 troopers and 20 'gentlemen that bore arms'[88]. Among such 'gentlemen volunteers' in the Royalist armies were included many of the highest estate, such as the Secretary of State Lord Falkland,

'Present & give Fire'; cuirassier discharging wheel lock pistol, held with lock uppermost to assist transmission of spark through touchhole into barrel (engraving after Cruso's *Militarie Instructions*)

Shabraque and holster cover, probably dating from the Civil War era

killed at First Newbury whilst riding with Byron's Horse. Typical troop composition was: one troop commander (captain or field officer), one lieutenant, one cornet (standard bearer), one quartermaster (commissioned officer), three corporals, two trumpeters, one farrier, and 60 troopers. Royalist regiments usually had three field officers and Parliamentary regiments had two, a colonel and a major, with the colonel's troop being commanded by a 'captain-lieutenant'. In the early part of the war at least, troops would often serve independently, the process of regimentation not being universal. A few examples may be quoted to show how widely divergent organization of horse could be. At Edgehill, Royalist regiments varied from eight troops to three, with totals from 500 to 150; troop strength ranged from 150 (the two troops of Lifeguard) to only 15 (Major Legge's troop of Prince Rupert's regiment). Parliamentary troops seem to have averaged about 50, save Essex's Lifeguard which was 100 strong. In Fairfax's army in the Marston Moor campaign, troops seem to have averaged only 25 men each, whilst the proportion of troopers to officers was sometimes as low as six; in mid 1644, for example, Colonel John Dalbier's regiment comprised four troops, totalling 43 officers and 267 men.

A few regiments kept up their strength remarkably: in December 1642 Prince Rupert's comprised 465 men and 630 horses (including Rupert's Lifeguard, which soon after became independent) in seven troops; in March 1644 it had 10 troops, was 500 strong at Marston Moor, and 400 in eight troops in May 1645, doubtless maintaining its strength because of the popularity of its commander. In the Eastern Association strengths varied from Sir John Norwich's three troops to Manchester's 11 and Cromwell's 14; Cromwell's 'double regiment' (i.e. double-strength) became two regiments upon the formation of the New Model, those of Sir Thomas Fairfax and Edward Whalley. In September 1644 the Eastern Association had 40 troops of horse (including one of 'reformadoes', officers without regiments) in five regiments, averaging 99 per troop. Organization of Scottish horse was similar to that of the English, except that eight troops per regiment was usual, and like the Royalists their regiments had lieutenant-colonels, plus sometimes additional staff such as adjutant and scrivener.

The tactics of horse were based on two styles, Dutch and Swedish. The former, or *Reiter* tactic, consisted of a regiment advancing in about six ranks towards their enemy and each successive rank halting to fire their pistols or carbines, then retiring for the next rank to do the same and so on until the enemy was sufficiently broken for a final charge with the sword. The Swedish fashion consisted of charging home with the sword in about three ranks, reserving fire for the pursuit, and was the style used increasingly throughout the war under the influence of Rupert and others; as early as Edgehill he instructed his horse to reserve their fire until in mêlée. Later experience altered the tactic of receiving a charge with fire to countercharging at 'a good round trot', as in one description: 'we stood and moved not till

Deployment of regiments of horse (from Sprigge's plan of Naseby)

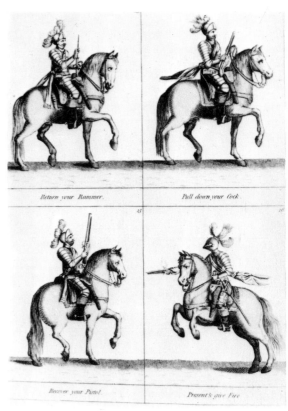

Pistol exercise on horseback, showing cuirassiers (engraving after Cruso's *Militarie Instructions*)

they had fired, which made Gerrard swear (God damn him), "The rogues will not stir". Upon those words we clapped spurs to our horses, and gave him such a charge ... routed him and pursued him and made him fly ...'[89]. The madcap charge, leaving all disorganized, which has been associated with Rupert, is sometimes exaggerated, for he was a skilled leader; nevertheless, the less-disciplined regiments (including many of the Royalist corps composed of gentlemen-volunteers who could hardly be expected to submit to discipline) would make a wild dash which carried them out of the action and

perhaps took days to reorganize. On the day following Edgehill, for example, the Royal horse was so disordered that there were no regiments or troops, only a vast body incapable of ordering itself and totally indisciplined.

Dragoons were mounted infantry: 'their service is on foot, and is no other than that of Musketeers'[90], and were thus equipped as foot, with firelocks and swords. They were regarded as foot soldiers made mobile by riding, and companies of foot were often converted to dragoons; yet they were 'reckon'd as part of the Cavalry' and could even charge as such, as did Okey's regiment at Naseby, though their mounts (ponies of about 14 hands) were invariably of the poorest quality and 'least price, the use thereof being but to expedite his march, allighting to do his service'[91]. Organization was in companies and regiments, though exact establishments are uncertain until the New Model's dragoon regiment of 1,000 men in 10 companies was set up; but as dragoons had existed in the militia for some time (Cambridge and Ely mustered as many dragoons as horse in 1628, for example), there were also independent companies, sometimes attached to regiments of horse.

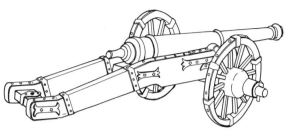

Fieldpiece upon split-trail field carriage

Cuirassier loading his pistol, holding ball in mouth until inserting it in barrel. Note fabric interior of holsters, which could be drawn closed over mouth of holster, protecting pistol from dampness (engraving after Cruso's *Militarie Instructions*)

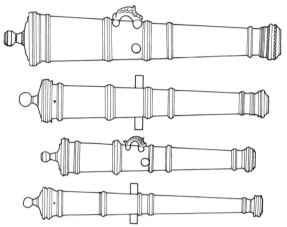

Comparative sizes of cannon-barrel from top to bottom: cannon, demi-cannon, culverin, saker. The decorative lifting handles were often cast in the shape of stylized dolphins

ARTILLERY

'Artillery' in the seventeenth century did not have the same meaning as it does today, but described any missile weapon, as in I Samuel xx, 40: 'And Jonathan gave his artillery unto his lad ...'; thus Bariffe's *Military Discipline, or the Yong Artilleryman* (1635) is concerned only with the musket and pike, and Niccols' *London Artillery* (1616) is so termed because 'the French word Infanterie would be scarce intelligible to any common Reader'[92].

Civil war cannon were clumsy, difficult to move and of limited effect except in siege warfare and in damaging morale; Turner quotes Monluc: '*Il fait plus de peur, que du mal*' (it frightens more than it hurts)[93]. Nevertheless, an army's artillery train was regarded not as lumbering impedimenta but as a vital part of the army, and although many varieties of cannon existed the most common are listed below:

Name	calibre (in./mm)	weight (lb./kg)	length (ft./cm)	weight of shot (lb./kg)	weight of powder (lb./kg)	team (horses/men)	
Robinet	$1\frac{1}{4}$/32	120/54	3/91	$\frac{3}{4}$/0.3			
Falconet	2/51	210/95	4/122	$1\frac{1}{4}$/0.6			
Falcon	$2\frac{3}{4}$/70	700/318	6/183	$2\frac{1}{4}$/1	$2\frac{1}{2}$/1.1	2	16
Minion	3/76	1,500/680	8/244	4/1.8	$3\frac{1}{2}$/1.6	4	20
Saker/Drake	$3\frac{1}{2}$/89	2,500/1,134	$9\frac{1}{2}$/290	$5\frac{1}{4}$/2.4	5/2.3	5	24
Demi-Culverin	$4\frac{1}{2}$/114	3,600/1,633	10/305	9/4.1	9/4.1	7	36
Culverin	5/127	4,000/1,814	11/335	15/6.8	18/8.2	8	50
Demi-Cannon	6/152	6,000/2,722	12/366	27/12.3	25/11.3	10	60
Cannon	7/178	7,000/3,175	10/305	47/21.3	34/15.4	12	70
Cannon Royal	8/203	8,000/3,629	8/244	63/28.6	40/18.1	16	90

The mortar 'Roaring Meg' (Hereford City Museums; photograph by Jonathan Cooter)

(Nomenclature varied: for alternative statistics see *The Compleat Gunner* (London, 1672; reprinted Wakefield, 1971) p. 40.) The 'team' quoted above refers to the number of horses or men required to drag the piece.

Missiles were principally iron (or even stone) balls, though case shot could be used at close range; the rate of fire was slow (eight shots per hour from a cannon, 10 from a demi-cannon, 12 from a saker, etc.), and gunnery was frequently inaccurate. For example, so unskilled were the gunners at Blackburn at Christmas 1642 that although a demi-culverin blasted away 'most of the night and the day following ... the greatest execution it did ... a bullet shot out of it entered into a house ... and burst the bottom of a fryen pan', after which the Royalists withdrew 'that they might eate their Christmas pyes at home....'[94]. Artillery crews consisted, for example, of three gunners and six matrosses (assistants) for a demi-cannon and two gunners and four matrosses for a culverin.

Different in efficacy was the mortar, which dropped explosive shells from a high trajectory into beleaguered garrisons, often with the greatest physical and morale-damaging effects. At Lathom House, for example, these pieces 'struck most fear with the garrison ... The mortar peece was that that troubled us all. The little ladyes had stomack to digest canon, but the stoutest souldiers had noe heart for granadoes ... The mortar peece ... had frightened 'em from meat and sleepe'[95]. Different again was the petard, an explosive, bell-shaped device which had to be fixed manually against a gate or even a wall to blow a hole through it; the petardier, even if he survived the attentions of the garrison, risked being killed by the explosion, or 'hoist with his own petard'. Before the petardier George Cranage blew down the door of Oswestry Castle with his petard, he had to be 'well lined with sacke'[96] before he would attempt it, the qualities required of a petardier being akin to those of the leader of the assault squad on Hereford, one Berrow, whose resolution was 'answerable and yet his understanding not so piercing as to affright him with the enterprise'[97]!

Draught animals (with collar, traces and even carters) were often impressed, though the New Model purchased their own; horse teams were ponderous enough, but teams of oxen, used when horses were unavailable, were even slower. An interesting practice was to give individual cannon their own names; at least two were called 'Roaring Meg', and two huge demi-cannon were both known as 'The Queen's Pocket Pistol', whilst other names included 'Gog', 'Magog', 'Sweet Lips' (named after a renowned whore), and 'Kill-Cow'.

ENGINEERS

The many sieges and fortifications involved in the Civil Wars were often organized by professional engineers, including a number of continentals like Manchester's Rosworm. Although pioneers had been recruited before (in 1590 there were supposed to be 20 armed pioneers per 100 soldiers, and in Norfolk in 1640 Lieutenant-Colonel James Calthorp was directed to muster his company with 10 pioneers per 100 men with sufficient tools and two carts), pioneer duties were regarded as below the dignity of a soldier and thus the task of impressed civilians or defaulters. The Earl of Northumberland's ordinances of war (1640) noted that if a regiment broke before coming to grips with the enemy it was to 'serve for pioners and scavengers, till a worthy exploit take off the blot', as were soldiers who lost their equipment 'by negligence or lewdness, by dice or cards'[98]. Some pioneers were, however, rated sufficiently highly to be classed as soldiers, such as those of the Eastern Association who doubled as the firelock guard for the artillery. Soldiers could be detailed as labourers, or civilians impressed, the latter practice unpopular as witness the instruction that each 100 pioneers should have a clerk to call the roll every morning to discover those 'sick, deade, or ronne awaie'[99]. Civilians were compelled to assist in the fortification of their towns (under a fine of 1s. at Oxford, for example), even including 'the ordinary sort of women'[100] who worked on the defences of Worcester. Engineering tools were comprehensive, whether impressed from civil authorities or bought; the New Model purchased some 3,000 spades and 1,900 pickaxes of various types in 1645. Ward's *Animadversions of Warre* recommended such tools should 'have the marke of the gallowse set on them, in token of deathe to them that steale them...'[101].

TACTICS

Although numerous military manuals specified the most precise details of tactical manoeuvre, all depended upon disciplined troops capable of performing them, not easily found, at least in the early years of the war. In theory, two systems were used, depending upon the experience or preference of the commander – the Dutch, and the more complex Swedish tactics evolved by Gustavus Adolphus. The simpler Dutch system, with men in eight ranks, was probably more practical than the Swedish array, though doubtless the best elements from both were utilized, for example in the Swedish tactic of forming flank guards of mixed horse and musketeers to disorder the enemy horse when it charged. The normal practice was to draw up the foot in one or two lines, with a reserve if possible, with horse on the flanks and artillery interspersed between the various blocks of troops. Terrain features were not always used to anchor the battleline; indeed, Waller was taunted that 'hils, boggs, hedges, ditches, these you must grant him, hee'll not fight else'[102]. In the confusion and smoke, however, commanders usually lost control, so that battles depended upon subordinate officers and the morale of their men. Though routs were common, morale was surprisingly high in armies of what were largely inexperienced civilians; 'The naturall courage of English men, which prompted them to maintain their ground, tho' the rawness and unexperience of both parties had not furnished them with skill to make the best use of their advantages', as James II wrote[103]. This determination was reflected in gallantry like that of the Whitecoats, dying at White Syke Close in a hopeless position, and even affected provincial actions, the Parliamentary stand at Whalley (Lancashire) in April 1643 only occurring because 'many of the Musketiers being resolut men replyed to the Captaines bouldly bidding them take what course they pleased for their safeties yet they would adventure themselves, see the enemie and have one bout with them ...'[104].

On the other hand, discipline was often atrocious, officers having to cudgel or threaten their men into standing firm, in which case the men 'stood together more like a flock of sheep'[105]. Some showed the reasonable desire 'to see their own Chimneys'[106] and others were so ignorant of drill, like Essex's Lifeguard at Powick Bridge, 'not understanding the difference between wheeling about and shifting for themselves ... retired to the army in a very dishonourable manner'[107], perhaps an ironic comment! Though armies became more professional as the war progressed, early vehemence waned, so that, combining all these factors, there was great truth in Lord Eythin's comment upon seeing Rupert's plan before Marston Moor: 'By God, sir, it is very fyne in the paper, but ther is no such thing in the ffields'[108].

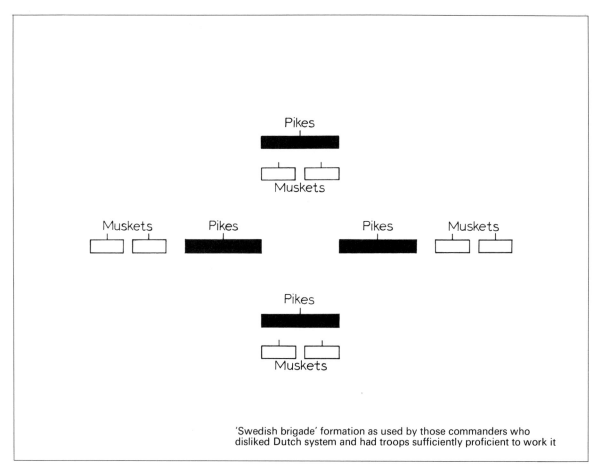

'Swedish brigade' formation as used by those commanders who disliked Dutch system and had troops sufficiently proficient to work it

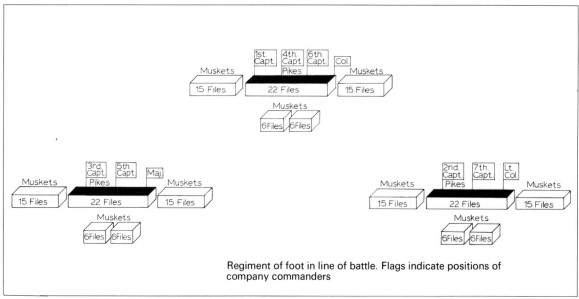

Regiment of foot in line of battle. Flags indicate positions of company commanders

4 THE FIRST CIVIL WAR 1642-3

The King's standard was raised on 22 August 1642, but Charles I had lost his first battle three and four months before, when Sir John Hotham with Parliamentary and naval support had denied him access to the munitions at Hull, withstanding a Royal attempt to take them by force. Loss of armaments, there and at London, and of the navy's support, cost the King and the Royalist faction dearly. Nevertheless, the embryo Royal army received a significant reinforcement in early August when Princes Rupert and Maurice and other European military experts slipped past the Parliamentary navy and landed a cargo of munitions from Holland. Prince Rupert of the Rhine, son of Charles' sister and the deposed King of Bohemia, was aged only 22 when given command in the Royalist army, but possessed some seven years' military experience and far greater skill than he has sometimes been credited with. Shortly after his arrival the Royal standard rose above Nottingham and the war had begun officially.

The army raised by Parliament was commanded by Robert Devereux, third Earl of Essex, previously the King's lieutenant-general against the Scots, a man said to be devoid of ambition, only wishing 'to be kindly looked upon and kindly spoken to, and quietly to enjoy his own fortune'[1], and to whom rebellion against the anointed King was distasteful. His opinions echoed those of many Parliamentary supporters at this time: their fight was not against the King but against those 'malignants' and Papists who sought to separate him from his Parliament. As the Parliamentary despatch of Edgehill read, they fought against 'the Cavaliers, and ... those evil persons, who ... ingaged His Majestie in a ... bloody fight against His faithfull Subjects, in the Army raised by Authority of Parliament, for the preservation of His Crowne and Kingdome'[2]; that the King was *with* the 'Cavaliers' in this fight was somehow overlooked.

Leaving London for Northampton on 9 September, Essex (accompanied by his coffin and winding sheet) gathered a sizeable force, 20 regiments of foot, six of horse (regimented from semi-independent troops) and one of dragoons, plus Essex's own cuirassier Lifeguard. Against this largely amateur army was arrayed an even poorer Royalist force; at the beginning of hostilities Sir Jacob Astley told the King 'that he could not give any assurance against his majesty's being taken out of his bed if the rebels should make a brisk attempt to that purpose'[3]. Nor were Royalist fortunes prospering else-where; the vital port and fortress of Portsmouth surrendered to Parliament on 7 September with a suspicion of treachery on the part of the Parliamentary-appointed Royalist governor, George Goring, and the withdrawl of the supposed relief force.

Charles rallied support from Cheshire and the Welsh Marches and a sizeable Royal army came into being, encouraged by their first success at Powick Bridge on 23 September, when Rupert, the King's General of Horse, beat up and routed a small Parliamentary force under Nathaniel Fiennes whilst covering the evacuation

Earl of Essex. Note use of single gauntlet, with helmet probably shown simply to emphasize the quality of subject (engraving by Wenceslaus Hollar, 1644)

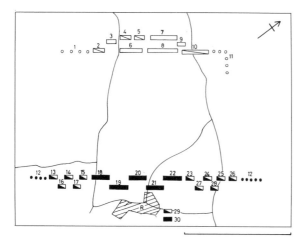

EDGEHILL

Parliamentary Army

1 dragoons or musketeers **2** Lord Fielding's Horse **3** Sir William Fairfax's Regt. **4** Sir Philip Stapleton's Horse **5** Sir William Balfour's Horse **6** Sir John Meldrum's brigade **7** Thomas Ballard's brigade **8** Charles Essex's brigade **9** Denzil Holles' Regt. **10** Sir James Ramsey's Horse **11** dragoons or musketeers

Royalist Army

12 dragoons or musketeers **13** Lord Wilmot's Horse **14** Lord Grandison's Horse **15** Earl of Carnarvon's Horse **16** Lord Digby's Horse **17** Sir Thomas Aston's Horse **18** Henry Wentworth **19** Sir Nicholas Byron **20** Richard Feilding **21** John Belasyse **22** Charles Gerard **23** Prince Maurice's Horse **24** Prince Rupert's Horse **25** Prince of Wales' Horse **26** King's Lifeguard **27** Sir John Byron's Regt. (part) **28** Sir John Byron's Regt. (part) **29** Gentleman Pensioners **30** William Legge's Firelocks *R: Radway village*
The scale represents one mile (1.6 kilometres)

of Worcester. Leaving Shrewsbury on 12 October, the King marched towards London, causing Parliament to begin the formation of a new army for the defence of the capital, based upon their excellent trained bands. Meanwhile, Essex's army attempted to find the King, but such was the inexperience of both sides that neither knew where the other was. On 22 October the King was at Edgecote, 40 miles (64 kilometres) west of Bedford, when he learned that Essex was only seven miles (11 kilometres) distant, and on the following day Charles drew up his army on Edgehill, dominating the Warwickshire plain. Awaiting the Parliamentarians, the Royal army was split by internal dissent; Rupert, though only General of Horse, insisted that he receive his orders only from the King, not the General-in-Chief, the Earl of Lindsey; and when Charles ordered the battle line to be arrayed by Patrick Ruthven, Earl of Forth, a Scottish veteran who 'dozed in his understanding', an immoderate drinker, almost illiterate and deaf [4], Lindsey resigned all command save that of his own regiment, with which he fell in the coming battle. The Royal army numbered almost 3,000 horse, about 10,000 foot and 1,000 dragoons; Essex's strength was about 2,000 horse, 12,000 foot and 700 dragoons.

Charles doubtless hoped that Essex would attack him uphill, but Essex, probably not wishing to initiate the first battle of an unprecedented war, remained immobile, so on the early afternoon of 23 October 1642 the Royalist army rolled down the hill, three brigades of foot in the centre and horse on the wings, meeting the Parliamentary army similarly arrayed. On the Royalist right, Rupert swept down upon Essex's left-flank horse who, demoralized by the defection of Sir Faithfull Fortescue's troop which changed sides *en masse*, broke and fled, pursued by the Cavalier horse which set about looting the Parliamentary baggage. A similar rout occurred on the other flank, though at least one Royalist commander, Sir Charles Lucas of Caernarvon's regiment, attempted to check the mad pursuit and gathered some horse around him. In the centre, nearly half the Parliamentary foot ran away before a blow was delivered, but the remainder held on tenaciously and, reinforced by Balfour's and Stapleton's Horse (both having avoided the rout on their flank), actually pushed back the Royalist foot. At this juncture the King's sons were in danger, the 13-year-old Prince of Wales (later Charles II) and his brother James being present in the King's entourage; ordered to escort them to safety, the Earl of Dorset told the King that 'he would not be thought a Coward for the sake of any King's Sons in Christendom' [5]. Young Charles wanted to fight, but they were escorted away by the commander of the Pensioners, but not before a Parliamentary cuirassier had attempted to kill or capture them. By the time Rupert returned with his horse, expecting to find an overwhelming victory, he found a stalemate. The survivors stayed put through the night, but the imminent approach of fresh Parliamentary troops (including the regiment of John Hampden) compelled the Royal army to withdraw. Neither side had much to acclaim, for the first battle of the war was both confused and amateurish. The Banner Royal had been captured upon the death of its bearer, Sir Edmund Verney, but had been recovered for the King; and though both armies were temporarily shattered, Essex had at least forestalled the King's march on London, though the Parliamentary army also retired. On balance, the pendulum of victory edged slightly towards the Royalists.

Charles was urged by Rupert and Lord Forth (the

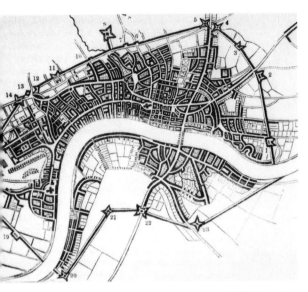

Civil War fortifications: defences of London, 1643, showing batteries and 'sconces' numbered 1–23

new General-in-Chief) to march immediately upon London, but fearing it might alienate too many subjects, he hesitated, occupying Oxford (to be the Royal headquarters throughout the First Civil War) and only then moving on London. Rupert surprised and, after a fierce fight, captured Brentford on 12 November. On the following morning he found his route to the city barred at Turnham Green by Essex and 24,000 Parliamentarians, with the London trained bands as the heart of the defence. Though Clarendon claimed that many of these would have defected had the Royalists attacked, the trained bands, arrayed 'in their brightest equipage'[6], saved the war for Parliament by what S.R. Gardiner termed 'the Valmy of the English Civil War'[7], as the Royal army retired rather than fight.

As the campaigning season of 1642 drew to a close, the King possessed not only the loyal local forces in various parts of the kingdom, but three field armies: his own Edgehill army, now in the Oxford area; a force in the north under the Earl of Newcastle; and in Cornwall Sir Ralph Hopton was in the process of forming an army which was to include the best infantry of either side. Hopton, an ex-mercenary with Mansfeldt and a Somerset landowner, had been a reform-minded M.P. who had led the delegation which presented the Grand Remonstrance to the King in 1641, but by the beginning of 1642 his traditional loyalty led him to support the attempted arrest of the 'five members' and resulted in a spell of imprisonment in the Tower upon Parliament's order. Appointed Lieutenant-General of Horse in the West, Hopton (with the support of the great Cornishman Sir Bevile Grenvile, 'the generally most loved man

of that county'[8]) rallied the county trained bands and evicted the Parliamentary forces; but before an invasion of Devon could be undertaken, new 'voluntary' regiments had to be organized, the trained bands being unwilling to leave their own county. In the north, the Earl of Newcastle marched south and occupied York, aided by an able Scottish general, James King (later Lord Eythin), against whose nationality some prejudice was exercised, and as Lieutenant-General of Horse, George Goring, ex-governor of Portsmouth, who according to Clarendon was an uncontrollable drunkard whose appointment with Newcastle was engineered by the Queen.

To finance the war, Parliament imposed a property tax or assessment (generally five per cent) on all counties under their control, and Pym proposed an excise tax; though unpopular, these measures (and the sequestration of Royalist property) enabled Parliament to provide most of the needs of its forces. Charles, however, was forced to rely on voluntary loans, levied contributions from Royalist areas, and on money the Queen had borrowed in Holland. Parliament's superior financial resources proved vital in the outcome of the war, which in 1643 was fragmented into a number of 'fronts'. Peace negotiations, which continued until March, broke down due to the stringency of the conditions which Parliament attempted to impose upon the King.

It is debatable whether Charles had any deliberate grand strategy in 1643; a three-pronged assault on the capital directed from Oxford, from the north and southwest may have been envisaged but the evidence is scant, and there seems to have been little attempt at coordination. If anyone attempted a cohesive strategy it was Parliament, which established a Committee of Safety to coordinate efforts, and during 1643 began to form 'associations' of counties to overcome the raging localism which often prevented the troops of one county from setting a foot beyond its borders. Most successful of these organizations were the Eastern Association, combining the forces of Cambridge, Essex, Norfolk, Suffolk, Hertfordshire, Huntingdonshire and Lincolnshire, with an army under the Earl of Manchester; and the South-Eastern Association combining the forces of Hampshire, Kent, Surrey and Sussex under Sir William Waller. Nevertheless, only Essex's national army was ever free of local bias, its funds and directions depending entirely upon the central government and not the committees of an association.

Fighting in the south-west continued through the winter of 1642–3, Hopton's brief excursion into Devon drawing the local Parliamentary forces over the border into Cornwall and to defeat at Braddock Down, near Liskeard, on 19 January. Parliament's campaigns in this theatre were hampered by the incompetency of their commander, the Earl of Stamford, who left the Welsh Marches to take control of Devon, allowing the Marquis of Hertford's Welsh regiments to pass unhindered to reinforce the King at Oxford. A temporary local truce was arranged between Devon and Cornwall, reflecting again the localized character of the combat in that area.

In the north, Newcastle's progress was slow though he was able to cut communications between the Parliamentary garrison of Hull and their adherents in the West Riding; despite the efforts of Sir Thomas Fairfax, perhaps Parliament's most able commander of the entire war, Newcastle succeeded in establishing a garrison at Newark, thus securing a crossing over the Trent, vital if the munitions acquired by the Queen on the continent were to reach the King at Oxford. Fairfax's capture of Leeds assured Parliament's hold on the West Riding, but sporadic fighting in Lancashire, Cheshire and Staffordshire only occasionally influenced the main theatres of war. The Queen with her cargo of munitions from Holland evaded Parliament's fleet and landed at Bridlington, at first joining the Earl of Newcastle at York but later, with her own army and styling herself 'Her she-majesty, generalissima', joined the King in July.

Following a Royalist success at Nantwich (28 January 1643), intermittant fighting spread into the Midlands, with local and largely untrained troops skirmishing without decisive result, but with some Royalist gains of towns like Lichfield, Tamworth and Stafford, which if allowed to develop could assist the juncture of Newcastle and the King. Parliament thus despatched Lord Brooke as commander of the forces of the associated counties of Warwick and Stafford to redress the situation, and though he secured Stafford he was killed on the morning of his planned assault on Lichfield, shot through the eye as he sat at his own window. Parliament thus lost a staunch supporter and an able soldier, but only 17 days later (19 March) the Royalists also lost a valued commander. The recapture of Lichfield by Parliament led to the despatch of the Earl of Northampton from Oxford; he defeated a Parliamentary force at Hopton Heath, two miles (3.2 kilometres) from Stafford, but in the course of the action was dismounted and surrounded by enemies. Attired in cuirassier armour, he was impervious to their attack until his helmet was knocked off, whereupon he was offered quarter. Refusing to accept such from 'base rogues' [9] he was killed by a halberd blow to the head, and Lichfield remained Roundhead.

In the west, an attempt on 7 March by Rupert to capture the vital port of Bristol (with the connivance of Royalists within) was foiled, and some Parliamentary success was enjoyed by Sir William Waller, who was appointed commander of the armies of the Western Association (Somerset, Gloucester, Shropshire, Wiltshire, Worcester). Waller, who had seen considerable campaigning in Europe, posed such a threat to Wales that Prince Maurice was sent from Oxford to threaten his rear, at which Waller withdrew to Gloucester. Further Royalist success occurred in the north when Sir Hugh Cholmley, Parliament's governor of Scarborough,

Edward Montagu, 2nd Earl of Manchester (portrait by Sir Peter Lely, c. 1661–5; The National Portrait Gallery, London)

declared for the King and prompted Sir John Hotham and his son, holding Hull, to consider the same course. Parliament's commander in east Yorkshire, Lord Ferdinando Fairfax (Sir Thomas' father), abandoned his headquarters at Selby and retired on Leeds, his son's covering manoeuvre meeting a reverse at Seacroft Moor at the hands of Goring's horse.

Attempting to open a route for the Queen's munitions from the north to Oxford, Rupert moved northward, capturing the small Puritanical town of Birmingham and the Parliamentary stronghold of Lichfield (21 April), but then returned to Oxford as Essex was on the move. Maurice was also recalled from the west, but not before Waller had attempted to intercept him; the Governor of Gloucester, Sir Edward Massey, was able to destroy Maurice's bridge of boats across the Severn, but Waller was routed by Maurice at Ripple Field, three miles (4.8 kilometres) north of Tewkesbury, on 13 April. The threat from Essex materialized as Parliament's main

Helmet, breast- and backplates reputedly worn by Lord Brooke when killed at Lichfield, 1643 (engraving by T. Hamilton)

Pl 47

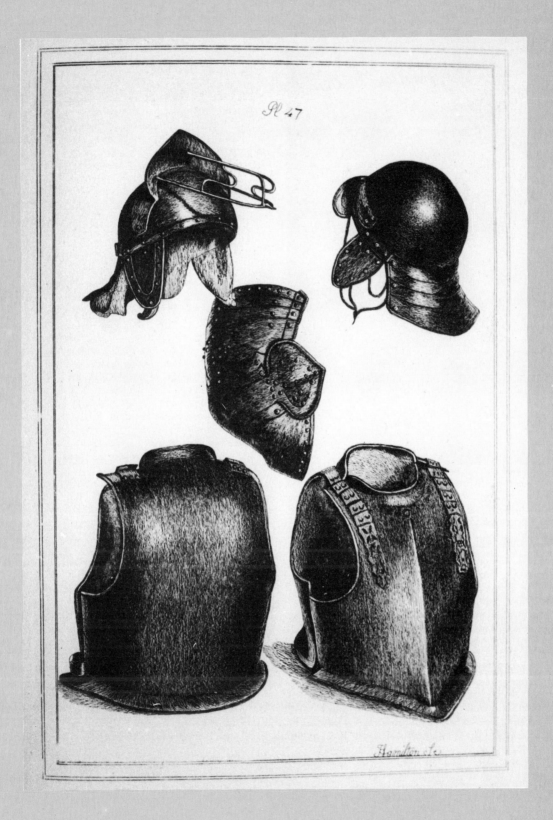

Hamilton Sc.

Ferdinando, 2nd Baron Fairfax. Illustrates use of a cassock (portrait by Edward Bower; York City Art Gallery)

result; in an attempt to explain his defeat, Stamford accused his subordinate, Major-General James Chudleigh, of treason. Chudleigh, captured whilst attempting a vain counterattack, promptly changed sides and was to die fighting for the King at Dartmouth later in the year.

In the north, Parliament made another attempt to capture Newark, and though inflicting a reverse upon the Royalists, the Parliamentary forces of Lord Willoughby of Parham, Sir John Hotham and Oliver Cromwell were too mauled to continue their attempt on the city. On 20 May 1643 Sir Thomas Fairfax attacked Wakefield, defeating the Royalists after confused fighting in the town; the Royal horse escaped but its leader, Goring, was captured. The hard-won town was later abandoned.

As Parliament's lord-general, Essex, began his move upon Oxford, a Royalist raid was launched under Prince Rupert to attack any target which presented itself; it was guided by John Urry, a Scottish deserter from Parliament's army who changed his allegiance probably more than anyone else in the war. Aiming to attack a convoy with £21,000 en route to pay Essex's army, Rupert's 1,000 horse, 350 dragoons and 500 musketeers instead rode over several disorganized parties of Parliamentary troops and then fought an action against the troops pursuing them at Chalgrove Field on 18 June. Its significance is largely due to the mortal wounding there of John Hampden, hero of the ship-money case, a leading Parliamentarian and friend of Pym. Tradition has it that he died of a bullet wound in the shoulder, but it is possible that his wound was inflicted by the explosion of his own pistol, an ever-present danger; as William Garrard wrote, 'He that loves the safety of hys owne person ... choose rather to pay double money for a good Peece, then (sic) to spare hys Purse and endanger hymselfe'[10], but in Hampden's case it was perhaps caused by the pistol being overcharged[11]. After Chalgrove, Essex withdrew his attempt upon Oxford and offered to resign his command, but it was not accepted.

Similar Royal success came in the north; as Newcastle advanced upon Bradford, Lord Fairfax (in overall command, now joined with his son) attempted, with a greatly inferior force (3,000 against at least 10,000), to surprise Newcastle at Adwalton Moor, some five miles (eight kilometres) east of Bradford. The Parliamentary advance was so delayed that Newcastle met them with his entire force in order of battle, but despite the disparity in numbers Fairfax's army held against the Royalist assault. Newcastle was contemplating withdrawal when one Colonel Skirton, 'a wild and desperate man', led a charge with his pikes which broke Fairfax's centre

field army (16,000 foot and 3,000 horse) moved against the Royal stronghold of Reading, a ruinous fortification held by Sir Arthur Aston with 3,000 foot and 300 horse. The King was marching to its succour when, the day after Rupert joined him, he learned that Reading had capitulated, Aston having been incapacitated by being struck upon the head with a roof tile dislodged by a roundshot, and the surrender arranged by his deputy, Colonel Richard Feilding, who narrowly escaped the King's sentence of death for his conduct, and then only by the intercession of the Prince of Wales.

The Royal cause prospered better in the south-west, despite an invasion from Devon under the Earl of Stamford which threatened to swamp Hopton's outnumbered Cornishmen. Stamford took up a strong position atop a hill at Stratton, but though heavily outnumbered (Hopton's field army comprised 2,400 foot and 500 horse against Stamford's 6,800) and short of ammunition and food, Hopton attacked before 1,200 horse unwisely detached by Stamford could rejoin. The battle raged from early morning until mid-afternoon, until Hopton's ammunition had all but run out, but his Cornish foot took the hill at a charge and routed Stamford, who abandoned his artillery and munitions in the flight. This astonishing victory had an equally unusual

Sir Thomas Fairfax, later 3rd Baron Fairfax, shown in cuirassier armour, wearing medal awarded for Naseby. The Fairfax arms are borne on horse's breastplate; in the background are horse and foot in battle array (engraving by Englehard after Bowers; York City Art Gallery)

SIR THOMAS FAIRFAX Knight
General of the Forces raised by the Parliament

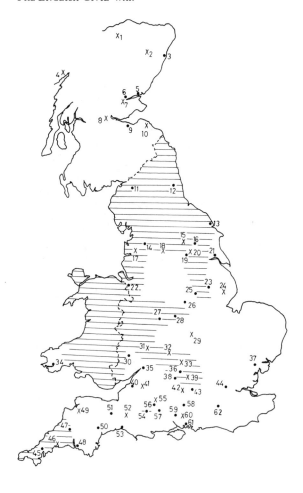

MAY 1643

1 Auldearn 2 Alford 3 Aberdeen 4 Inverlochy 5 Dundee
6 Perth 7 Tippermuir 8 Kilsyth 9 Edinburgh 10 Dunbar
11 Carlisle 12 Newcastle 13 Scarborough 14 Skipton
15 Marston Moor 16 York 17 Preston 18 Adwalton Moor
19 Pontefract 20 Sherburn 21 Hull 22 Chester 23 Lincoln
24 Winceby 25 Newark 26 Nottingham 27 Lichfield
28 Ashby de la Zouch 29 Naseby 30 Hereford
31 Worcester 32 Edgehill 33 Cropredy Bridge
34 Pembroke 35 Gloucester 36 Oxford 37 Colchester
38 Abingdon 39 Chalgrove Field 40 Bristol 41 Lansdowne
42 Newbury 43 Reading 44 London 45 Truro
46 Lostwithiel 47 Launceston 48 Plymouth 49 Torrington
50 Exeter 51 Taunton 52 Langport 53 Lyme Regis
54 Wardour Castle 55 Roundway Down 56 Devizes
57 Salisbury 58 Basing House 59 Winchester 60 Cheriton
61 Portsmouth 62 Reigate
Shaded portion represents territory in Royalist hands in May 1643

and through which poured the Royal horse, routing the left wing as well. Only Sir Thomas Fairfax, on the right, was able to withdraw his troops in some order and join his father in Bradford. Lord Fairfax marched to Leeds, followed by Sir Thomas when Bradford could no longer be held, but as Leeds was no more secure, the whole force fought its way to Hull, Sir Thomas being wounded at Selby. That Hull remained Parliamentary was only due to the discovery of a plot that the Hothams were preparing to turn over the city to the King. But by mid-July all Yorkshire, save Hull, was in Royalist hands, and the Fairfaxs' only consolation was that Sir Thomas' wife, captured in the flight from Bradford, had been returned with characteristic courtesy by Newcastle.

Royal fortunes continued to improve in the west, as Hopton (now Lord Hopton of Stratton) was reinforced by the Marquis of Hertford and Prince Maurice from Oxford, who joined Hopton's force as the United Army of the West at Chard on 4 June 1643. Though small in size (4,000 foot, 2,000 horse and 300 dragoons) it included Hopton's five 'voluntary' Cornish regiments which were of the highest calibre, though some of the foot and part of the horse were inexperienced, one regiment of the latter being exchanged for Sir James Hamilton's corps from Devon where its unruly behaviour had been turning the inhabitants against the King! Command of the United Army presented a problem, as Hertford was the senior and in nominal control; it was resolved by Hopton receiving command in the field with Maurice commanding the horse. Opposing them was Parliament's 'William the Conqueror', Sir William Waller, who received an early reverse at Chewton Mendip on 10 June, when a cavalry action was turned into a Royal victory by the Earl of Caernarvon, 'who always charged home'[12], rescuing the wounded Prince Maurice. Shortly afterwards, Hopton communicated with his old friend, suggesting a meeting; Waller replied in one of the most moving documents of the war:

... my affections to you are so unchangeable, that hostility itselfe cannot violate my friendship to your person, but I must be true to the cause wherein I serve: The ould limitation usque ad aras holds still, and where my conscience is interested, all other obligations are swallowed up ... That great God which is the searcher of my heart, knows with what a sad sence I goe upon this service, and with what a perfect hatred I detest this warr without an enemie, but I looke upon it as opus domini, which is enough to silence all passion in mee. The God of peace in his good time send us peace, and in the meane time fitt us to receive it: Wee are both upon the stage and must act those parts that are assigned us in this Tragedy: Lett us do it in a way of honor and without personall animosities ...[13]

Waller attempted to hold the route to Bath, but was forced to fight a delaying action until he could concentrate his forces on Lansdown Hill some three miles (4.8

kilometres) north-west of the city, a strong position befitting the 'best shifter and chooser of ground', as Major Slingsby of the Cornish Foot termed him. So strong was it, in fact, that Hopton declined an immediate attack and on 5 July began, with his entire army and encumbered by baggage, to bypass Waller and march towards Oxford to effect a juncture with the King. This Waller could not allow and sent his horse into the charge, 'the boldest thing that I ever saw . . . for a party of less than 1,000 to charge an army of 6,000' [14]. As the Royalist rearguard faltered more of Hopton's army became engaged, until the Cornish Foot, who did 'believe noe men theire equals' according to Slingsby, cried out 'lett us fetch those cannon'. Hopton duly launched his horse and foot upon Lansdown Hill, the former with little success, some 1,400 out of 2,000 bolting. But the indomitable Cornish Foot cleared the crest of the hill, though with the grievous loss of Sir Bevile Grenvile, who died at the head of his pikes which stood 'as immovable as a rock' [15]. After a fight of the utmost ferocity, Waller withdrew and, after some musketry during the night, left the Royalists in possession of the hill, a position so precarious that, wrote Slingsby, one charge might have rolled them back down the hill like a rock.

Next day Hopton was looking at some prisoners of war seated on an ammunition cart when it exploded, perhaps as a result of deliberate sabotage or simply carelessness; in any event, Hopton was burned, temporarily blinded, and the Royalists carried him with them in a withdrawal upon Devizes, followed by the tenacious Waller. So short of ammunition were the Royalists that Hopton had to order the collection of all bed cords in Devizes to turn into match, and with Waller about to invest the town, a council of war was held at Hopton's lodging, to which the wounded general was carried in a chair. It decided that Hertford, Maurice and the horse should break out to Oxford, with Hopton and the foot holding Devizes until relieved. The horse escaped just in time, and for three days the Parliamentary artillery bombarded the beleaguered town. Relief was extremely rapid; the horse left Devizes around midnight on 10/11 July, and on 13 July a relief force of 1,800 horse under Lord Wilmot, the King's Lieutenant-General of Horse, and Sir John Byron, compelled Waller to march and face them at Roundway Down.

Cavalry combat; apart from the fact that most wear cuirassier armour, this is a good representation of a fight between two bodies of horse during Civil War (engraving by Jacques Callot from *Misères et Malheures de Guerre* (1633))

Wilmot first routed Haselrig's brigade of Waller's horse (including Haselrig's own cuirassier regiment), and as Waller advanced with the remainder of his force, Byron charged that and scattered the remaining Roundhead horse. Breaking off the pursuit, Wilmot and Byron challenged Waller's foot but were unable to break them until the sight of Hopton's Cornish Foot coming up from Devizes caused the Parliamentarians to withdraw. Their formation broken, they fell prey to the rallied Cavalier horse. Waller's army was destroyed totally.

This resounding victory persuaded the King's council of war to make a further push in the west, attempting to capture both Bristol, a port second only to London, and Gloucester, which protected a crossing of the Severn. Rupert was duly despatched from Oxford to join the Cornish army before Bristol; Waller, with a remnant of his force having taken shelter in Gloucester, slipped away to London. Bristol's defences were arranged in two rings, a series of forts connected by a wall and an inner defence around the city centre, but the Royalist engineer Bernard de Gomme, who had travelled from the continent with Rupert, reported that in places the wall was only $4\frac{1}{2}$ feet (1.4 metres) high and the ditch at some points less than five feet (1.5 metres) deep. Furthermore, Colonel Nathaniel Fiennes' garrison numbered only 1,500 foot and 300 horse, somewhat inexperienced but with the support of many of the citizens of a predominantly Parliamentarian city. Opinions in the Royalist camp were divided; the Cornish favoured an investment, there being no prospect of a Parliamentary relief of the city, but Rupert preferred an immediate assault despite the casualties it would entail. His opinion prevailed and the assault went in on 26 July in the early hours. The Cornish attacked with great bravery, but failed to penetrate the defences despite heavy casualties, including the leaders of all three assault columns, Sir Thomas Basset (Major-General of the Cornish army) being wounded and the others killed; Colonel Buck (slain by a halberd as he scrambled to the top of the wall) and Sir Nicholas Slanning, who with his friend Colonel John Trevannion (killed at the same moment), were 'the life and soul of the Cornish regiments' [16]. Rupert's assault was successful, however, breaching the outer defences and fighting to the city centre before Fiennes surrendered, but at the cost of young Viscount Grandison, Colonel-General of Rupert's Foot, who was mortally wounded and greatly lamented; 'court or camp could not shew a more faultless person' [17], but he paid for his reckless bravery.

The capture of Bristol was perhaps the highest point of Royalist fortunes during the war, for not only had the port been secured, but within it the nucleus of a Royal fleet, and furthermore, some of Fiennes' defenders changed sides and took up arms for the King. In the north, Parliament resumed the offensive against Newcastle's army, Lord Willoughby of Parham capturing Gainsborough in Lincolnshire, a vital point lying be-

PLATE 11

26 Sir Charles Lucas, officer, Royalist horse
27, 28 Officers, Royalist horse

The left-hand figure is based upon William Dobson's portrait of Sir Charles Lucas, with the addition of a *zischagge*-style 'Dutch pot' helmet with fixed peak and sliding nasal bar. The buff-coat's leather sleeves open down the front like a cassock, and the lace aiguilettes at the shoulders are relics of the 'arming points' which used to lace the sleeves to the body of the garment. The sash has its tails tucked out of the way.

The central figure is based in part upon a portrait by Gerard Soest. The buff-coat is fastened by metal clips, and includes an interesting feature in the leather flap laced to the skirt by a red ribbon, from which flap a pistol is hung by means of a belt hook attached to the stock; the pistol has a firelock action, no trigger guard and the old-fashioned knob as a trigger. The pole-hammer or axe is known to have been carried by officers of horse in the early part of the war, if only as a version of the infantry 'leading staff'. Poleaxes were the distinctive weapon of the Gentlemen Pensioners, who served as a unit at Edgehill and used their axes in action. It is not known whether they wore livery, as one of the few records of their costumes dates from the restoration of Charles II, when it was ordered that they 'be not obliged to wear or use any other habit or give any other livery than such as they themselves shall think fit' [1], though it is not clear whether this implies that each dressed as he pleased or whether the corps had freedom to choose its own uniform. Later illustrations show the poleaxes with very small halberd blades or plain partizans. The duty of the Pensioners at the start of the war was to escort the King and ensure that 'none of mean condition, or unknown to them, to come near His Majesty's Person' [2].

The right-hand figure is based loosely upon a portrait by William Dobson, with the addition of a sash worn from personal preference rather than as an expression of loyalty to any faction. He carries a wheel lock pistol (the key slung over his shoulder on a cord), these being common despite Ward's assertion that 'Most of our peeces goe with English lockes' [3].

NOTES
1 Lawson, C.C.P. *History of the Uniforms of the British Army* (London, 1940) vol. III, p. 15
2 *Ibid.*, p. 14
3 *Animadversions of Warre* (1639); see Eaves, I. 'Some Notes on the Pistol in Early 17th Century England' *Journal of the Arms and Armour Society* VI (1970) 277–344

tween Newcastle and the Royal garrison of Newark. A Royalist expedition to recapture Gainsborough, led by Newcastle's young cousin, Charles Cavendish, encountered a body of Parliamentary horse south of Gainsborough near the village of Lea. The Roundheads charged and routed part of the Royal horse, but Cavendish's own regiment, held in reserve, then drove off the Parliamentarians; whereupon the Parliamentary

PLATE 11

26 Sir Charles Lucas   27 28 Officers, Royalist horse

Oliver Cromwell (portrait by R. Walker, c. 1649; The National Portrait Gallery, London)

reserve, kept back by Colonel Oliver Cromwell, fell upon Cavendish's rear, 'which do so astonish him'[18], broke his regiment and pursued him into a bog where Cavendish was killed by Cromwell's captain-lieutenant. Though Newcastle's main army came up, recaptured Gainsborough on 30 July and pushed on to Lincoln and Stamford, Cromwell's military reputation was founded upon his defeat of Cavendish.

Instead of contemplating a combined advance upon London, the King decided to swing the weight of his forces against Gloucester, virtually the only Parliamentary stronghold between Bristol and Lancashire, and the capture of which would secure the routes to the Royalist support in Wales. Meanwhile, after a delay caused by a dispute between Hertford and Rupert over the governorship of Gloucester, the Earl of Caernarvon and Prince Maurice were sent into Devon to extinguish Parliamentary resistance. Caernarvon gave generous terms to those surrendering or changing allegiance, but when Maurice ignored the terms already granted, Caernarvon stormed off in indignation to the King, whilst Maurice joined Sir John Berkeley in the siege of the Parliamentary stronghold of Exeter. An attempt at its relief by sea having failed, Parliament intended to draw a force from the garrisons of Plymouth, Barnstaple and

Bideford to relieve it by land. Berkeley despatched Sir John Digby with 300 horse and 600 to 700 foot to intercept the Roundheads, but Digby had only 150 horse with him when he encountered the enemy at Torrington. Leaving these to hold their position until his remaining troops could come up, Digby and four or five officers alone charged the Parliamentary advance guard; this, a 'forlorn hope' of 50 foot, threw down their muskets and fled, and were followed by the entire body as panic spread, after which Digby's horse pursued them 'till their swords were blunted with slaughter'[19]. This incredible charge by a half-dozen men had even more profound effects, for both Bideford and Barnstaple surrendered upon receiving the news, followed by Exeter on 4 September.

With these Royalist successes, Parliament was placed in a difficult position. Already internal dissent suggested that Waller should replace Essex as overall commander, but Pym achieved a compromise, Essex remaining as Lord-General and commanding the army to attempt the relief of Gloucester, while the Earl of Manchester's army of the Eastern Association remained virtually independent of Essex. At the same time, Pym endeavoured to reach an alliance with the Scots, at the instigation of the Marquis of Argyll, a saturnine Presbyterian who feared an invasion of Scotland by Royalists from the north of England and Ireland. Pym duly despatched a deputation to Edinburgh led by Sir Henry Vane, who not being a Presbyterian might have been expected to uphold the independence of the other English Puritans.

The King arrived before Gloucester on 10 August 1643 and, being gamely resisted by Edward Massey, the governor, declined Rupert's plan of a storm as at Bristol because of its cost in lives, preferring a regular investment. Essex, meanwhile, left London with a relief force including some of the London trained band regiments. Fending off attempts to bar his path, including a large attack by Rupert at Stow-on-the-Wold, Essex brilliantly negotiated his path to Gloucester and entered the city on 8 September, not a moment too soon as the garrison had only three barrels of powder remaining. Resupplying the defenders, Essex now began his withdrawal back to London, but swung north to Tewkesbury to deceive the Royalists about his true intention. The ruse worked, for Essex doubled back, captured a Royal convoy at Cirencester (which replenished his failing supplies) and was well on his way home to Reading, via Swindon and Newbury, before the King could stop him. Chasing Essex along an almost parallel line of march, Rupert swung across country and made a sharp attack on Essex's left flank at Aldbourne, which, though driven off, persuaded Essex to leave the main Reading road and swing slightly south to put the River Kennet between him and the Royalists. The tired, wet and hungry Parliamentarians intended to rest at Newbury, a sympathetic town, but arriving before it on 19 Sep-

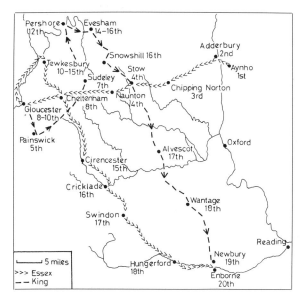

Manoeuvres of Essex's relief of Gloucester, and King's pursuit leading to first battle of Newbury. Numbers below place names indicate date in September 1643 on which the armies reached each town

tember discovered that a rapid march had brought Rupert there first. Essex was cut off from his road home and had to fight.

Essex's army comprised some 4,000 horse in the conventional two wings, and 10,000 foot in four brigades, with the six London trained band regiments in reserve (the Red, Yellow and Blue Regiments and Red, Blue and Orange Auxiliaries); despite their inexperience they were Parliament's best foot and were to stand 'as a bulwark and rampire to defend the rest' [20] in the coming action, but due to their 'part-time' service were available only for specific operations, at the conclusion of which they expected to go home no matter what the situation. Essex's second-in-command was Sergeant-Major-General Philip Skippon, a tough and vastly experienced professional soldier who had risen from the ranks in the Netherlands, 'a man of order and sobriety' though 'altogether illiterate' [21], who had been appointed Major-General of the London militia. Against this army, Charles I commanded the Royalists, with his Lord-General, the Earl of Forth, as his deputy and Rupert commanding the horse. The King's army was about equal in numbers but with a greater preponderance of horse, about 6,000, generally far superior to that of Parliament where conditions suited their deployment – but at Newbury they did not.

Essex was moving before daybreak on 20 September, stealing a march upon the Royalists and securing the dominant feature of the terrain just south of Newbury,

the 'Round Hill', which the Royal army had been sufficiently lax not to occupy on the previous day. The surrounding country was intersected with lanes and hedgerows, excellent cover for the foot but quite unsuitable for the employment of horse. Though the Royalists had some success against Essex's horse, their foot in the centre made little progress and horse was called up. The Royalist cavalry leader Sir John Byron made sterling efforts to penetrate the hedge-covered country (during which the Secretary of State, Lord Falkland, riding as a volunteer with Byron, was killed in what was probably a suicide bid caused by his distress at the horror of civil war [22]), and Essex's foot was even pushed back; but when Skippon committed his trained band reserve, the exhausted Royal horse had to pull back. Had they been supported by their own foot, Round Hill might

---

PLATE 12

29 Officer, trained bands 1642
30 Musketeer, trained bands 1642
31 Pikeman, trained bands 1642

Excepting the officers, trained band equipment was frequently wretched. Often stored within the church, parish arms were often ill-kept and ancient; in 1613, for example, the armour in Durham had been bought in 1569 and 1588, and by the Civil War much armour of this type was more than a century old. Another drawback to central parish armouries was that when the trained bands assembled 'there in a hubbledehuffe disorderlie to arme themselves, whereof ... little men doo put on great or tall mens armore, and leave litle mens armors unfit for great men to put on ...' [1]. The appearance of some trained bands may be gathered from the order issued to Hertfordshire men to 'weare their armor Just and Close to their bodies, Soldeor Lyke, and neate and fit and not neggligentlie or Looselye as though thei carried it in a fayre or market to sell it' [2], whilst others may have resembled Ben Jonson's knight, 'so hung with pikes, halbets, petronels, calivers, and muskets that he looks like a justice of peace's hall' [3]!

The officer illustrated wears an old-fashioned burgonet helmet and rather outdated baggy *pluderhosen* or 'cloak-bag' breeches and narrow-topped boots; his 'leading staff' has an ornamental, gilded head and large tassels as shown in a portrait of Sir Nicholas Crisp by Cornelius Jansen. The musketeer has a leather jerkin atop his doublet and a cabasset helmet dating from about 1600; he carries a short-barrelled caliver with an old-fashioned stock. The pikeman's equipment is even more antique, an Elizabethan morion and simple armour, the breastplate with a flange bolted to the bottom edge instead of tassets, and a single buff-leather gauntlet.

NOTES
1 Smythe, Sir J. *Instructions, Observations and Orders Mylitarie* (1595) p. 217; see Boynton, L. *The Elizabethan Militia 1558–1638* (Newton Abbot, 1971) p. 23
2 Quoted Boynton, pp. 25–6
3 *Ibid.*, p. 21

PLATE 12

29 Officer, trained bands 1642   30 Musketeer, trained bands 1642   31 Pikeman, trained bands 1642

PLATE 13

32 Ensign, Red Regt., London trained bands 1643   33 Sergeant, Red Regt., London trained bands 1643

PLATE 13

32 Ensign with 4th captain's colour, Red Regt., London trained bands 1643
33 Sergeant, Red Regt., London trained bands 1643

The ensign's costume is typical of an officer of foot, a buff-coat over a doublet, with a metal gorget, and a cassock, an overcoat with sleeves which could be unbuttoned down their entire length, allowing the sleeves to hang loose. His boots have plain black 'boot-hose' inside; many preferred much more decorative hose. The hairstyle with a curled fringe on the forehead enjoyed some popularity. The colour of the fourth captain of the Red Regiment was plain red with the usual St George's canton, the five white flames or piles wavy indicating the regiment's fourth captain; that with a single pile wavy indicated the major.

The sergeant is taken in part from a rare depiction of an N.C.O. on the window of Farndon Church. Sergeants' uniform was frequently as fine as that of the officers proper, with metallic decoration; Sergeant Nehemiah Wharton mentioned having a 'soldier's sute for winter, edged with gold and silver lace', presumably to replace 'a scarlet coate lined with plush' which had been a gift for saving a justice from being pillaged, and which was subsequently stolen by some Parliamentary horse[1]. The halberd was as much a badge of rank as a weapon, and remained so into the following century. To allow the sword to hang vertically, the scabbard could be removed from the lower baldric loop, suspending it from the upper loop only.

Although both figures wear similar colouring, the title 'Red Regiment' referred not to the uniform colour but to that of their flags, as with all London trained band corps, whose uniforms are unknown. Both men wear a sprig of green foliage as a field sign in the hat, as used (for example) by the Parliamentary forces at First Newbury, where the Red Regiment was engaged.

NOTES
1 Wharton, N. 'Letters' ed. Ellis, Sir H. *Archaeologia* XXV (1853) 322–3

Lord Falkland (engraving after a portrait by Van Dyck)

well have fallen and Essex defeated, but although Byron's uncle, Sir Nicholas Byron, held the ground gained, his foot refused to advance; they 'play'd the poltroons extremely'[23], wrote an exasperated Sir John.

By seven o'clock that evening the fighting subsided, and at a council of war (at which Sir John Byron and Rupert wished to fight on), Charles was informed that he had but 10 barrels of powder remaining. The Royalists therefore retired on Oxford, leaving Rupert to make a final thrust at Essex's rearguard as the Parliamentary army marched to Reading and home to London. First Newbury may be seen as the turning point of the war, for the capital might have capitulated had Essex's army been destroyed. As it was, Essex's relief of Gloucester and the extrication of his army mark him as a general of considerable skill, and he

received deserved praise and public rejoicing on his return to London for the conduct of his campaign, 'amongst the most soldierly actions of this unhappy war'[24]. No such praise was accorded the Royal foot, and to complete the Royalists' grief not only had Falkland fallen at Newbury but also the Earl of Sunderland, a volunteer attending 'upon the King's person under the obligation of honour ... and ... taken away by a cannon bullet'[25], and the gallant Earl of Caernarvon who, having 'charged home', was run through and killed by a Parliamentary straggler who recognized him as he made his way back to rally his men. That day, 20 September 1643, was a black one for the Royal camp.

In the autumn of 1643 John Pym used his diplomatic talents to cement an alliance between Parliament and the Scots; it was his last service, for he died of cancer in December, 'always a man of business' and good character, 'yet not of those furious resolutions against the Church'[26]. In August 1643 a Solemn League and Covenant was drawn up (not to be confused with the 1638 National Covenant which repudiated the King's interference with the Kirk). The Solemn League swore to preserve the Church of Scotland and reform the religion of England and Ireland 'according to the word of God and the example of the best reformed Churches' and to protect 'the rights and liberties of parliaments'. On 25

September it was accepted by the House of Commons and the Assembly of Divines formed on 1 July to advise Parliament on religious reform; Parliament had already abolished bishops, but it was noted by the Congregational minister Philip Nye that they were not committed to imitate exactly the structure of the Scottish Kirk. For the cost of its maintenance, paid by Parliament, a Scottish army, 21,000 strong, began to march south in January 1644. A Committee of Both Kingdoms now ran the war for Parliament, concerting strategy and including members like the army and navy commanders the Earls of Essex and Warwick, M.P.s like Oliver Cromwell and Sir Henry Vane, and four Scottish representatives.

As Parliament sought Scottish aid, so the King looked to Ireland, ordering his Lord-Lieutenant, the Marquis of Ormonde, to arrange a peace with the Irish rebels to allow loyal troops to be sent from Ireland to reinforce the King in England. Peace was concluded on 15 September 1643 and the first troops from Ireland began to arrive before the end of the year. In Scotland, the King had a staunch servant in James Graham, Earl of Montrose, himself a Calvinist but loyal to the Crown, 'celebrated amongst the most illustrious persons of the age in which he lived'[27], and probably the greatest general of the Civil Wars. Appointed the King's Lieutenant-General in Scotland in February 1644, Montrose hoped that the Royalist faction in Scotland, supported by troops from Ireland, could create sufficient havoc to force the return of any Scottish force operating on Parliament's behalf in England.

Weakened by the loss of his London regiments, whose members returned to their shops and businesses, Essex was unable to prevent the capture of Reading, but London provided seven more regiments to attempt, under Essex and Waller, to retrieve the town. As Essex started, however, he diverted his course to Newport

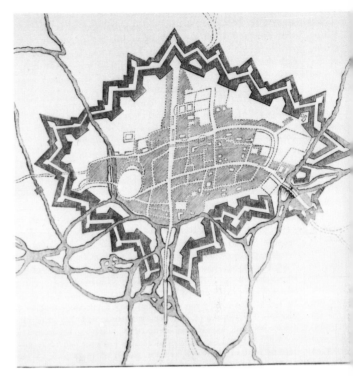

Above: Civil War fortifications: plan of defences of Oxford (engraving after Anthony Wood)

Below left and centre: Colours of 2nd and 3rd captains of Tower Hamlets Regiment (illustrations from contemporary manuscript; National Army Museum, London)

Below right: Colour of Edward Hooker, 2nd captain of Red Regiment of London trained bands (illustration from contemporary manuscript; National Army Museum, London)

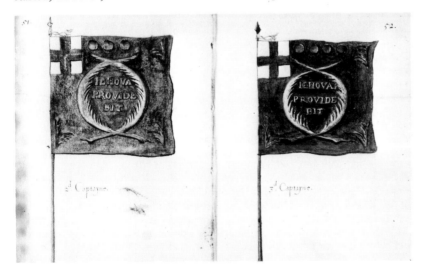

Pagnell, recently captured for the King and an important link in Royal communications with Newcastle's army in the north. The town remained in Royalist hands for less than a fortnight as its commander, Sir Lewis Dyves, withdrew without a fight due to a mistake in the orders from Oxford.

Royalist strategy at this point seems to have divided their effort when their resources were only sufficient for a single major campaign. Instead of securing the north in the face of imminent Scottish arrival (which would in turn have threatened the Eastern Association and curtailed an offensive from that quarter) whilst containing other Parliamentary forces, the King decided to attack Waller in the south-east with an army under Hopton, and send another force under Lord Byron (*ci-devant* Sir John) to clear Parliamentary forces from Shropshire, Cheshire and Lancashire and then, with assistance from Ireland, either attack the Eastern Association or assist Newcastle.

On 4 November 1643 Waller was appointed commander of the army of the South-Eastern Association (Sussex, Surrey, Hampshire and Kent) and made an unsuccessful attempt upon the Royal stronghold of Basing House, the defence of which was one of the truly remarkable sagas of the war. During November Waller's old friend (and adversary) Lord Hopton arrived in the area with an army of 1,500 horse and 3,000 foot, but without the Cornish Foot and including half-trained and mutinous troops. The original intention was for Hopton to contain Waller over the winter, but Waller's withdrawl, the Royal capture of Winchester and unfortunate reports that Sussex and Kent were ready to rise for the King, persuaded Charles to reinforce Hopton with 1,000 foot commanded by Sir Jacob Astley, a brave, plain and honest man, 'as fit for the office ... of major general of foot as Christendom yielded'[28], and order Hopton to take the offensive. He duly captured Arundel on 6/9 December 1643, but Waller (reinforced by two London regiments and 600 horse from the Earl of Essex) fell upon a Royalist detachment at Alton on 13 December, taking 875 prisoners (of whom half changed sides) and forcing Hopton to retire. Slain at Alton was the Royalist commander Sir Richard Bolle, upon the news of whose death the King called for a 'mourning scarf', for 'I have lost one of the best commanders in this kingdom'. Bolle and a few staunch Royalists had made their last stand in Alton Church, Bolle being killed in the pulpit as the Parliamentarians stormed in. Arundel fell to Waller on 6 January 1644.

Parliament's fortunes improved in the north towards the end of 1643, Hull defying the Marquis of Newcastle (he had been elevated in the peerage for Adwalton Moor). In early September the Earl of Manchester despatched the Eastern Association horse under Cromwell from the siege of Lynn to resupply Hull; Cromwell was joined by Sir Thomas Fairfax and his own horse who had escaped from the besieged town. Together, 'Old

PLATE 14

34 Ensign with 1st captain's colour, Charles Gerard's Regt. 1642

35 Pikeman, Charles Gerard's Regt. 1642

Charles Gerard's Bluecoats was one of the better Royal regiments of the Edgehill campaign, being 10 companies strong, recruited from Lancashire, Cheshire, Flint and Montgomery. The ensign illustrated wears a rather old-fashioned dress of a pikeman's corselet and helmet, with refinements of gilded stud decoration on the tassets, gilded shoulder straps and a helmet with flexible earflaps and a sliding nasal bar. Ward's *Animadversions of Warre* (1639) notes that an ensign should 'be gallantly apparelled, with a faire sword and brigandine' befitting his responsibility, some 'that rather they would undergoe the dishonour of losing their colours ... have chosen rather to wrappe them about their bodyes, and have leapt into the mercilesse waters, where they have perisht with their colours ...'[1]; when the colour represented not only a rallying point but also the honour of the company, its capture or preservation was always paramount. The colour illustrated is carried on a short staff about $9\frac{1}{2}$ feet (2.9 metres) high; in theory it should have been borne in one hand, leaving the other free for the sword, but the large size of the flag must have made this difficult in strong wind, even with the butt resting on the ensign's thigh. Gerard's colours were of simple design, having the usual St George's canton and the field divided into alternate blue and yellow segments, the design varying with the company; that illustrated is divided diagonally into triangles, the upper and lower blue and those at the sides yellow, with a gold wreath in the centre.

The pikeman wears an old-style helmet of semi-cabasset shape, with earflaps, and a corselet complete with gorget, a feature probably seen but rarely in the early stages of the war and hardly at all thereafter; the whole suit is enamelled black, and he wears a buff-leather gauntlet on his left hand and an ordinary wrist glove on the right.

NOTES

1 See Grose, vol. I, pp. 256–7

Noll' Cromwell and 'Black Tom' Fairfax laid siege to Bolingbroke Castle, to be joined by Manchester after he had captured Lynn. The Royalist governor of Newark, Sir John Henderson, attempting to relieve Bolingbroke, was roundly beaten by Cromwell and Fairfax at Winceby (11 October), only a few of the Royalists regaining Newark. This action proved not only the deterioration in the quality of the Royal northern horse but also the great improvement in that of Parliament, in particular Cromwell's Eastern Association horse. At Hull, too, the Cavaliers had problems, with perhaps as much as half Newcastle's army (filled with impressed conscripts) deserting to return home. Newcastle was too weak to resist a counterattack by the Hull garrison and retired, and on 20 October Lincoln fell to Parliament.

PLATE 14

34 Ensign, Charles Gerard's Regt. 1642   35 Pikeman, Charles Gerard's Regt. 1642

5 THE FIRST CIVIL WAR 1644

The year 1644 began inauspiciously for the Royalists in Cheshire, for although Lord Byron had been reinforced from Ireland and had besieged the last Parliamentary garrison in the county, Newcastle's failure in the north-east released more Parliamentary troops. Sir Thomas Fairfax was joined in Manchester by the local Round-head commander, Sir William Brereton, and a relief of Nantwich was mounted in mid January. On 25 January Fairfax fell upon Byron as the Royal forces were divided by the swollen River Weaver, and though Byron managed to unite his troops, the Irish fled. Byron escaped with his horse but the remainder were captured, more than half changing sides. Among the prisoners was George Monck, a Devonian veteran of the Dutch wars who had commanded a regiment in Ireland but had been removed from command due to his doubtful loyalty. He rejoined his regiment before Nantwich after a reconciliation with the King, but insisted on serving as a private volunteer pikeman. Committed to the Tower after his capture, he eventually agreed to serve Parliament in Ireland and was to play a major part in the restoration of Charles II. Having defeated Byron, Fairfax sat down to besiege the last major Royal stronghold in Lancashire, Lathom House, ably defended by Charlotte de la Trémoille, Countess of Derby.

On 19 January 1644, 21,000 Scots crossed the Tweed, commanded by Alexander Leslie, Earl of Leven, an elderly but experienced soldier who had been appointed Field-Marshal of Sweden in 1635 after a distinguished career under Gustavus Adolphus. A poorly educated man, this 'old, little, crooked souldier'[1] was probably past his best, but his army gave Parliament a vital advantage. Newcastle, fearing attacks from the Scots to his north and the Fairfaxes to the south, pleaded for assistance to both Prince Rupert and the King, rightly claiming that the Scottish threat must take priority over all other operations. Newcastle's 5,000 foot and 3,000 horse, partly ill-equipped, fell back on Durham with a threat on both sides; Newcastle was thus in no position to provide significant help to the Earl of Montrose who arrived at Durham on 15 March. All Newcastle could do was to call out the militia of Cumberland and Westmorland, provide Montrose with 100 horse and two cannon, and let him undertake an expedition to Scotland on his own.

Before Newcastle's appeal to the King, Rupert had already left Oxford for the north and began to form an army to relieve Newark, invested on 29 February by a Parliamentary force under Sir John Meldrum. Rupert cobbled together a force drawn from various Royal garrisons and defeated Meldrum outside Newark after a furious cavalry fight in which Rupert himself was almost killed. Meldrum's force surrendered and was allowed to go free, forfeiting their munitions, valuable acquisitions for the hard-pressed Royalists, and control of the area again passed to the Cavaliers; Lincoln and Gainsborough among other places again exchanged hands. But with his army having to return to their garrisons, and with no other troops to consolidate their gains, Rupert retired to Wales in search of another army.

In the south, Lord Hopton spent the winter training and recruiting his depleted army around Winchester, almost doubling his strength in comparative safety as the bad weather temporarily prevented Waller from pursuing the war. In March Hopton was joined by the elderly Lord-General, the Earl of Forth, who had requested the King that he be allowed to reinforce Hopton with 2,000 men rather than sit in winter quarters until spring. It was with some difficulty that Forth was persuaded to take command as the senior Royalist general. Hearing that the reinforced Waller was moving toward Winchester, the Royalist commanders advanced to make contact at Cheriton on 28 March. Though the Royalists were outnumbered (some 6,000 against Waller's 10,000), Waller held a council of war that night which resolved to retire. During the night he changed his mind and ordered his London brigade (the White and Yellow Regiments, both new to active service) to sieze the Cheriton woods. As the mist cleared in the morning, Hopton and Forth found themselves in for a battle instead of a pursuit, and set about clearing Cheriton woods. Outflanked, the raw London regiments retired. Hopton suggested an advance but Forth decided to hold their position, leaving Waller to advance or retire as he wished; probably in view of the disparity in numbers, Hopton complied. But Waller, with his eye for terrain, was so positioned that the Royal horse could only deploy in the advance by moving along a lane in the centre of their position, due to the hedgerow-covered country. The Royalists suffered an early disaster when young Sir Henry Bard, against orders, led his regiment into the Parliamentary ranks where it was destroyed utterly. Accounts of the Royal horse in the following

Marquis of Montrose (print by Fairthorne)

defeated the Royalists at Selby (11 April). Newcastle was thus compelled to move to York with his 6,000 horse and 5,000 foot and prepared for a siege, Leven following and joining the Fairfaxes at Tadcaster on 20 April. Despite its age, York was a strong fortification holding considerable supplies which were augmented by foraging parties sent out by the garrison until the besiegers became sufficiently powerful to impose a blockade. To husband his resources, Newcastle sent Goring with most of the horse into the Midlands, cavalry being of very limited use during a siege.

In the south, it was intended that Essex and Waller should unite at Aylesbury for a move against the King's headquarters at Oxford, Essex being supplemented by three London regiments, again 'loaned' for a limited period. The King, meanwhile, was assembling an army he intended to command in person, raising new regiments to garrison Oxford so that he could take his entire force with him. Unable to recall Prince Maurice from the siege he had commenced at Lyme, Charles withdrew

PLATE 15

36 Captain, Gamul's Regt.
37, 38 Officers, Royalist foot

The painted windows of Farndon Church provide one of the few contemporary (or near-contemporary) representations of the various ranks of a regiment, that of Sir Francis Gamul, perhaps the city trained band of Chester. A yellowcoat regiment (a colour perhaps derived from Gamul's arms), the men portrayed (including officers) all wear 'uniform' clothing, including yellow sashes and black bow trimmings for the officers, and perhaps even a form of rank distinction in the bands of lace around the breeches leg; the picture of Captain William Barnston of Churton, upon which this captain is based, has two bands of lace; senior officers had up to five. These rank badges (if such they are) may have been unique, for few other clues point to similar systems in use, though other badges are recorded, such as the embroidered crossed swords on the sleeve of members of the Provost-Marshal's staff. The partizan carried by the officer illustrated (with the tassel again in Gamul's livery) was also a badge of rank, rather more functional than the decorative 'leading staff', for example, when Sir John Owen was appointed colonel of the Caernarvonshire Militia in 1660, he bought two 'halberts' and a partizan costing £3, complete with tossells'.

The other officers wear suits with open sleeves, revealing the shirt; the redcoat carries a fine-quality wheel lock rifled musket, with which chosen marksmen might be equipped; his spanner for the wheel lock is suspended from a cord. The other officer carries a 'secrete', a velvet-lined steel cap worn underneath the soft hat.

NOTES

1 Tucker, N. *Royalist Major-General Sir John Owen* (Colwyn Bay, 1963) p. 125

action are conflicting, Clarendon claiming that they behaved ill, but others that they fought bravely; probably the fact that as the regiments passed down the lane and were defeated in turn as they tried to deploy demoralized the remainder, so that Hopton was able to rally only some 300, mostly the Queen's Horse which included many Frenchmen. During this furious mêlée Waller himself charged without his helmet and, though recognized by the enemy, survived. With the loss of their horse and their foot under severe pressure, Hopton and Forth broke off the action and managed to extricate their ravaged army in disorder and fell back on the Royalist stronghold of Basing House. Though the Royalist faction must have been thrown into despair (especially at the defeat of their much-vaunted horse), Waller was unable to press home the advantage as he might have wished as the London brigade, having completed the task they had agreed to undertake, went home.

In the north, Newcastle decided to attempt to retrieve Royalist control of the area, lost by the arrival of the Scots. Leven, however, refused to give battle and Newcastle withdrew to Durham, his cavalry leader Sir Charles Lucas inflicting a check upon the pursuing Scottish horse. Meanwhile, Sir Thomas Fairfax had returned from Lancashire and, reunited with his father,

PLATE 15

36 Captain, Gamul's Regt.

37, 38 Officers, Royalist foot

PLATE 16

39 Pikeman, Earl of Essex's Regt. 1642   40 Pikeman, Lord Brooke's Regt. 1642   41 Musketeer, Hampden's Regt. 1642

PLATE 16

39 Pikeman, Earl of Essex's Regt. 1642
40 Pikeman, Lord Brooke's Regt. 1642
41 Musketeer, Hampden's Regt. 1642

The pikeman of Essex's Regiment wears a complete corselet of the type probably seldom worn after the early engagements, the cumbersome gorget and tassets being discarded. Essex's Regiment wore orange coats (the distinctive colour associated with its colonel), the man illustrated also wearing the orange-tawny sash. Raised in Essex, the regiment was 1,500 strong in August 1642, one of the better Parliamentary corps, and served in Essex's army at Newbury and in Cornwall before merging with the New Model.

The pikeman of Lord Brooke's Regiment wears a knitted woollen (Monmouth) cap, his helmet hung from a hook on his backplate as recommended by Markham: 'if to the pikeman's head peece be fastened a small ring of iron, and to the right side of his back peece (below his girdle) and iron hooke, to hang his steele cap upon, it will be a great ease to the souldier, and a nimble carriage in the time of long marches'[1]. His helmet is of 'morion-cabasset' form, an older style than the wider-brimmed type; both pikemen carry 'good, sharpe, and broade swords (of which the Turkie and Bilboe are best), strong scabbards, chapt with iron'[2]. Raised in London, Brooke's Regiment wore purple coats and bore purple colours; it was about 1,000 strong at Edgehill, where it appears to have suffered heavily, and is believed not to have survived long after the death of Lord Brooke at Lichfield. Its second captain was John Lilburne.

Hampden's Greencoats was another fine regiment, raised in Buckinghamshire; one of its colonels following John Hampden's death was Richard Ingoldsby, the regicide, who took the regiment into the New Model. The musketeer illustrated has a matchlock musket and the usual bandolier, and carries a lighted match removed from the jaws of the lock. His hat bears a scrap of white paper as a field sign.

NOTES
1 *Souldiers Accidence*; see Grose, vol. I, p. 132
2 *Ibid.*

the force watching Gloucester (allowing the Parliamentary garrison to resupply), and ordered Rupert to join him from the north. Rupert pleaded successfully that he needed all his resources to attempt the relief of York, and recommended (unsuccessfully) that the King fortify Oxford and join Maurice in the west. Instead, Charles chose his own way, hampered rather than assisted by the council of war and his own lack of self-confidence: whilst Hopton could give sound advice, he was apt to change his mind in discussion; Forth was illiterate, deaf and had declined through excess of alcohol; General of Horse Lord Wilmot was an ambitious debauchee whose jealousy and dislike of Rupert led him to oppose anything the Prince suggested; Sir Jacob

Astley was never comfortable in conference; and the two Privy Councillors, Master of the Rolls Sir John Culpeper and Secretary of State Lord Digby, had little practical experience and, like Wilmot, were opposed to Rupert. This inauspicious group decided to dismantle the defences of Reading and add its garrison to the field army.

On 6 May Lincoln was stormed by the Earl of Manchester, and the whole county passed into Parliamentary control. Edward Montagu, second Earl of Manchester, had (as Viscount Mandeville) commanded a regiment of foot at Edgehill which was disbanded shortly after due to the speed at which it retired. Appointed General of the Eastern Association in August 1643, Manchester was no great commander and recognized the fact, being prepared to act upon the advice of those more experienced. 'Of a gentle and generous nature'[2] he was, with the Earl of Warwick, one of the leading English Presbyterians. His 'reverence and affection'[3] for the King, it has been suggested, prevented him from prosecuting the war to its utmost. With his forces free, Manchester moved to join the Fairfaxes and Leven in the siege of York, his men enabling the encirclement to be completed and the city starved into capitulation.

The Parliamentary stronghold of Lyme, besieged by Maurice, was of considerable tactical and moral value, for if it fell, Maurice reckoned that he could reduce the remaining Parliamentary fortress, Plymouth, and clear the area of their influence. Otherwise, Lyme had become something of a symbol as the little town was defended by the beleaguered garrison, led by the governor, Mayor Ceeley, and Colonels John Were and Robert Blake, the latter later winning fame as an admiral. On 23 May the Earl of Warwick, Lord High Admiral, arrived off the town with his fleet to replenish their supplies, and over the next two weeks reported to Parliament and the Committee of Both Kingdoms that the town's plight was desperate, that it must be relieved by land, and that its loss would severely damage morale in the entire south-west.

Due to the mutual antipathy of the commanders, it was probably with pleasure that it was decided on 19 May that the united armies of Essex and Waller should separate to operate against Oxford. The Committee of Both Kingdoms was dismayed by the decision, but as their military members were on active service and as Essex was the commander-in-chief with every right to give orders to his own subordinate (Waller), they had to be satisfied with it. In any case, Essex delayed the news of his decision until it was already implemented.

On 27 May a Royal council of war at Oxford agreed to follow a course proposed by Lord Forth (who was created Earl of Brentford on the same day), namely, to garrison Oxford as a secure base but to take the field army to manoeuvre against the Parliamentary forces, which, if Essex and Waller separated, might be overwhelmed in detail. Hopton was sent to take com-

Civil War fortifications: Micklebar Gate, York

Sir Richard Willys, showing the use of ceremonial blued-and-gilt cuirassier armour (portrait by William Dobson; Newark District Council)

mand of Bristol, as the King was concerned over the enthusiasm of its defence. The field army which left Oxford, however, was soon trapped between Essex and Waller and had to return to the Oxford defence lines. Charles slipped out under cover of darkness on 3 June with 5,000 horse and 2,500 foot and, in one of the most remarkable marches of the war, covered the 60-odd miles (97 kilometres) to Worcester by 6 June. The Parliamentary pursuit was interrupted by urgent instructions from London, prompted by Warwick, that Waller's army should perform the task for which it had been formed and march south-west to relieve Lyme. The two generals, however, decided that Essex's army should undertake this service, as Waller's men had not enlisted for general service and might be unwilling to stray so far from their Association. Leaving Waller to cover the King, Essex began the 130-odd mile (210 kilometres) march to Lyme. The siege was lifted in the early hours of 15 June as the Royalists had notice of Essex's approach; the Parliamentary army must have covered about 110 miles (177 kilometres) in a week, an excellent speed given the artillery and baggage which accompanied a large army and the wretched state of many of the roads. From that point, Essex had three alternatives: stay put, advance into the west, or return to Waller. The first was pointless, but the second had the possibility of destroying Royalist support in the area, as Warwick thought the presence of a Parliamentary army would cause widespread defection from the King's cause. Essex decided to leave Waller to cover the King alone.

Learning of Essex's departure, the King determined to engage Waller as soon as reinforcements arrived from Oxford, despite Waller's attempt to prevent the juncture. The armies met near Banbury but Waller's skill for choosing his own ground had established the Parliamentarians in so strong a position that the King refused to engage and began to march away from Banbury along the Daventry road on 29 June. Waller followed along the opposite bank of the Cherwell, both armies in view of each other. Hearing of a body of Parliamentary horse two miles (3.2 kilometres) ahead, the Royal van and centre were ordered to speed their rate of march to intercept them, but apparently no similar order was received by the rear, thus opening a wide gap in their line of march, through which Waller plunged across Cropredy Bridge and a ford across the river. The Royalists counterattacked, taking the ford but failing at the bridge, which was defended stoutly by Weldon's (or the Kentish) Regiment and the Tower Hamlets Regiment of the London brigade. Despite the near success of Waller's attack, he had suffered a sharp reverse and his army began to deteriorate through declining morale and desertion; it had always been less disciplined than Essex's army, and its commander was never as popular. Essex and his army regarded each other with mutual affection and their good discipline made them popular in the country areas where loyalties could be swayed by the treatment received from whichever army was currently in occupation. Waller's army, however, was now unable to prevent the King's return to Oxford or the pursuit of Essex.

Whilst these operations were in progress, Montrose crossed into Scotland with his small force of about 1,300, soon depleted as the Cumberland and Westmorland militiamen deserted in droves because they objected to serving outside their own immediate area. Montrose arrived at Dumfries with only a few hundred men, as 2,000 promised reinforcements from Ireland were not forthcoming and in the face of a Covenant army, Montrose had to abandon his guns and retire to aid Royalist efforts in the north of England. On 6 May his patent as Marquis arrived from the King, and three weeks later (aided by guns from the Newcastle garrison) he captured Morpeth. He was strengthening the defences of Newcastle when he was called to assist Rupert, but before he could do so, Royalist fortunes in the north had been decided in battle.

The walls of York being sufficiently strong to withstand artillery bombardment, the Parliamentary forces attempted to open a breach by mining beneath the walls. Newcastle tried to buy time by parleying with the besiegers, but on the morning of Trinity Sunday (16 June) a mine was sprung under St Mary's Tower on the northwest of the defences, and an assault made upon the Manor, a great house which had been the headquarters of the Lord President of the North, and where Strafford had lived between 1628 and 1633. Whilst many of the garrison's officers were attending Anglican service in the Minster, the attack was made apparently on the orders of Major-General Laurence Crawford who commanded Manchester's foot. Whether Manchester was aware of the attack is uncertain, but the other generals were not, and Crawford's storm of the breach created by the mine was repelled with the loss of some 300 men as a corps of volunteer citizens and some of Newcastle's

---

PLATE 17

42 Pikeman, bluecoat regt., Royalist foot 1642
43 Pikeman, whitecoat regt., Royalist foot 1642
44 Musketeer, redcoat regt., Royalist foot 1642

The bluecoat pikeman wears armour of 'sanguined' or 'russeted' metal, rustproofing like the black enamelling often shown in contemporary pictures. The breast- and back-plates are not attached by the usual strap, bolted to each side of the backplate and buckled at the front, but by hasp-and-staple fittings at the bottom edges, similar to the fixing of the shoulder-scales to the breastplate. He carries a knapsack, apparently an 'issue' item as early as 1626, and which (sometimes under its alternative name, 'snap-sack') is mentioned frequently in contemporary documents, containing spare clothing as well as four or five days' provisions when available: 'daily two pound of Bread, one pound of Flesh, or in lieu of it, one pound of Cheese, one pottle of Wine, or in lieu of it, two pottles of Beer. It is enough, crys the Soldiers, we desire no more ...'[1].

The whitecoat exemplifies the shortages which beset the Royal army, though Clarendon's comment that not one complete corselet existed in the army seems an exaggeration. However, many regiments were chronically ill-equipped, the man illustrated having no defensive armour save a buff-coat and a leather cap reinforced with iron bands, like a 'secrete' in reverse, on the outside of the cap instead of inside.

The redcoat wears a uniform suit and Royalist hat band; his musket has an old-fashioned stock and small trigger, a style dating from the first decades of the century. Such might have been the dress of the King's Lifeguard at Edgehill, a redcoat regiment raised in Lincolnshire and recruited with Derbyshire miners and Cheshire men, and not a selected élite as its title might suggest.

NOTES
1 Turner, p. 201

PLATE 17

42 Pikeman, Royalist bluecoat regt. 1642   43 Pikeman, Royalist whitecoat regt. 1642   44 Musketeer, Royalist redcoat regt. 1642

(647)

MERCVRIVS AVLICVS,

Communicating the Intelligence and affaires of the Court, to the rest of the KINGDOME.

The fortie sixth VVeeke, ending Novemb. 19.

SUNDAY. *Novemb.* 12.

 E have this day discovered the way which the *Faction* intend for Reformation of the *Protestant Religion*, not in opposition to the *Brownists* and *Jesuites*, for they professe to be the former, and love the latter all besides the name; but in a faire complyance to *Mahomet* himselfe: In prosecution whereof, the Earle of *Stamford* (before he bestowed *Exeter* on Prince MAURICE) tooke divers *Turkes* out of *Lanceston* Gaole, which were committed thither for divers piracies and robberies by Sea, and listed them into the service of the pretended *Houses*, which being not sufficient to gratifie these tender conscienced *Turkes*, he set a farther marke of favour on them, and married some of them (before they were christened) to such maides as his wisedome thought most fit; but whether these women were of his owne family and traine, or what kinde of children these new couples will bring into the Church of *England*, I leave to *Cornelius Holland*, who said openly at a late Committee, that *the Cavaleirs in his opinion were ten times worse then Turkes*; onely,

Vvvv   next

Mercurius Aulicus, issue 46

---

(662)

upon the place, their fellowes hasting home, lest by staying too long they would have no home to goe to.

But their News-men must needs hold up still, who this week say, 1. *That the Marquesse of* Newcastle *sent a Letter to His Majestie for supply, else the North would be lost*; *which Letter was intercepted and read in the Close Committee,* (it was read in the Close Committee before it was intercepted.) 2. *That some of the Irish Army come over to* Bristol *will not fight against the Parliament,* (and yet you say they are all *Irish* Rebels.) 3. *That the Garrison of* Plimmouth *have taken a great Worke from the Cavaliers called* Mount Stamford, (that is, the Cavaliers have taken it from the Garrison.) 4. *That Sir* William Waller *hath onely two men lightly hurt at* Basing, (the rest were maymed and killed out-right. 5. *That many men of quality will pay no debts by reason of these hostile times,* (this *Lye* was never read, nor voted by the *Members.*) But another new Intelligencer is entered in haste, who calls himselfe the KINGDOMES WEEKLY POST: and he sayes (6.) *That the Parliaments Northerne Army is at least* 18000 *strong,* (is not this some Knight of the *Post?*) 7. *That on Thursday last,* 48 London Cavaliers robbed the French *Ambassadour,* (those Cavaliers had wondrous short haire.) 8. *That some of the Ambassadours Plate will in time be discovered,* (yes, if you looke in *Guild-Hall.*) 9. *That Sir* William Waller *lost onely three men at the siedge of* Basing, (were all the rest Apes?) 10. *That* 5000 Kentishmen *are risen up to releive Sir* William Waller, (that's halfe a Lye, for though *Waller* need *reliefe*, the Men are not risen up.) 11. *That the New Assembly goes on unanimously,* (that is, they are all *Covenanters.*) 12. *That they will conclude their Controversies to the good of all Christians as well as of themselves,* (yes surely, they will do others as much good as themselves: especially at their *conclusion.*) 13. *That divers men of quality of the Cavaliers in* Basing *Castle were slaine by Sir* William Waller, (onely two common Souldiers, who are men of quality, compared to your *Commanders.*) 14. *That the* Irish *daily landing at* Bristol *will make all* English *Christians suffer like dogges, but no doubt the curse of God will scatter them*: O Sir, now you see your destiny, you are angry.

FINIS.

Mercurius Aulicus, issue 46; one propaganda news-sheet criticizing another!

Whitecoats rushed to the defence of the Manor. Had the other generals been told and mounted diversionary attacks, the assault might have succeeded; as it was it served only to dispirit further the investing army which was now suffering from sickness and hearing rumours of the approach of Rupert with a strong relief force.

Rupert made for Lancashire upon leaving Oxford, gathering a force with which to relieve York; he had about 6,000 foot and 2,000 horse when he left Shrewsbury on 16 May, but after capturing Liverpool and relieving Lathom House, still defended by the Countess of Derby, he was joined on 30 May by Goring with 5,000 of Newcastle's horse and 800 foot, and a few days later received a further 500 foot from Derbyshire. Around York, the besieging generals received Sir Henry Vane, an emissary from the Committee of Both Kingdoms, urging them to divide their forces and recover Lancashire (and, perhaps, it gave Vane an opportunity of

canvassing the generals about the establishment of a republic when the King was beaten, but this is uncertain). Wisely, the generals decided that as Rupert was obviously coming to them, their forces should remain united and await him.

On 14 June Charles I wrote a somewhat ambiguous letter to Rupert, in which the instructions even now are not completely clear. The significant part read:

If York be lost I shall esteem my crown little less; unless supported by your sudden march to me; and a miraculous conquest in the South, before the effects of their Northern power can be found here. But if York be relieved, and you beat the rebels' army of both kingdoms, which are before it; then (but otherwise not) I may possibly make a shift (upon the defensive) to spin out time until you come to assist me.

It is clear that the relief of York was uppermost in the

(201)   Numb. 26

A Perfect Diuinall

OF SOME

PASSAGES

IN

PARLIAMENT:

And from other parts of this Kingdom, from Munday the
15. of Iannary, till Munday the 22. of Iannary, Anno 1643.

Collected for the satisfaction of such as desire to be truly informed.

Printed for *Francis Coles* and *Laurence Blaikelock*: And are to be sold
at their Shops in the *Old-Baily*, and at *Temple-Bar*.

Munday the 15. of January.

Here was a Conference of both Houses this morning, upon occasion of a Letter from the Lord *Roberts* to his Excellency the Earle of *Essex*, for some supplies of money for the Army, which was left to the consideration of the Commons. And they accordingly taking the same into consideration, agreed in an order for the speedy raising of 10000 pound, out of the profits of the Excise Office, or to be procured upon loane for the present supply of the Army, untill such time as the said summe can be raised out ot the Excise Office. And they appointed a Committee to treat with the Commissioners for Excise this afternoone about the same.

There was also another Conference of the Houses about the Earle of *Holland*, touching which the Lords gave the Commons to understand, that they have been often sollicited by petition and otherwaies, for the restoration of the said Earle of *Holland* to his place in their House againe; and more particularly, received a petition on the Saturday before by the Noble Admirall the Earle of *Warwicke* in his behalfe; with much submission acknowledging his errour for his former deserting the Parliament, upon the grounds and reasons faithfully related, in his

Cc

A Perfect Diurnall of some Passages in Parliament; issue 26

King's mind, but later instructions that Rupert was to join him if the city could not be relieved point towards a view that Charles did not intend Rupert to fight at all costs. Lord Culpeper saw a copy of the letter shortly after it had been sent, and was aghast: 'Why, then', he said, 'before God you are undone, for upon this peremptory order he will fight, whatever comes on't'[4]. Whatever the case, Rupert carried the letter with him for the rest of his life to justify his conduct in the operations to relieve York.

By 30 June Rupert was at Knaresborough, some 12 miles (19 kilometres) from York. The Parliamentary generals, fearing being sandwiched between Rupert and the city garrison, marched out to meet him, barring his path from Knaresborough to York. By the simple expedient of a circuitous route, Rupert evaded the combined army and lifted the siege. This was all he had been instructed to do, but the Prince seems to have been determined to fight, irrespective of the true meaning of the King's letter. He seems not to have entered the city itself, but instead sent Goring to instruct Newcastle to draw his army out of York and join Rupert for an encounter with the Parliamentary and Scottish armies. Had Newcastle been able to read the King's instructions for himself, reason might have prevailed; as it was, some 17,000 Royalists (many hungry and dispirited by 10 weeks' siege) prepared to take on perhaps 28,000 (though other estimates put their opponents' strength at around 22,000).

Influenced by the Scots, the Parliamentary commanders decided to withdraw to ground of their own choosing, retiring on Tadcaster and covering Rupert's two presumed routes, to join the King or invade the Eastern Association. But when Sir Thomas Fairfax, commanding the rearguard, saw the approach of the Royalist horse, the Parliamentary army was forced to deploy upon Marston Moor. Rupert was a more capable commander than he has sometimes been described, but at times seems to have shown limited tactical ability; instead of catching the Parliamentarians attempting to deploy from line of march, he spent the time drawing up his own battleline in preparation for a 'set-piece' action. It was not until about 4 p.m. on 2 July that the Parliamentary and Scottish armies settled into their positions in line of battle.

Their right wing, around 5,000 strong, consisted of the horse of Lord Fairfax's army, commanded by his son, Sir Thomas, with three Scottish regiments in reserve; the Swedish tactic of interspersing bodies of 'commanded' musketeers between units of horse was used by both sides. The Parliamentary centre was organized in four lines: the first and third composed of units of foot from each of the three armies, and the second and fourth entirely Scottish, totalling perhaps 11,000 or considerably more. Leven commanded the centre, but exact details are unclear; Lord Fairfax may have commanded his own foot, but as Manchester had a major-general for this purpose (Crawford), he may have exercised personal command over the Eastern Association troops in the third line. The left wing was composed of horse, Cromwell and that of Manchester's army in the first line, the Scottish horse under Major-General David Leslie in the third, and the second mixed; in all something over 5,000. Rupert's army had its right wing of some 2,600 horse and interspersed musketeers under Lord Byron. The bulk of the Royal foot occupied the centre, perhaps 10,000 in number, and the left comprised the northern horse, commanded by Goring, some 2,100 strong with 500 musketeers. Rupert held back a reserve of 700 horse, including his own and Newcastle's Lifeguard. But Rupert's dispositions were unsound; his line was within Parliamentary cannon shot and hampered by hedges and ditches. Newcastle's foot, his Whitecoats, were the last to arrive (rather uncharitably described as 'all drunk'[5] by Rupert),

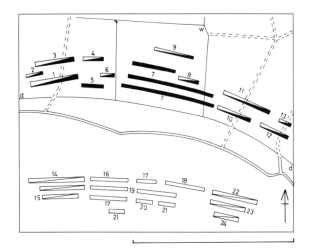

MARSTON MOOR

Royalist Army

1 Byron's Horse and musketeers **2** Tuke's Regt. of Horse **3** Molyneux's House **4** Rupert's Regt. of Horse **5** Napier's Foot **6** Trevor's Regt. of Horse **7** Eythin's Foot (commanded by Tillier & Mackworth) **8** Blakeston's Horse **9** Reserve Horse (Rupert's Lifeguard, Widdrington's & Porter's) **10** Goring's Horse and musketeers **11** Goring's reserve horse (Lucas & Dacre) **12** Langdale's Horse **13** Carnaby's Regt. of Horse

Parliamentary Army

14 Cromwell's Horse **15** Leslie's Scots Horse **16** Manchester's Foot (Crawford) **17** Lord Fairfax's Foot **18** Baillie's Scots Foot **19** Lumsden's Scots Foot **20** Scots Foot **21** Manchester's Foot **22** Sir Thomas Fairfax's Horse **23** Lambert's Horse **24** Eglinton's Scots Horse

d: ditches

w: White Syke Close

scale represents one mile (1.6 kilometres)

commanded by Lord Eythin (the Scottish professional soldier, General King, who may have commanded the Royal centre). Rupert showed him a plan of his dispositions; Eythin was appalled: 'By God, sir, it is very fyne in the paper, but ther is no such thinge in the ffields'.[6] Rupert offered to withdraw, but by then it was too late; as he had said to Newcastle that morning, 'Nothinge venture, nothinge have'[7], (though Rupert claimed he would have attacked earlier had he not been waiting for Newcastle).

The lateness of the day suggested that if battle were ever joined, it would be on the morrow; but Leven thought otherwise and called a conference of his generals. Probably Cromwell and Sir Thomas Fairfax were

PLATE 18

45, 46 Musketeers, Royalist northern foot
47 Sergeant, Royalist northern foot

Plate 18 illustrates the Marquis of Newcastle's gallant Whitecoat regiments immortalized by their 'last stand' at White Syke Close, Marston Moor.

Probably the white uniform colour was not intentional, but adopted simply because undyed cloth was more readily available than the red which Newcastle is believed to have favoured; a legend exists that the Whitecoats requested that their uniforms be left uncoloured, so that they could dye them in the blood of their enemies! Red uniforms were worn, however, as were unusual insignia (perhaps badges for valour), as noted in the following, concerning the siege of York in June 1644: ... a souldier of the Marquess of Newcastle was taken ... he was in a red suit ... Some more of the Marquesse his souldiers were taken prisoners also; they had white coats (made of the plundered cloath taken from the Clothiers in these parts) with crosses on the sleeves, wrought with red and blew silk, an ensigne wee conceive of some Po[p]ish Regiment'[1].

The musketeer wearing a buff-coat is shown blowing upon the match of his musket preparatory to firing, ensuring that it is glowing sufficiently to ignite the charge. The second musketeer is ramming down the charge of his firelock, with which some of Newcastle's troops are known to have been armed, including Percy's Regiment which provided the firelock guard for the artillery train. The sergeant wears a grey uniform (as may some of the Whitecoats) laced with silver and including a helmet, gorget and his badge of rank, a halberd.

NOTES

1 Ash S. & Goode W. *A Continuation of True Intelligence from the English and Scottish Forces* (London, 1644) issue no. 4; see Wenham, p. 46

still with their respective wings, and as Lord Fairfax and Manchester were comparatively inexperienced they must have bowed to Leven's recommendations. The probable absence of Cromwell and 'Black Tom' Fairfax would have had no great effect on the decision, for Fairfax never shunned a fight and Cromwell's Eastern Association horse, the 'Ironsides', were as reliable troops as existed. About seven in the evening the entire Parliamentary and Scottish line rolled down the gentle slope from their position towards the hedge and ditch in front of the Royal army. For the Royalists it must have been a great shock, both to the soldiers eating their supper and to the commanders; assured by Rupert that no action would occur, Newcastle was lighting his pipe in his coach when the attack began. It coincided with an immense thunderclap and a torrent of rain, extinguishing musketeers' matches and making the sight of the rapidly advancing Allied army even more terrifying.

The Allied centre rolled over the ditch and engaged the Royalist foot behind it with some success, but on

PLATE 18

45 Musketeer, Royalist northern foot   46 Musketeer, Royalist northern foot   47 Sergeant, Royalist northern foot

the right the attack went badly. Fairfax's horse came under heavy fire from the 'commanded' musketeers with Goring, and came off worst in the furious mêlée which followed; Sir Thomas received a cut on the cheek, and his brother Charles was mortally wounded. Part of the Cavalier horse pursued the broken elements of Fairfax's wing, whilst Sir Charles Lucas, who had executed a similar manoeuvre at Edgehill, prepared to charge the foot on the right of the Allied centre.

Cromwell's attack on the left achieved much more

Deployment of regiments of foot in alternate blocks of pikes and muskets, with artillery interspersed (from Sprigge's plan of Naseby)

'The Train guarded with Firelocks': the Parliamentary baggage camp at Naseby (from Joshua Sprigge's *Anglia Rediviva*)

than Fairfax's. Aided by a premature countercharge by Byron's horse, and even more by pressure from the impetuous Crawford's foot, Byron's first line was swept away by the Ironsides. Rupert, who had been eating his supper when the attack began, led his reserve in person to his right flank, where Byron was taking a beating; (the flight of that part of Byron's wing commanded by the triple-turncoat Urry should not be regarded as sinister; it was Urry's practice to change sides between battles, not in the middle of one). Newcastle himself attempted to rally some of the fleeing horse, but in vain; he then led Blakiston's brigade of horse against the Parliamentary centre, pushing them back and causing considerable havoc. Newcastle must have broken his sword in the fight, for he continued to lay about him with his page's sword, and as the Allied front collapsed a single pikeman made a one-man stand against the entire Royalist troop

Provision waggon (engraving by Jacques Callot)

PLATE 19

48 Pikeman, Earl of Manchester's Regt.
49 Musketeer, Col. Thomas Grantham's Regt.
50 Musketeer, Edward Montague's Regt.

Plate 19 illustrates members of Parliament's forces, *c.* 1643–4, all with a white field sign in the form of a handkerchief or slip of paper. The pikeman wears the green uniform, turned up with red, of the Earl of Manchester's Regiment of the Eastern Association; there is no evidence that the Earl's Edgehill regiment, when he was Lord Mandeville, wore the same colouring. The pikeman illustrated wears a breastplate with a flange on the bottom edge, instead of tassets, and has his helmet hung from a hook on his backplate.

The musketeer of Thomas Grantham's wears the regimental russet uniform; none of the early Parliamentary corps had more professional officers (at least nine with military experience, including a captain who had held that rank as early as the Rhé expedition), but the regiment disappeared in early 1643. The musketeer has wrapped his musket lock in cloth to protect it on the march, and carries a leather water bottle, which had to be acquired by the individual as no official issue was made despite the frequent scarcity of drinking water.

The musketeer of Edward Montague's Regiment wears its red uniform with white lining, the latter visible at the turned-back cuffs. He carries a firelock and a bandolier incorporating a scalloped-edged, buff-leather flap protecting the tops of the cartridge tubes from the weather. The somewhat archaic shape of the musket butt suggests that it may be a conversion from an earlier matchlock; many styles of butt and stock may have been used within the same regiment, at least judging from the collection of muskets preserved at Oxford which, with the collections at Apethorpe, Northamptonshire, and Littlecote, represents a remarkable survival from the mid seventeenth century. The Oxford muskets have barrel lengths ranging from 41 to 49 inches (104 to 124 centimetres); the Council of War in 1630 quoted 48-inch (122-centimetre) barrels, though the ordnance officers in 1639 recommended a reduction to 42 inches (107 centimetres); Turner notes that 'The longer a Musket is (so it be manageable) the better, for she shoots the further ... and experience daily teacheth what advantage a long Musket hath of a short one'[1]. The Oxford muskets have all manner of butts, from the 'French' (straight upper edge) to the crooked Spanish-style, the 'club' type or the modern shape; the carving 'OX' on the butts of some seems to denote a connection either with the regiment formed with the University's assistance in 1642, 'with such weapons as they had trained up and down the streets'[2], or by the University company raised during the Monmouth rebellion, in which case some of the muskets would have been very archaic.[3]

NOTES

1 Turner, p. 175
2 Quoted in Ffoulkes, C. *European Arms and Armour in the University of Oxford* (Oxford, 1912) p. 12
3 See Spencer, Dr M.G. 'Early English Muskets in the Town Hall at Oxford' *Journal of the Arms and Armour Society* IX (1977) 10–17

PLATE 19

48 Pikeman, Earl of Manchester's Regt.   49 Musketeer, Col. Thomas Grantham's Regt.   50 Musketeer, Edward Montague's Regt.

PLATE 20

51 Officer, Parliamentary greycoat regt.   52 Fifer, Parliamentary foot   53 Drummer, Parliamentary foot

PLATE 20

51 Officer, greycoat regt., Parliamentary foot
52 Fifer, Parliamentary foot
53 Drummer, Parliamentary foot

The greycoat officer wears a uniform of which the cut, shape of hat, sidearm and very voluminous sash are taken from one of the figures shown on the Farndon Church window. His gloves have fringed cuffs, turned back onto the hand.

The drummer's traditional rôle was like that of the cavalry trumpeter: to convey orders by drum beat (Turner noted that a proficient drummer should be able to beat a 'Gathering', march, alarm, charge, retreat, 'Travaille or Dian' and 'Taptoo') and to 'carry a message wittily to an enemy' [1]. Among marches in use was the ancient 'English March', dating probably from the Hundred Years War, which Charles I ordered to be resurrected in 1632. The French Marshal Biron said this tune, beaten on a drum, was slow, heavy and sluggish; 'That may be', replied Sir Roger Williams, 'but slow as it is, it has traversed your master's country from one end to the other!' [2]. Fifers occupied a less important place, Turner remarking that 'With us any Captain may keep a Piper in his Company, and maintain him too, for no pay is allowed him, perhaps just as much as he deserveth' [3], but he is in error in stating that 'here as home was acknowledg no such Creature' as 'Drummer-Major' [4], as drum-majors are mentioned before, during and after the Civil War.

Musicians traditionally wore elaborately-laced uniforms; for example, in 1587-8 Norwich purchased for their drummer a green kersey coat with eleven yards of lace and six yards of 'pointing', and spent 10s. on five yards of green and white Levant taffeta for their flute player, but few contemporary pictures are extant; the drummer and fifer portrayed in the Farndon window are copied from French engravings. Two carved figures from the staircase of Cromwell House, Highgate, show musicians wearing short coats open at the front, the fifer with a hat and the drummer wearing a cap similar to that illustrated, probably a type of montero with folded peak. The one extant picture of a Civil War drum, shown in the portrait of the King and Sir Edward Walker upon which Plate 2 is based in part, shows a brown wooden shell decorated with brass nails, red rims, and a coloured painting of the Royal Arms on the front, perhaps indicating that it belonged to the Lifeguard. Drums were usually carried on a sling as illustrated, with the skin almost vertical. The Cromwell House fifer carries a fife case on the right hip, slung from a shoulder belt.

NOTES
1 Turner, p. 219
2 Grose, vol. II, p. 44
3 Turner, p. 219
4 *Ibid.*, p. 224

---

which Newcastle headed (Sir John Metham's corps of gentlemen-volunteers). This anonymous, gallant man stood-off the Marquis of Newcastle but fell beneath the weight of the troop. At the same time, or just after,

Lucas made repeated charges against the Allied foot on the right, until he was unhorsed and taken prisoner.

With his centre apparently shattered and his right under what seemed intolerable pressure, Leven decided the day was lost and quit the field, as did Lord Fairfax; and on the left, Rupert's counterattack fell upon Cromwell's men at a time when they were probably without their commander, who may have retired to have a wound dressed. There is still doubt about Cromwell's part in the action, and even the nature of his wound, some saying that he was accidentally shot in the neck by one of his own men. Whatever his injury, several witnesses testified to his absence, and that his troops were led either by David Leslie or Laurence Crawford. Denzil Holles' *Memoirs* (written by a man who detested Cromwell) repeats a story that, at the critical moment, Crawford roundly cursed Cromwell's troopers for their inactivity, whereupon Cromwell appeared, 'and in a pitiful voice said, "Major General, what shall I do?"'. Crawford replied, 'Sir, if you charge not all is lost', whereupon Cromwell indicated his wound (Holles says a pistol burn) and left Crawford to lead the charge [8]. Holles' antipathy to Cromwell clearly puts this story in some doubt, at least to the degree if not the fact of Cromwell's absence. Whatever the case, Rupert's counterattack failed largely as a result of being charged in the flank by David Leslie's horse (Cromwell's reserve), which Cromwell somewhat ungraciously mentioned only as 'a few Scots in our rear' in a letter to his brother-in-law, Colonel Valentine Walton (in which he also communicated the following piece of news: 'Sir, God hath taken away your eldest Son by a cannon-shot. It brake his leg. We were necessitated to have it cut off, whereof he died' [9], a message not as terse as sometimes quoted, for he paid great tribute to the young man in the remainder of the letter). Whatever the truth of Cromwell's absence, however, he *did* ensure that not all his horse pursued the broken Royal regiments, but formed up in close order to menace the Royal foot in the centre, who were withdrawing following the patching up of the Allied centre.

As night came on, fugitives from both sides were scurrying away panic-stricken; both commanders were out of action, Leven having fled and Rupert, cut off even from his Lifeguard, hiding in a beanfield. The Royal foot was still largely intact and Goring had a body of horse with him on their left, whilst in the centre Manchester, alone of the three Allied commanders, held his place gamely. Despairing of retrieving the Allied right, Sir Thomas Fairfax took from his hat the 'field sign' (a piece of paper or white handkerchief used to distinguish friend from foe) and rode the length of the battlefield to Cromwell's horse, perhaps taking with him the remnants of his own command, including some Scottish lancers. Thus reinforced, the left-wing horse supported the centre as the Allied army wheeled east and struck the Royal foot, Cromwell apparently passing along what had been the rear of the Royal position to smash Goring's command and drive it from the field. He then turned and slammed into the rear of the Royal foot, already under pressure from the Allied foot. Not all were routed; Newcastle's Whitecoats and a regiment of greencoats (Broughton's or Tillier's regiment) fought bravely, the Whitecoats making an incredible 'last stand' in White Syke Close, a ditched enclosure, refusing quarter until, after an hour's futile resistance, they were all but annihilated.

By 11 p.m. the fires of battle were extinguished and the Earl of Manchester, the only Allied commander to stand his ground, was touring his victorious but shattered forces. His men were exhausted and famished but called that they would wait three days longer for sustenance if he would stay with them; in his own way the quiet, gentle commander of the Eastern Association was something of a leader. The captive Sir Charles Lucas passed over the field, identifying the corpses of his friends, saying 'Alas for King Charles. Unhappy King Charles'. It was said that 4,550 men were buried in White Syke Close. Next morning the wife of Colonel Charles Towneley, a Lancashire Royalist, came to look for his body. A Roundhead officer begged her to leave the scene of such carnage, where she could find only distress, and gave her a trooper to take her to safety. She later discovered that the officer was Oliver Cromwell; the hard exterior masked a heart.

Scoutmaster Watson of Manchester's army thought that the final charge at Marston Moor had decided the business of the kingdom. Perhaps it had, for the north was lost to the King. Rupert gathered what horse he could and departed, leaving the veteran governor of York, Sir Thomas Glemham, to hold out for as long as he could; he capitulated on 16 July. The Marquis of Newcastle, having expended a fortune and fought nobly for his king, quitted the war altogether, taking ship at Scarborough for Hamburg rather than 'endure ye laughter of ye Court'[10]. With him gone, there was no-one left capable of rallying Royal support in the north.

Charles I was in pursuit of Essex when he learned of the catastrophe. Given his letter stressing the value of York, it was difficult to understand why such disaster had occurred, but it probably added urgency to the King's campaign to destroy Essex. With the north gone (though Glemham's garrison was to be allowed to march out unimpeded to Chester), a victory in the south was imperative to attempt to redress the balance. Additional pressure might be put upon the Scottish alliance if Montrose could cause sufficient trouble in Scotland to compel the recall of their army from England, but when he met Rupert at Richmond two days after Marston Moor, Montrose was able to extract nothing from the despondent Prince, though he begged for 1,000 horse to take into Scotland.

On 23 July Essex reached Tavistock and wrote to the Committee of Both Kingdoms that he was intending to relieve the Parliamentary garrison of Plymouth, and

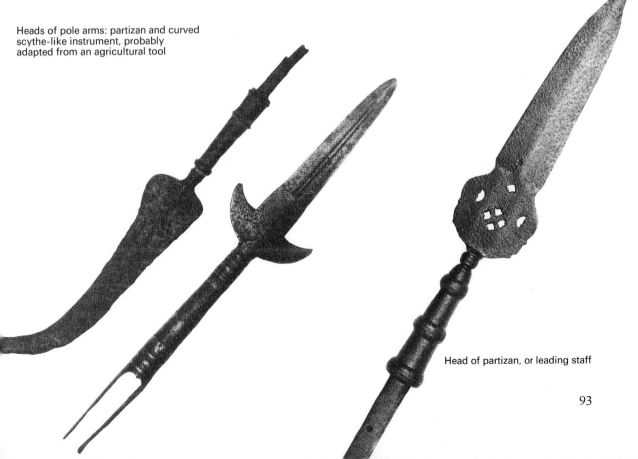

Heads of pole arms: partizan and curved scythe-like instrument, probably adapted from an agricultural tool

Head of partizan, or leading staff

93

hoping that Waller was following the King. After relieving Plymouth he had a choice: face the King or advance into Cornwall. Essex chose Cornwall, believing that the county would turn against the King and that the south-west could thus be cleared of Royalists. As Essex advanced, with Warwick's fleet cooperating offshore, he probably had 10,000 men, deducting troops left in garrison. The King, including the forces of Prince Maurice and the local Royalist leader Sir Richard Grenvile, could muster about twice that number. Essex pushed on into Cornwall, Grenvile retiring before him, but with the King at his heels. Essex hoped to capture Truro and Falmouth (the latter being one of the few contacts between the Royalists and the continent now that Newcastle was unusable, and the port from which was exported the tin which helped to buy the necessary munitions for the Royal war effort), but as this was no longer practical he withdrew to Lostwithiel in the hope of being resupplied – or evacuated – by Warwick's fleet via the port of Fowey. But due to contrary winds, Warwick never arrived. With empty sea at his back, short of provisions and in a hostile land (for the Cornish had not risen for Parliament), Essex's future was bleak. His only hope was to hold the King long enough for a relief force to break through and sandwich the Royal forces, but the necessity of holding both Fowey and sufficient land for his army to live off stretched his resources too thinly.

At this juncture a minor crisis occurred in the Royal command, for Baron Wilmot, Lieutenant-General of the King's Horse, had been urging that negotiations be opened with Essex, and Parliament, to put an end to the

Pikeman and musketeer in Civil War costume (from 18th-century document of Honourable Artillery Company)

PLATE 21

54 Musketeer, bluecoat regt., Royalist foot
55 Pikeman, greencoat regt., Royalist foot
56 Pikeman, yellowcoat regt., Royalist foot

The musketeer wears a cloth cap, probably a type of montero, in a colour matching his coat, a practice which is suggested by several contemporary references. His buff-coat is really only a short jerkin, and his short sword typical of those carried by musketeers but upon which critics like Turner poured scorn: 'the Butt-end of their Musket may do an enemy more hurt than these despicable Swords'[1]. He carries a modern-looking firelock with a carved butt like one of those in the Oxford collection, and has the cartridge tubes of his bandolier painted red. Both he and the greencoat have a sprig of foliage in their hats as a field sign.

The greencoat, from a regiment such as Broughton's or Tillier's Irish, has buff-leather lining to his armour instead of a buff-coat, and carries a bag resembling a sack with a strap attached at top and bottom, an alternative to the satchel-type knapsack. He bears his pike levelled at shoulder height in the normal posture for both attack and defence and known as 'Charge your Pike'. The yellowcoat, wearing a more classic pike armour including tassets and helmet, is in the posture of preparing to receive a charge of cavalry, crouching with the pike braced against the right instep, the head at horse's-breast level, and sword half-drawn.

NOTES
1 Turner, p. 175

war. Wilmot was a hard drinker and a haughty character, but was a capable officer and never allowed his drink to interfere with business. His remarks on negotiation, however, led to his arrest for treason and his replacement by Goring, whose immoderate drinking probably *did* affect his work.

Waller sent a small relief force of 2,000 horse under Lieutenant-General Middleton to help Essex, but it was repelled at Bridgwater. As the Royalist ring tightened around Essex it was obvious that his army was doomed, and on the night of 29/30 August Sir William Balfour broke out of the encirclement with 2,000 horse, reaching the Parliamentary garrison at Plymouth with the loss of only some 100 men, a considerable achievement. An attempt to retire on Fowey, where Warwick's ships might arrive, met with little success despite a valiant rearguard action by the veteran Skippon, and Essex decided to leave his army in its hopeless position, for as Parliament's commander-in-chief his capture would only aggravate the disaster. Leaving by fishing boat for Plymouth, Essex turned over his command to Skippon, who proposed a last attempt to cut his way out, but his regimental commanders reported that their troops were too exhausted. On 2 September the surviving 6,000 Parliamentary troops surrendered on generous terms, the

PLATE 21

55 Pikeman, Royalist greencoat regt.

54 Musketeer, Royalist bluecoat regt.   56 Pikeman, Royalist yellowcoat regt.

King being anxious to settle the matter before Parliamentary reinforcements might arrive in his rear. The defeated army surrendered their weapons (except the officers) but was allowed to march away on the proviso that they should not take up arms until reaching the Parliamentary garrisons of Portsmouth or Southampton. In a terrible march, the exhausted soldiers fell prey to angry civilians at Lostwithiel (who took most of their clothing) and, half-starved, large numbers perished from exposure. Clarendon claims that not a third of the army reached safety, but this may be an exaggeration; estimates vary from 4,000 to only 1,000 survivors. Essex reached Plymouth before Balfour's escaped horse, and was soon in London where his presence was greeted with relief.

The remnants of the Royal army in the north comprised some 3,000 in Cumberland and Westmorland, and Rupert with about 5,000 horse at Chester. Thus presented with little threat, the victorious Marston Moor army broke up, Leven to besiege Newcastle (which city presented a threat to his communications with Scotland), Fairfax to reduce Royal strongholds in Yorkshire, and Manchester to protect his own Eastern Association. The Committee of Both Kingdoms urged Manchester to attack Rupert in Chester, but he declined as his army had been badly mauled, and in any case his Association would refuse to support the army if it could no longer protect its home. Manchester, however, moved south shortly after Rupert took the same direction.

Leaving Plymouth blockaded, the King started his return to Oxford where his exhausted army might recuperate; they had been marching for almost half a year, were under-fed, unpaid and dispirited, and the horse were upset by Wilmot's dismissal. By the end of September Rupert had arrived to present a personal account of Marston Moor; the King ordered him to take his 2,000 horse and around 2,000 foot from Wales into Gloucestershire, hoping this would cause the Parliamentary command to divide its forces, for now Waller, Essex and Manchester were hoping to unite. On 15 September the King's army reached Salisbury, the horse 'most lamentable spectacles' according to the agents of the Parliamentary Scoutmaster-General Sir Samuel Luke. At Salisbury the King learned that Waller was at Andover, Manchester was approaching Reading with 5,000 troops and awaiting four London regiments, and that Essex's 3,000 were near Portsmouth. Rupert was still collecting his forces and it appeared doubtful that he could be of immediate help to his uncle; however, Parliament's forces were slow to concentrate, Manchester delaying as Royal marauders were at large in Lincolnshire, which Manchester's army was supposed to protect.

Instead of retiring to Oxford, the King (apparently persuaded by Goring) decided to attack his nearest enemy in the hope of defeating the opposing armies in

Pikeman's corselet with tassets, bearing armourers' marks of Commonwealth period, proving the continued use of tassets, though unpopular during the Civil War (Wallis & Wallis)

detail. He chased Waller out of Andover on 18 October, but the Roundhead escaped to join Manchester at Basingstoke. Charles had hoped to relieve the Royal garrison of Basing House, but on 21 October Essex joined Manchester in the vicinity, making relief impossible without fighting a major action. On 22 October Charles marched towards Newbury, already the site of one battle. The Committee of Both Kingdoms had appointed no overall commander, but left the campaign in the hands of a council of war, which in effect gave Manchester the command as Essex was ill.

At Newbury the King's army was well deployed, resting upon three strongpoints, Shaw House, Donnington Castle (held by the Royalists for over a year) and Speen village. The King commanded in person, with old Lord Forth (now Brentford) his deputy, Hopton in command of the artillery, Goring the horse and Astley the foot of the Oxford army; Prince Maurice was also present with part of his western army. Despite the advantage of numbers (perhaps around 17,000 to Charles' 10,000), the Parliamentary commanders decided not to risk a frontal assault on the Royal position, but embarked upon an enterprising but dangerous manoeuvre: the army was to divide, Waller to perform a circuitous march at night to attack the King from the rear, whilst Manchester would storm the Shaw House area of the Royal line. It was a plan fraught with danger, for if Waller's force were discovered the King could have overwhelmed Manchester before having to face Waller. Nevertheless, Waller set off on the evening of 26 October, swung past the Royal left and, though seen by Royalist scouts, some ineptitude allowed him to pass without impediment; nor was the King's army warned of the danger to the rear. At about 3 p.m. Waller's attack fell on Speen village, taking Maurice's troops completely by surprise; aided by the guns of Donnington Castle they put up a good defence until finally ejected. Maurice's horse was scattered, but Goring's horse repelled first Waller's right-wing horse (under Balfour) and, as it came up, his left (under Cromwell). Manchester, whose troops had been engaged in desultory fighting before Shaw House since daybreak, was apparently unable to recognize the noise of Waller's attack for what it was, and delayed his own assault until about 4 p.m., when it ran out of steam before Shaw House could be stormed.

By nightfall the fighting subsided, both sides thinking themselves beaten. As a Parliamentary attack the following day might have been successful, the King retired during the night, going to Bath to inform Rupert of the situation, leaving Maurice and Astley to extricate the army. The Roundheads were not even able to occupy Donnington Castle, much less prevent the retreat of the Royalists to Oxford. Combined with the disaster at Lostwithiel, this battle proved that Parliament needed a totally reorganized army and, perhaps, more determined leaders.

Before leaving the campaigning season of 1644 with an account of Montrose's actions after Rupert refused to help him following Marston Moor, it is necessary to sketch events in Ireland during the first years of the Civil War. Internal warfare had been in progress some time before the war in England; less clear-cut than the Civil War, aims and allies varied with circumstance. It began with a rebellion in October 1641 by the native Irish and 'Old English' Catholics (i.e. descendents of the English settlers) against the Protestant government; war in England divided the government of Ireland between Royal and Parliamentary factions, and the Scots in the north-east followed their own line. The King's Lieutenant-General in Ireland, the Marquis of Ormonde, had insufficient forces to control the guerrilla tactics of the Irish, and by the outbreak of war in England the rebels had won almost all of Cork and Limerick; the Scots in the north controlled the

NOVEMBER 1644

Royalist Garrisons in Parliamentary areas
1 Carlisle **2** Bolton Castle **3** Scarborough **4** Greenhalgh Castle **5** Knaresborough **6** Latham House **7** Pontefract **8** Sandal Castle **9** Beeston Castle **10** Newark **11** Belvoir Castle **12** Lichfield **13** Ashby de la Zouch **14** Crowland

Parliamentary Garrisons in Royalist areas
15 Montgomery **16** Abingdon **17** Taunton **18** Lyme Regis **19** Plymouth
Shaded portion represents territory in Royalist hands in November 1644

Carrickfergus area. In the summer of 1642 a number of Irish mercenary officers returned from service in the Spanish army, notably Owen Roe O'Neill and Thomas Preston, the former the most skilled soldier in Ireland. Both took service against Ormonde, Preston being appointed to command the army in Leinster by the Supreme Council of the Catholic Confederates, though their nominal adherence to the King made no immediate difference to the war. In 1643 the Supreme Council of the Confederates appointed the Earl of Antrim a general, and in November of that year he returned to Oxford (where he had spent the previous winter) with a proposition: that the King should appoint

him general-in-chief of the Confederate forces whilst he raised 10,000 troops to serve under Royal command in England and 3,000 in Scotland. Pressure was temporarily removed in Ireland as two months before Ormonde had negotiated a 12 months' armistice with the Confederates. Charles was unimpressed by Antrim's claims, as clearly O'Neill would never accept him as overall commander; but, given Antrim's influence in Scotland and the desperate need for troops, the King accepted the offer of men, never expecting any for use in England. The Supreme Council, indeed, was not enthusiastic, but agreed to send 2,000 troops to Scotland, formed in three regiments under Antrim's kinsman Alasdair Colkitto Macdonnell, whose Scottish ancestry might be expected to win support in that country. The three regiments (Alasdair Macdonnell's own, James Macdonnell's and Colonel O'Cahan's) were three-quarters Irish and the remainder Scots or English; all had served under O'Neill, all were Catholics, and they proved to be among the best foot on either side.

In early July Alasdair Macdonnell landed in Argyllshire and attempted to rally support from the west Highland clans, but met with limited success due to the predominance of the Covenant forces. The saturnine Presbyterian Archibald Campbell, Marquis of Argyll, raised his clan and destroyed Macdonnell's ships, leaving him isolated. Macdonnell managed to recruit 500 Gordons, but wrote in desperation to try and contact Montrose, who at this point was roaming the area of Perth and Dunkeld endeavouring to drum up support. Montrose and Macdonnell united at Blair, where Montrose unfurled the Royal standard. Montrose's force comprised only the Irish 'brigade', if it may be so termed, and some 1,200 Highlanders, the latter ill-disciplined and armed with bows and broadswords, but his opponents were not much better off – Highlanders and largely untrained local levies. Three Covenant armies faced him, Lord Elcho in Perth, Argyll's Campbells in the west and Lord Burleigh at Aberdeen, so Montrose set about defeating Elcho before he could be joined by Argyll. Montrose's small force met Elcho (7,700 strong, though 500 of his archers had changed sides the previous day) at Tippermuir on 1 September. Short of ammunition, Montrose arrayed the Irish in three ranks (instead of six) to enable them to deliver one massive volley which he hoped would be enough; the Atholl clansmen he commanded in person had only

Loading artillery; the lower cannon is being cooled by cloths or skins soaked in water (from *Les Travaux de Mars* by A.M. Mallet, Paris, 1684)

Equipment belonging to Sir Francis Rhodes of Barlborough Hall, Derbyshire, including buff-coat with white tape lacing and silver-wire buttons, carbine belt and swivel, sword and belt, arm defence made of three skins of leather and one of pasteboard, fixed to buff-leather glove, and 45-in. (114-cm) 'Toledo' (rapier) associated with 'a suit of common iron armour, with a barred helmet', believed to date from 1620 (engraving by T. Hamilton)

stones to throw. It was more than enough, for Elcho's horse charged, was devastated by musketry, broke and fled; Montrose's whole force followed and utterly routed the remaining Covenant troops.

Perth surrendered immediately, but Montrose lost almost all of his army save the Irish, the Highlanders following tradition and, after winning a battle, returning home with their loot, a problem which was to dog Montrose for the remainder of his career. Not daring to await the junction of Argyll and Burleigh, Montrose set off to defeat the latter, recruiting some 75 invaluable horse on the way. On 13 September he routed Burleigh before Aberdeen, the indifferent Covenant levies proving no match for the Irish brigade. Still with insufficient strength to meet Argyll, Montrose retired, leaving a remarkable success behind him, having defeated two and evaded one of the three armies sent to annihilate his small force.

6 NEW MODEL: THE FIRST CIVIL WAR 1645

Parliament capitalized not at all upon the second battle of Newbury; they called upon the governor of Donnington Castle, Sir John Boys, to surrender, or they threatened not to leave one stone upon another. Boys replied that he was not responsible for the upkeep of the castle, but if they did pull it down he would still defend the ground on which it stood. The Parliamentary attack upon it failed and they retired, choosing not to pursue the King.

Charles I reorganized his army, replacing old Forth with Rupert as his senior general, which Clarendon thought thoroughly unwise, though the Prince possessed better qualities than might have been apparent. Despite a half-hearted attempt to prevent it, the King relieved Donnington Castle in early November, and Basing House later in the month. With desertion rampant, the Parliamentary army retired into winter quarters around Reading and Farnham, and the King to Oxford. Elsewhere, 1644 drew to a close with several Parliamentary gains; on 27 October the Scots captured Newcastle, whilst Fairfax mopped up Royal garrisons in Yorkshire. On 1 November Liverpool surrendered, the morale of its Royalist garrison having collapsed as its Irish members believed they would be murdered if the city were stormed. They siezed their officers and surrendered on the condition that they were transported home; it was only just in time, for on 24 October an ordinance had been passed to the effect that all Irishmen taken in England or Wales were to be executed, an attempt to end the recruitment of such 'mercenaries' into the Royal army.

Despite Royal reverses in the north, it was now painfully obvious that Parliament could only achieve total victory by a drastic reorganization of their forces and military leadership. The central necessity was for the creation of a 'general service' army, one unhampered by local loyalties and commanded by those prepared to prosecute the war to its utmost. The more extreme members of Parliament tended to shift all blame onto Essex, Manchester and Waller, whose Presbyterian beliefs saw the King as the supreme authority, without whom the social order would dissolve into anarchy. This, it was contended, caused such members of the Presbyterian 'aristocracy' to seek not the defeat of the King, but merely an accommodation which would end the war with the King remaining as the country's figurehead. Thus Waller's failure to exploit Cheriton might be seen

as an attempt to avoid defeating the King completely; thus might be explained Manchester's apparent lethargy in his march to Second Newbury. One incident following Second Newbury could be quoted in evidence: John Birch, a Parliamentary colonel, heard a report that the Earl of Forth's personal baggage train might be intercepted, and reported as much to Manchester. Manchester replied that he was resting and could give no instructions until morning; scandalized, Birch gathered 47 'resolved horse' and charged off after Forth, who managed to escape, though losing all his baggage. Birch's reception with his booty was decidedly cool. Was this simply courtesy on the part of a general towards a beaten opponent, or evidence of a lack of desire to prosecute the war to its ultimate? Cromwell thought the latter, that Manchester believed 'that this war would not be ended by the sword ... but it would be better for the Kingdom if it were ended by an accomodation'[1]. Adherence to the King on the part of some Parliamentary commanders only maintained the original aims of the war, which (waged in the name of the King) precluded an all-out offensive, as the war was being conducted *on behalf of* the King, at least in theory; as the *Souldiers Catechisme* claims, 'I am for the King and Parliament ... *But is it not against the King that you fight in this Cause? No surely: yet many do abuse the world with this base and absurd objection ...*'[2]. Even the Scottish *Articles and Ordinances of Warre* (1644) noted as Article V, 'If any shall speak irreverantly against the Kings Majestie & his authoritie, or shall presume to offer violence to his Majesties Person, he shall be punished as a Traytor', which even if never enforced at least maintained the facade of fighting on behalf of the King. The charges made against Essex, Manchester and Waller had some foundation; Essex said that 'rather than they would consent to make the King a prisoner, they would all die'[3], and Waller numbered among his principles that 'the person, dignity, and honor of the King preserved, and the peace and safety of the Kingdom settled'[4].

The problem was complicated by personal feelings. Cromwell's dislike of his immediate superior, Manchester, originated before the war and perhaps coloured his appraisal of the situation and (as a member of the Committee of Both Kingdoms and an M.P. – and incidentally a far better commander than Manchester), he accused the Earl of hesitating deliberately at Second

Newbury on the grounds that 'if we beat the King ninety-nine times yet he is King still, and we subjects still; but if the King beat us once we should be hanged and our posterity undone'[5]. Waller supported this criticism, though Manchester may have been no more than an over-cautious general. Coupled with this was a belief in some quarters of Parliament that their successes were so limited due to God's displeasure at their lack of radicalism, and that 'Man's power doth execute what God decrees'[6] and success would only follow when God's supposed will had been implemented, i.e. the overturning of what might be termed the 'establishment' by the more radical Protestant sectaries. Steps had already been taken in January 1645 with the abolition of the *Book of Common Prayer* in favour of a Presbyterian directory of worship, and, on 10 January, the execution of Archbishop Laud for treason he had not committed.

After his initial attack on Manchester, Cromwell's tone moderated, though his beliefs remained unaltered: that the war should be won not only to ensure constitutional reform but to reshape the Church. Manchester, though the King's leading critic in the House of Lords before the war, still favoured reconciliation. Parliament's solution was framed in the Self-Denying Ordinance, suggested by Cromwell to quash criticism that

'the Members of both Houses have got great places and commands, and the sword into their hands; and, what by interest in Parliament, what by power in the Army, will perpetually continue themselves in grandeur, and not permit the War speedily to end, lest their own power should determine with it'[7]. The Ordinance stated simply that no member of either house should hold military command (later amended to the effect that all should resign their commissions, but with nothing to stop their reappointment). Its critics saw it as a way of removing Essex and Manchester from their commands without dismissing them outright; and though the House of Lords (those supporting Parliament, that is, for the Royalists naturally could not attend) put up a fight, the Ordinance was passed on 3 April 1645; to save unpleasantness, both Essex and Manchester resigned their commissions just before the Ordinance came into effect. Parliament's revised 'New Model Army' could now settle down under its new commander, Sir Thomas Fairfax, the only senior Parliamentary officer not affected by the Ordinance. The claims of this capable, modest but somewhat inarticulate and unpolitical general had been advanced by Cromwell, whose advice was accepted; the position of commander of the foot went to the veteran Skippon, and the equivalent position for the horse was earmarked for Cromwell, temporarily barred by the Ordinance.

The New Model (or rather, Parliament's army 'new modelled') was neither totally new nor always termed so; 'the Army under Sir Thomas Fairfax' was a common designation in contemporary documents, and officially

'Lobster-tail' helmets, with triple-bar face guard and hinged peak (left), and sliding nasal bar and fluted skull (right) (Wallis & Wallis)

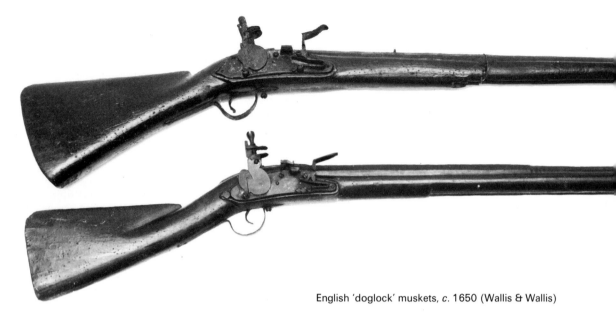

English 'doglock' muskets, c. 1650 (Wallis & Wallis)

it ceased to exist in 1647 when Parliament created a standing army with Fairfax as commander-in-chief of all land forces, local forces hitherto remaining independent of the New Model. Even before the passing of the Self-Denying Ordinance, a total reorganization of Parliament's forces was under way in order that the campaigning season of 1645 could commence without giving the Royalists an advantage. Nominally, the New Model Army was to comprise 22,000 men in 11 regiments of horse, 12 of foot and one of dragoons; precise establishments were set, but there is some doubt whether all were raised. Formation of the new army was based upon those of Essex, Manchester and Waller, with regiments transferred en masse, reorganized or formed of impressed men to make up the numbers, and in some cases members of more than one army combined in the same regiment, for example Aldrich's Foot, later Lloyd's. Some regiments were transferred directly whilst others were reorganized completely, and Cromwell's 'double regiment' of horse split into two new ones, those of Fairfax and Whalley. In the formation of the old Eastern Association army, experienced soldiers had been attracted from afar, some of the horse, for example, having served previously with Fairfax and Waller, in Liverpool, Cheshire or with the city brigade, attracted by prospects of promotion or of joining an army where religious Independency was in favour. The recruiting of experienced men thus improved the quality of the Association forces, especially the horse, and it was from here that most of the New Model's horse was taken. The foot came largely from Essex's army, though Waller's and Association regiments were also represented.

Coming from existing armies, the newly organized army was not as radical as has sometimes been asserted, at least not at this stage. The officers commissioned into the New Model do not seem to have depended upon religious persuasion or patronage, but upon 'antiquity or merit', and at least at the start there appears to have been little connection between the radical religion in the army and radical political activity; certainly some regiments (particularly horse) became renowned for extreme views, such as Cromwell's ex-Ironsides, now the regiments of Fairfax and of Cromwell's cousin, Edward Whalley. Fleetwood's Horse had a number of fanatical Independents in its ranks, and included at one period the Fifth-Monarchist Thomas Harrison. Much of this religious radicalism emanated from Manchester's old army, though the criterion for an Eastern Association recruit was an 'honest Godly' spirit without specific conformity. The accusation of the 'low birth' of New Model officers (especially after 1647) is probably largely untrue, though in the Association horse, for example, only Manchester's Lifeguard was composed of what Mercurius Aulicus termed 'the gentler sort of rebels'[8], and Cromwell himself reported difficulty in getting 'men of honour and birth'[9]; Manchester's army was officered by experienced professionals (including one French colonel and a number of New Englanders as well as Scots), and, at least initially, local dignitaries were commissioned as often as officers like Cromwell's 'plain russet-coated captain that knows what he fights for and loves what he knows'[10]. The same was probably true of the New Model, though by this time length of service and ability had become primary considerations. There is little evidence of religious discrimination; the House of Lords objected to two colonels and 40-odd captains from Fairfax's original list of proposed commissions, some because they were Independents but others on the grounds of patronage. Essex led the fight against their inclusion, but objections were withdrawn when a vote ended in a dead heat, until a proxy from Essex's brother-in-law, the Earl of Clanricarde, was disallowed due to his being a Catholic.

Discipline in the New Model, certainly superior to that of the previous armies (notably Waller's, renowned for pillaging), was largely a development over years of war rather than new policy, though the popular belief that the New Model was composed of sombre, psalm-singing Puritans is quite misleading; as Sir Samuel Luke noted, 'I think these new modelles kneads all their doe with ale, for I never saw soe many drunke in my life in soe short a tyme'[11]. The combination of experienced officers and well-trained, disciplined veterans leavening the recruits or impressed men made the New Model into a formidable force; as the *Souldiers Catechisme* claimed, 'fresh-water souldiers are commonly faint-hearted souldiers; whereas they that have been used to the Warres are usually of undaunted spirits[12] . . . a few well-trained Soldiers are better then (sic) a multitude of raw, unexperienced men . . . Every souldier should seeke God by prayer . . . for it is the blessing of God that makes men to profit in any profession . . .'[13]

It is possible, indeed, to overestimate the religious bigotry present in the Civil War armies; whilst it is generally true that the more radical Protestants supported Parliament and most Catholics took the King's part, only certain regiments were affected seriously by religious fanaticism, though its effect was sometimes profound. For example, the decision to declare Basing House a Catholic garrison, depriving it of some 500 excellent (but non-Catholic) Royalist troops and their energetic leader, Sir Marmaduke Rawdon, was a major contributory factor in its fall, and the interference of the ministers in the running of the Covenant armies against Montrose had similar dire results. Turner's remark that a chaplain's duty 'is to have *Curam Animarum*, the care of Souls, and it is well if he meddle with no other business . . .'[14] was probably made with the knowledge of the results of such interference. Over-zealous religious beliefs led to misguided views on both sides; for example the *Souldiers Catechisme* claimed that the Royalists were 'for the most part Papists and Atheists . . . generally the most horrible Cursers and Plasphemers (sic) in the World . . . for the most part, inhumane, barbarous and cruell . . .'[15], 'men so loose, lewd, and wicked, as most of your Cavaliers are . . .'[16], whilst explaining why 'there are so many lewd and wicked men in the Parliaments army . . . Because Commanders in Chief are not more carefull in choosing godly Officers . . . honest religious men are not more forward to put forth themselves . . . Order and Discipline is not more strictly executed by Superiors . . . Officers in Towns and Countries aim to presse the scumme and refuse of men, and so by easing themselves, pesture our Armies

with base conditioned people'[17]. Religious fanaticism could be manifested in an altogether more distasteful manner; for example, in the final storm of Basing House, the Royalist Major Robinson (in civilian life a Drury Lane comedian) was one of a number murdered in cold blood. He attempted to surrender to Thomas Harrison, the fanatical major of Fleetwood's Horse, who shot him dead, crying 'Cursed be he that doeth the Lord's work negligently!'[18]. Harrison also killed another of the garrison's officers, Major Caffaud, whilst the latter was running away. How different from Essex's instruction, 'I shall desire . . . that you avoid cruelty, for it is my desire rather to save the life of thousands, than to kill one . . .'[19]. The belief that 'Almighty God declares himselfe a friend to our Party'[20] could lead to as unpardonable excesses as could the behaviour of 'lewd and wicked men', or to simple blood lust as exhibited at Colchester in 1648, when the death of Colonel Needham caused his Tower regiment to go berserk, 'killing and slaying in a terrible manner'[21] so that 'they will hardly admit of quarter'[22].

Before resuming an account of the events of 1645, mention should be made of a growing movement around this time called the 'clubmen'. Supplies for an army were usually garnered from the area in which it was situated as there was comparatively little transportation of food and fodder over large distances. Local acquisition could be accomplished amicably when the army had cash to buy provisions, but as pay on both sides was often weeks or months in arrears, food was often acquired by payment with a ticket redeemable from the army's administrators, or simply by theft. The habit of plundering friend and foe alike afflicted most armies and in some cases was allowed to proceed unchecked, though only the ransacking of opponents' property (or that of 'neuters') would usually be permitted officially. The large numbers of men who enlisted simply for loot, coupled with 'legitimate' plundering for food and weaponry, created widespread destruction. This ruination of the lives of innocent civilians is described in numerous documents:

The Cavaleers are extremely outragious in plundering . . . puting no deferanc at all betweene friends and supposed enemis . . . taken al that hath been usefull for them and ript up fetherbeds and throwne the feathers in the wind to be blowen away for sport and scaned all the barrels of beere and wine and spilt it in their sillers. They have kild of one mans 1,000 sheepe and throwne away much of it they could not eate, many other outrages they commit to large to exspres this way . . .'[23]

Even officers in positions of responsibility succumbed to the temptation to plunder; during the Scottish siege of Newcastle, for example, the Scottish officer Sir John Lesley wrote to Sir Thomas Riddle of Gateshead, offering to prevent the plunder of Riddle's house in exchange

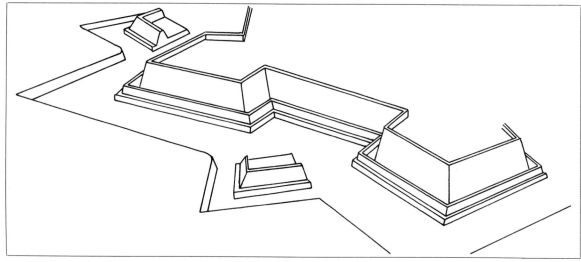

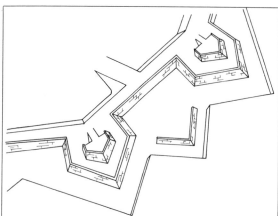

Civil War fortifications: two bastions connected by a stretch of *enceinte* (curtain wall) which is protected by ravelins (V-shaped fortifications) in ditch. A low wall runs around foot of ramparts

Civil War fortifications: aerial view of double bastion with masonry facing. On each bastion is constructed a higher gun-platform or 'cavalier', and set in ditch is a ravelin or V-shaped fortification to protect exposed length of curtain wall between the two bastions. Earthen ramps lead up to curtain wall, and from rampart to cavaliers, to facilitate the moving of ordnance

Civil War fortifications: cross sections through ditch and rampart of earthwork fortification. Top: rampart protected by palisade of vertical stakes. Bottom: rampart protected by a 'fraise', a line of horizontal stakes

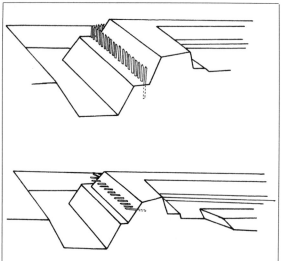

Civil War fortifications: design of earthwork 'sconce', a four-bastioned fort

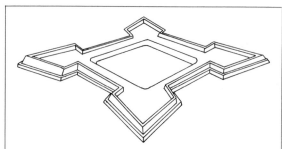

for a £30 bribe, some barley, a horse and Riddle's chiming clock: 'I maun hae the tagg'd tail trooper that stans in the staw, and the wee trim gaeing thing that stans in the newke of the haw chirping and chirning at the newn tide o'the day ...'[24]

Results of such looting were twofold; firstly, it alienated the local population and drove them to support the opposite faction (as late as 1648 it was noted that a unit of Essex foot fought especially hard as they were 'much incensed against Goring and his party'[25] for bringing the war to their county); and secondly it gave rise to self-defence associations of 'clubmen', which themselves sometimes took on political bias, the majority of these swinging towards Parliament. As early as 1642 it was reported that 'the country meet, and not only intend to stand upon their guard, but to disarm all the papists and malignants within their precincts ... The men of Blackburn, Padiham, Burnley, Clitheroe, and Colne, with those sturdy churls in the two forests of Pendle and Rossendale, have raised their spirits, and are resolved to fight it out rather than their beef and fat bacon shall be taken from them ...'[26], protecting their homes from the most likely marauders, the Royalists. Some wished to oppose whichever side tried to plunder; John Williams, Archbishop of York (who changed sides from Royalist to Roundhead) claimed that by fortifying himself at Penrhyn, 'I kept my House neither against the King or Parliament, but to prevent Surprizells'[27], a policy exemplified by the mottos inscribed on the flags of the clubmen:

If you offer to plunder or take our cattel,
Be assured we will bid you battel.[28]

Despite their poor arms (typical weaponry was described as carried by an anti-Royalist mob in Devon in 1642, 'some with Muskets loaden, some with Halberts and Black Bills, some with Clubs, some with Pikes, some with dung Evells, some with great Poles, one I saw had heat the calke of a sive [scythe] and beat him right out and set him into a long staffe ...'[29]), they were sufficiently numerous to harrass an army, especially after some had decided to support one faction or the other instead of being simply anti-war.

In the winter of 1644–5, before the New Model Army was operational, Parliament managed to relieve Lyme, but elsewhere ran into problems. A surprise attack captured Weymouth in early February 1645 and Waller was ordered to recover it; his foot, however, previously of Essex's command, hated him and refused to proceed under his orders. They agreed to march when Cromwell joined them, but their action hastened the Lords' acceptance of the New Model Ordinance. Goring's forces at Weymouth were held up by the Parliamentary garrison of Melcombe (reinforced by a landing party of sailors) and retired before the approaching Waller. Waller and Cromwell, however, made little impression in the area

Petard used to blow down a gate (engraving from Grose)

and suffered a sharp reverse at Dorchester. A notable Parliamentary success occurred on 22 February when Shrewsbury was captured, severing direct Royalist communications with Chester, itself besieged, and a relief force under Prince Maurice was checked at Nantwich. Rupert arrived to assist his brother but retired southwards on the approach of Scottish reinforcements for the Parliamentary commander Brereton. In Wales Parliamentary success was shorter lived, as the return of Gerard's Welsh troops after the King's withdrawal to Oxford stabilized the Royal position, leaving only Pembroke and Tenby in Parliamentary hands in south Wales. Isolated Royal garrisons like Chester and Scarborough still held out in the north, in which direction marched Sir Marmaduke Langdale's northern horse, from Newcastle's old army, having wintered near Shrewsbury. After a passage marked by the most appalling indiscipline and brutal plundering, they relieved Pontefract (aided by the mass desertion of Sandy's Horse, the second wholesale defection of this unit; it had originally been a Royal corps), and then joined Rupert and Maurice in Cheshire.

In the Highlands, Montrose rallied support from those clans with old enmity towards the Marquis of Argyll's Campbell clan, and was supplemented further by the defection from Argyll of 150 Gordon horse. Taking the war to Argyll's homeland, Montrose pillaged the Campbell capital, Inverary, and created such consternation that some of Leven's army was drawn northwards out of England, thus achieving Montrose's primary objective. William Baillie, one of Leven's generals (aided by Urry, who had deserted the King before Second Newbury) commanded a force at Perth, Argyll headed the main body of his army, the Earl of Seaforth led another corps at Inverness, and a Covenant garrison held Aberdeen. To prevent the union of Argyll and Seaforth, Montrose decided to attack the former by a hill route, difficult enough in summer but almost impossible in mid winter, surprising and routing Argyll's army at Inverlochy. The Campbell clansmen received no quarter in payment for years of oppression; as the Gaelic poet Ian Lom Macdonald wrote,

No harp in the highlands will sorrow for you;
But the birds of Loch Eil are wheeling on high,
And the Badenoch wolves hear the Camerons' cry –
'Come feast ye! come feast where the false-hearted lie!'[30]

For Montrose's loss of about a dozen men, it was claimed that around 1,500 Campbells were killed in the pursuit or drowned in Loch Linne and Loch Eil.

Having recruited his army to about 2,500 foot and 200 horse, Montrose intended to strike at the Lowlands, but as before, with each victory, his Highlanders melted away home with their booty, forcing him to retire north to reorganize. Before going, Montrose sacked Dundee, but whilst his troops were looting he learned that Baillie's Covenant army was but a mile (1.6 kilometres) away. Commanding a rearguard of 200 sober Irish, Montrose managed to get the remainder of his drunken, disorganized troops away before Baillie arrived. Baillie divided his forces in an attempt to trap Montrose (always a hazardous manoeuvre against so skilful an adversary), Urry with four good Lowland regiments and some mediocre levies (totalling about 4,000) being tempted to assault Montrose's 1,000 Irish foot and 650 Gordons at Auldearn, two miles (3.2 kilometres) east of Nairn, on 9 May. When the Gordon horse led a counterattack against Urry's regulars the Covenant army was overthrown, with only Urry and 100 horse escaping after a 14-mile (22.5-kilometre) pursuit.

Part of the New Model Army was organized and ready to march at the opening of the campaigning season of 1645, though not all Parliamentary forces were included in it; the major independent commands were those of the energetic Massey in the west and the army of the Northern Association (five regiments of horse, one of dragoons and seven of foot) under Major-General Sydenham Poyntz, a mercenary lately in service in Holland and Germany. The continuance of the war was inevitable following a conference between the two factions held at Uxbridge in the first half of May, 1645,

the King refusing the stringent demands of Parliament; these were that he should accept Presbyterianism as the religion of England, and that permanent control of the army and navy be in Parliament's hands, as well as sole responsibility for waging war against the rebels in Ireland.

Parliament, anxious to relieve Taunton (besieged by Goring), ordered Sir Thomas Fairfax to accomplish it with part of his New Model, the young general (aged only 33) having come from Yorkshire in February though his appointment was not approved until April. Royalist strategy was confused, and was upset by Cromwell's impounding of the available draught animals around Oxford, depriving much of the King's artillery of its mobility. With the young Prince of Wales (not yet 15) appointed Captain-General in the West, it was intended that Goring should reinforce the main Oxford army to meet Fairfax before the New Model had settled into its new organization; but Rupert, due partly to his hatred of Goring, persuaded the King to march north instead, returning Goring to the west, which plan Goring approved as he enjoyed exercising independent command. Rupert envisaged attacking Leven's army in the north, now depleted by troops sent to oppose Montrose, and was supported by Langdale, whose unruly northern horse disliked fighting anywhere except near their homes in Yorkshire. The King, as ever trusting too much on the advice of others, agreed, and disaster followed.

Fairfax sent a detachment to relieve Taunton (it was reinvested as soon as Goring returned to the west) but kept the remainder of his forces under his own command, making clear from the outset that the New Model had no privileged units; even his own regiment had to take its turn in the rear of the army, a departure from the usual custom that the general's own regiment always occupied the van on the march and the right of the line when drawn up for battle.

As the King marched north, the Committee of Both Kingdoms instructed Fairfax to besiege Oxford, hoping that the Royal cause would collapse with the fall of its capital, whilst Leven could deal with Charles. Lord Fairfax, commanding in Yorkshire, urged Leven to march south as the sieges of Chester and Hawarden Castle were relieved, but Leven determined to advance via Westmorland where he hoped he could both support Brereton's Parliamentarians in the north and cover the King's route to Scotland, an invasion of which he feared. This decided the King to march north via Yorkshire, hopefully to evade Leven in Westmorland and recruit in Yorkshire, where Leven's forces had made themselves highly unpopular. Charles ordered Sir Charles Gerard from Wales and Goring from the west to join him, but on learning that Oxford was running short of supplies, diverted Goring to attempt the city's relief. On 26 May Massey stormed Evesham, severing direct communications between Oxford and the King's army. Charles' plan was now formulated: if Oxford could hold for six or eight weeks, he would continue north and throw Leven back across the border; if not, he would return and rendezvous with Goring between Oxford and London, and whilst awaiting a reply from Oxford was persuaded by Rupert to assault Leicester, the nearest Parliamentary town. It was stormed on 30 May and sacked, much to the King's distress, but its fall threw Parliament into panic. Fairfax was instructed to abandon the siege of Oxford and march against the King, and Parliament began to consider terms of peace. Morale in the Royal army was high and at this stage the prestige of the New Model was low; furthermore, Leicester was an excellent place to await the arrival of Gerard and Goring. Then everything went wrong, as 'the evil genius of the kingdom in a moment shifted the whole scene'[31].

Not knowing that Oxford was free, the council of war (probably influenced by Rupert) began to march the army towards Oxford on 4 June, despite the fact that some were scattered after the looting of Leicester and that Langdale's mutinous northern horse were 'all discontented, and could hardly be kept from disbanding or returning home in disorder'[32]. Sir Thomas Fairfax and the New Model moved nearer the King, determined to engage; Fairfax also requested Cromwell as his Lieutenant-General of Horse if the House of Commons could spare him. It could, and the architect of the Eastern Association's fine horse was sent to join the army with whose creation he is often linked. Apart from his earlier training of the horse and his political endeavours, however, the New Model was the work of other hands.

Fairfax's scouts found the King's army east of Daventry, but the Royalists began to retire on Market Harborough before an engagement could be brought, Charles having decided to fall back upon Leicester to await reinforcement, as his army was inferior in numbers (and quality). Against Fairfax's 13,000 or more, estimates of the King's strength vary from 7,500 to over 10,000; probably a figure between the two is more accurate. In the early morning of 13 June Fairfax called a council of war which resolved to engage the King; midway through its session Cromwell arrived with 700 additional horse. Pressing after the Royalists, Colonel Henry Ireton with his own regiment of New Model horse surprised and beat up elements of the northern horse eating their supper at the village of Naseby, south of Market Harborough. Realizing that Fairfax was nearer than he had believed, the King called a midnight council of war. The consensus of opinion was that the Royal army could not disengage successfully, so would stand and fight.

In the morning the King's army was arrayed on rising ground about a mile (1.6 kilometres) south of Market Harborough, a good position to stand off a superior enemy; Lord Astley commanded the foot in the centre, Rupert the 2,000 horse on the right wing, and Langdale

Henry Ireton (engraving after Samuel Cooper)

his northern horse plus a small detachment from Newark on the left, totalling around 1,600. Held in reserve were 800 foot from the King's Lifeguard and Rupert's Regiment, plus the Lifeguard of Horse about the King. Fairfax sent out reconnaissance patrols to ascertain whether the King was standing or retreating; the withdrawal of one such patrol may have persuaded Rupert that Fairfax was retiring, but for whatever reason he convinced the King to leave his strong position and advance. When this desperate error was realized, it was too late to do anything but draw up as best they could on high ground north of Naseby.

Fairfax assembled his army in Swedish fashion, two lines of foot with the second-line regiments covering the gaps between those of the first; Fairfax commanded the centre in person. Ireton's horse on the left was drawn up in two lines, and Cromwell's on the right in three; both wings included units of (independent) Eastern Association horse. On the Royal right flank, Okey's New Model dragoon regiment was strung out in what might later have been termed 'skirmish order'. Adumbrating Wellington's favourite practice, Fairfax drew back most of his army beyond some high ground, out of sight of the Royalists, who (taking it for a withdrawal) advanced; Fairfax brought his army back onto the crest of the hill,

THE DESCRIPTION OF THE ARMIES OF H

S.ʳ Thomas Fairefax his Excellency, as they wer draw

the Foverto

Dust Hill

Prince Rupert   Prince Maurice

Sir Barnard Astly   The Fort.

The Left Wing Commanded by
Comiss. Generall Ireton.

The King

Maior Generall Skippon

Coll. Pickton Regiment   Earle The Tormidgate   Maior Generall
commanded by the Skippo
Recruits

Com.ni Generall
Ireton   Maior   Generalls

Harden   Waller

Coll. Lewis Regiment

Coll. Sir Richard Regiment   guardement   free

Regnite Hill

Farmy Hill

The Mill Hill

Lens Cotch hill

The traine guarded with firelockes.

NASBYE

Printed for John Patridge

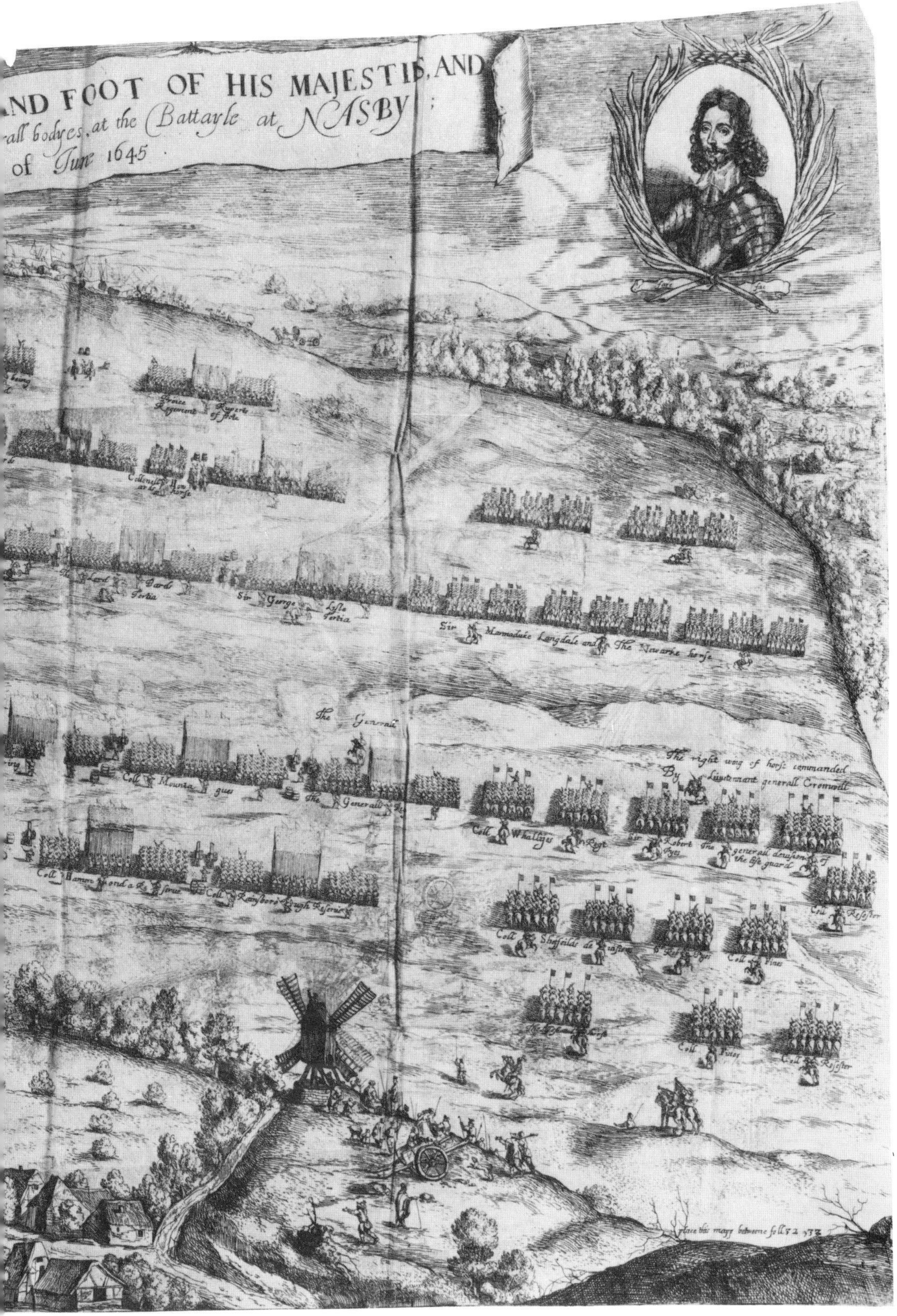
ND FOOT OF HIS MAJESTIS, AND
rall bodyes, at the Battayle at NASBY
of Jun 1645
Sir Marmaduke Langdale and The Newarke horse
The Generall
The right wing of horse commanded
By Lieutennant generall Cromwell

The opposing armies arrayed at Naseby (illustration from Joshua Sprigge's *Anglia Rediviva*; National Army Museum, London) and battle was joined at about 10 a.m. on 14 June 1645.

Langdale's northern horse, opposing Cromwell on the Parliamentary right, were countercharged by the New Model horse, the old Ironsides of Whalley's Regiment making first contact. With the advantage of charging downhill, Cromwell's troops withstood a volley of pistol fire, engaged and scattered the Royalists who were both outnumbered and outflanked, and 'fled farther and faster than became them'[33]. In the centre, though, the Royal foot moved so quickly that the New Model regiments had time to fire only one volley before their first line was sent spilling backwards onto the second line, Astley's foot being no doubt more experienced than some of the impressed New Model men.

On the Royal right, the horse of Rupert and Ireton approached each other somewhat disorganized by the hedges and ditches in their path. Despite suffering the musketry of Okey's dragoons on their flank, Rupert's men had the best of the encounter; Ireton was brought down and captured as he attempted to relieve the pressure on the foot of the Parliamentary left-centre, and only two formed regiments escaped the onrush of Rupert's charge. In a repeat of Edgehill, Rupert pursued the fugitives almost two miles (3.2 kilometres), to the Parliamentary baggage park, instead of reforming and taking the Roundhead foot in flank and rear. By the time he recovered his command, he was too late to save the day and could only join the King who was attempting to rally Langdale's broken horse at the rear.

Their advance stopped by Fairfax's second line, the Royal foot were now bereft of cavalry support. How different from Rupert's behaviour was that of Cromwell, who instead of careering off after Langdale, detailed sufficient horse to watch the broken Cavaliers and then turned his command inwards to assail the flank of the Royal foot. Only instilled discipline could control victorious horse in this way, discipline originally imbued in Cromwell's Eastern Association horse, and which now virtually won the war for Parliament; as the different character of the Royal horse would have made the imposition of such strict discipline much harder, Rupert does not, perhaps, deserve all the criticism which has been levelled at him. As remnants of Ireton's horse began to reform, Okey's dragoons mounted and charged the right of the Royal foot, which under pressure on three sides at last gave way, one brigade standing firm until Fairfax personally led his own regiments of horse and foot against it. At the rear of this debacle, the King made as if to lead a final charge at the head of his Lifeguard, for whatever his failings he never lacked courage. The Earl of Carnwath siezed the King's bridle 'and swearing two or three full-mouthed Scots' oaths . . . said, "Will you go upon your death in an instant?"'[34] and pulled the King's horse round, whereupon the Lifeguard turned and bolted. It might have been better had the King fallen a hero amidst the wreck of his army at Naseby.

When Rupert's horse returned, an attempt was made to rally into some order, but the field was abandoned when Fairfax marshalled his army. Charles' foot was smashed, his entire artillery lost, Royalist morale severely dented, and his papers captured, revealing a plan to bring over an Irish army and give preference to Roman Catholics, which served only to strengthen the 'war party' in Parliament at the expense of those desiring a settlement. Yet the King remained optimistic and journeyed to Hereford to raise another army. Although it grew in numbers until it almost replaced the Naseby losses, the quality of recruits was indifferent and its leaders no more certain of what course to adopt; torn between joining Montrose or Goring, the King went instead to recruit in Wales. After the recapture of Leicester on 18 June, Fairfax set off to relieve Taunton. Carlisle having fallen to David Leslie on 28 June (causing mixed feelings in Parliament, for a Scottish garrison was installed in the old Border fortress), Parliament intended Leven to cover the King by besieging Hereford whilst Fairfax cleared up in the west. But Leven refused to go further than Nottingham until his army had been paid, and furthermore was concerned over the order to execute all Irish prisoners, fearing the Royalists might in retaliation order the same fate for captured Scots. Even with an English reinforcement, Leven's force at Nottingham numbered only about 7,000, having been depleted by casualties, garrisons and detachments sent to chase Montrose.

As Fairfax and Cromwell advanced on Taunton, Goring raised the siege and prepared to meet them in the open. He attempted to deceive Fairfax into dividing his command by sending a strong force of horse towards Ilminster. It *did* cause a division of Fairfax's command, but backfired when Goring's detachment was destroyed at that place on 9 July. Attempting to evacuate his baggage and artillery, Goring made a stand at Langport on 10 July. Fairfax launched a cavalry charge along a lane which bisected the Royalist position (the remainder of Goring's front was marshy and unsuitable for cavalry); led by a composite regiment of Fairfax's and Whalley's horse – the old Ironsides – the charge split Goring's position and drove off his army in chaos. Two miles (3.2 kilometres) further on Goring made a last effort to save his artillery and baggage, but by now morale had gone and his army ceased to exist. The Parliamentary forces made equally short work of pacifying the local clubmen, who simply wished to protect their own homes.

Only in Scotland was the King's party having any success, and that due entirely to the efforts of one remarkable general. After Auldearn, Montrose consistently outmanoeuvred a harrassed Baillie, whose plans were interfered with constantly by advisors attached to his army by the Committee of Estates, the ruling Covenant body. Another army was also formed around Perth, commanded by Lord Lindsay. Having sent away Alasdair Macdonnell to recruit, Montrose had only

O'Cahan's regiment and loyal Highlanders when he encountered Baillie at Alford on 2 July. Spurred on by his travelling committee, Baillie attacked unwisely and came to grief as Lord Gordon, commanding Montrose's horse and incensed at the sight of captured Gordon cattle with Baillie's army, charged prematurely and, followed by the rest of the army, routed the Covenant force, though Gordon himself was killed in the fight. Baillie's resignation was refused for the second time and he was given a new army, mostly untrained levies, and, to ensure disaster, another travelling committee under Argyll. Engaging Montrose at Kilsyth, midway between Stirling and Glasgow, on 15 August, he met with no more success than before; Montrose broke Baillie's centre whilst containing his right, then turned upon that and destroyed the army. Argyll fled as far as Berwick-upon-Tweed and others fled to Carlisle.

Bad as the Royalist situation was in England, the King was still optimistic; in reply to Rupert's advice to conclude peace, Charles said: 'If I had any other quarrel but the defence of my religion, crown and friends, you had full reason for your advice; for I confess that, speaking as a mere soldier or statesman, I must say there is no probability but my ruin; yet, as a Christian, I must tell you that God will not suffer rebels and traitors to prosper, nor this cause to be overthrown ...'[35]. Yet there were few glimmers of hope. After Langport, Goring seems to have taken to drink completely and made little effort to reform his shattered forces; a plan to ship the King's army from Cardiff to join Goring had failed when the Parliamentary navy captured the transports, and on 23 July the Royal stronghold of Bridgwater went down under the New Model, severing communications between the King and his supporters in the west. Pontefract fell on 21 July, Scarborough four days later; the Royal strongholds in Pembrokeshire went after the victory of a combined Parliamentary army and naval force at Colby Moor. On 5 August the King left Cardiff with some 2,200 horse and 400 foot to attempt the march to Montrose, but found his way barred by Poyntz. The Royalists raided Huntingdon (Cromwell's birthplace), and Leven raised his siege of Hereford, as more Scots raced home to deal with Montrose, enabling the King to enter the city in triumph on 4 September, thanks to the heroic efforts of his great general in Scotland.

After the fall of Bridgwater, Fairfax captured Sherborne Castle (14 July) and Bath (30 July), and then moved on Bristol, held by Rupert, who tried to buy time by negotiation. On 10 September the New Model – which now seemed invincible – stormed part of the outer defences despite a fierce resistance. Fairfax then offered terms and Rupert accepted, the city being virtually indefensible with the forces he had. Furious at his nephew's supposed negligence, the King relieved him of all appointments and ordered him to go overseas.

The King attempted to assist the beleaguered Chester, his last point of disembarkation of reinforcements from

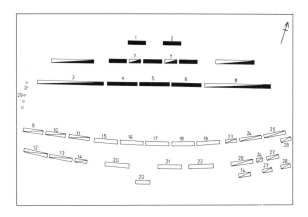

NASEBY

Royalist Army
1 King's Lifeguard **2** Prince Rupert's Regt. **3** Right-wing horse (Rupert & Maurice) **4** Sir Bernard Astley's tertia **5** Lord Bard's tertia **6** Sir George Lisle's tertia **7** Howard's Horse **8** Left-wing horse (Langdale)

Parliamentary Army
9 Butler's Regt., Ireton's horse **10** Vermuyden's Regt., Ireton's horse **11** Ireton's Regt., Ireton's horse **12** Rich's Regt., Ireton's horse **13** Fleetwood's Regt., Ireton's horse **14** Association Horse **15** Skippon's Regt. **16** Sir Hardress Waller's Regt. **17** Pickering's Regt. **18** Montague's Regt. **19** Fairfax's Regt. **20** Pride's Regt. **21** Hammond's Regt. **22** Rainborough's Regt. **23** Whalley's Regt., Cromwell's horse **24** Pye's Regt., Cromwell's horse **25** Fairfax's Regt., Cromwell's horse **26** Sheffield's Regt., Cromwell's horse **27** Fiennes' Regt., Cromwell's horse **28** Rossiter's Regt., Cromwell's horse **29** dragoons

Ireland, but Langdale's northern horse was overthrown by Poyntz and the besieging force at Rowton Heath on 24 September. Unable to help, Charles and his 2,400 surviving horse rode away next day. In Scotland, Montrose's hopes to raise the Border landowners for the King proved unfounded; his Highlanders drifted homeward and with a disintegrating army Montrose encountered David Leslie (returned from England) with about 6,000 men (and Argyll's travelling committee) at Philiphaugh near Selkirk on 13 September. Outnumbered perhaps ten to one and assailed by a surprise attack out of a fog, Montrose's force was annihilated. The general himself cut his way free with a few companions, but the last remnants of the Irish brigade, commanded by O'Cahan, surrendered on a promise of clemency from Leslie. The ministers in the Covenant army protested at this leniency; the few surviving Irish troops were then massacred, including some 300 camp followers, and O'Cahan was later hanged in Edinburgh. It was a shameful end to a heroic campaign.

The King rested at Newark, attempted to go north again until he learned of Montrose's disaster, then retired to Oxford where he arrived on 5 November. There had been a temporary reconciliation with Rupert, the King having been convinced that the surrender of Bristol had not been treasonous, but he refused to employ his nephew again. On 13 October the famous Royal stronghold of Basing House was stormed by the New Model with great loss of life amongst the garrison, and excesses by the fanatics amongst the stormers; six priests in the garrison died in the assault and four were hanged later. The famed architect Inigo Jones, captured at the fall of the stronghold, was plundered so completely that he had to go away in a blanket. On 1 November the last hope of Chester's relief was de-stroyed with a Royal defeat near Denbigh, Parliament gaining control of nearly all of Wales; Newark was invested by Leven and Poyntz, and in the west the Prince of Wales was assembling the last Royal army, largely untrained levies from an area whose sympathy had been lost due to the excesses of Goring's troops. Included in this force was Wentworth's wretched horse, whom 'only their friends feared, and their enemies laughed at; being only terrible in plunder and resolute in running away'[36]; the Cornish trained bands ran away home on the pretext that they feared this rabble would plunder their houses, even though both were on the same side. Goring himself, his health broken by defeat and debauchery, left for France in November.

Basing House after siege, showing effects of investment

7 BETWEEN THE FIRST AND SECOND CIVIL WARS 1646–7

The campaigning season of 1646 opened with the Royalists in a totally hopeless position. In the west, the Prince of Wales appointed the faithful Hopton commander-in-chief, but it was only to negotiate a surrender as the New Model rolled onward, storming Dartmouth on 18 January; Fairfax sent home the Cornish garrison with 2s. each, attempting to win the favour of the Cornish people. Hopton was beaten at Torrington on 16 February and, his ammunition destroyed in an explosion, surrendered to Fairfax on 14 March. The Royal western field army was disbanded six days later, the Prince of Wales having sailed to join his mother in France at the beginning of the month. Chester had capitulated on 3 February, and on 21 March Astley's last 3,000 men, en route to Oxford, were beaten at Stow-on-the-Wold, Astley and Lucas being taken. Old Astley remarked to his captors, 'You have done your work and may go play, unless you will fall out amongst yourselves'[1].

The King slipped away from Oxford in disguise and gave himself up to the Scottish army besieging Newark, which surrendered on the day after his arrival, on 6 May. Exeter had yielded on 9 April, St Michael's Mount on the 15th. On 22 June Princes Rupert and Maurice left Oxford and two days later the garrison was disbanded. The last Royal strongholds were Pendennis Castle, held by 80-year-old John Arundel of Trerice, who was prevented by his own garrison from blowing it up in a last gesture of defiance, and Raglan Castle, captured three days after Pendennis Castle, on 19 August. Charles I was taken to Newcastle-upon-Tyne, where he refused to promise the Scots to accept Presbyterianism as the official English religion, or agree to the proposals put to him by Parliament, which eventually paid off the Scottish forces. The King was sent to comfortable captivity at Holmby House, Northamptonshire.

On 16 September 1646 the Earl of Essex died, 'in a time when he might have been able to have undone much of the mischieve he had formerly wrought; to which he had great inclinations; and had indignation enough for the indignities himself had received from the ingrateful Parliament, and wonderful apprehension and detestation of the ruin he saw like to befall the King and kingdom . . . he might, if he had lived, given some check to the rage and fury that then prevailed'[2], wrote Clarendon, his enemy. Perhaps he was correct; how much it was to be lamented that one of Parliament's most capable generals, and certainly the most beloved by his troops, should die in shadows.

The socioeconomic consequences of the First Civil War were probably limited, excluding those families which suffered loss of property or life. London became more puritanical, with numerous fast days decreed during the war in an effort to guarantee divine support for Parliament's cause. Some areas had suffered severely from the presence of marauding armies, causing the formation of organizations like the clubmen; but local government appears to have changed little, and though Royalist landowners had their holdings sequestered until the fines levied upon them were paid in full, no great changes of ownership seem to have occurred over

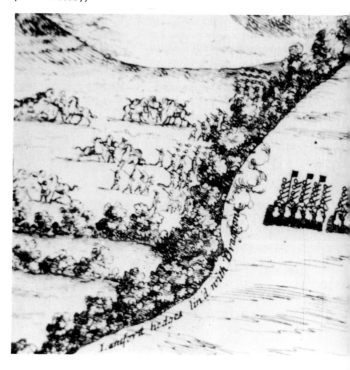

Okey's dragoons concealed in ambush behind hedges, assailing Royalist flank with musketry; note men detached as horse-holders at the rear of the hedge (from Sprigge's plan of Naseby)

the country as a whole. In some areas the demands of war had caused full employment, but new taxes (particularly the excise levied upon ale) were unpopular. The many 'ordinary' people now standing victors over some of the greatest families in the land showed little vindictiveness to their erstwhile masters, though the undermining of Royal and Church authority allowed radical ideas to develop.

With hostilities ended, Parliament had to attempt a settlement with the King, and find some way of disbanding their armies. The former was made impossible by the King's attitude; had he agreed that Presbyterianism be accepted as the national religion for three years, and that Parliament control the armed forces for ten, he might have been restored to his throne immediately. But he prevaricated.

Dealings with the army were no more successful. To be rid of them, Parliament decided that half should be disbanded (including all officers above the rank of colonel, apart from the commander-in-chief), and that the rest should be sent to Ireland or kept in security duties in England, no clear provision being made for payment of arrears of pay. By keeping the army under command of officers they could trust, the 'peace party' hoped to retain enough power to ensure that the King kept to the constitutional settlement they hoped to arrange. Not unnaturally, the army objected to demobilization without being guaranteed the pay owed them, and thus grew the conflict between the army and a majority of Parliament. A deputation from Parliament went to army headquarters at Saffron Walden in spring 1647, to be told that the army wanted more information about disbandment and the Irish expedition, and the rank and file presented to Fairfax a petition requesting arrears and that bereaved widows and orphans of soldiers should receive pensions. The perpetrators of these not unreasonable demands, thought Parliament, were in a 'distempered condition' and to be regarded as 'enemies of the State and disturbers of the public peace' [3] if they continued. A second deputation insisted that

'Siege-pieces' struck in Newark (engravings)

PLATE 22

57 Mercenary French musketeer
58 Mercenary officer of horse

The influx of foreign military experts, mercenaries and British officers returned from overseas would have resulted in the presence of foreign styles of arms and even costume. This musketeer wears French-style uniform, as illustrated (for example) in Lostelnau's *Le Mareschal de Bataille* (1647). The coat has sleeves open down the front seam and a contrastingly-coloured lining, and the very baggy breeches have a pleated bottom edge turned back and laced, showing the coloured lining. All items of costume are ornamented by ribbon bows, and the outer pair of stockings is cut and tied up with ribbons so as to resemble the shape of soft-topped boots. The French-style musket has a trigger in the form of a 'sear' bar, an old fashion which persisted into the later part of the century despite the introduction of more modern triggers, and the musketeer is encumbered with both a spiked-ended musket rest and a swine-feather. Combined rest and swine-feathers, musket rests with pike heads, were never in general use but did exist; see for example *European Arms & Armour: Wallace Collection* by Sir James Mann (London, 1962) vol. II, p. 620.

The officer wears a buff-coat with silver lace hoops on the sleeve, a not uncommon decoration misinterpreted by some later artists to give the impression that rugby shirts were worn during the Civil War! He wears a Polish-style *zischagge* helmet with fluted skull, sliding nasal bar and a small tube at the front on the left into which the plume was affixed. He has a knotted neckerchief as a field sign, and has tied his sword to his wrist with a leather thong.

Fairfax *order* his men to volunteer for Ireland, to serve under Skippon, who was trusted in London. Fairfax said he would express a wish, but would not give such an order, and the army said it would do nothing until arrears had been paid and an indemnity given. Parliament then voted six weeks' pay and sent four Members, including Cromwell, Skippon and Ireton, to speak to the army. They reported that the army was still dissatisfied at receiving six or eight weeks' pay when they were owed for more than a year, but would disband if a satisfactory arrangement could be made, but would not go to Ireland. Fairfax was told that his army wanted a general meeting, when 'agitators' from each regiment could put its case. On 4 June the whole force camped at Newmarket.

This disaffection in his enemies' ranks gave the King new heart; they were, as Astley had said, falling out amongst themselves. Charles told the Speaker of the House of Lords that he agreed to the proposals given him, but that he wished to come to Westminster to give the necessary Royal assent to the bills which would achieve the settlement. His plan, evidently to act as a symbol of national reconciliation or to profit from the

PLATE 22

58 Mercenary officer of horse

57 Mercenary French musketeer

split in his opponents' ranks, was spoiled by Cornet Joyce, a junior officer, who arrived at Holmby and told the King to accompany him to the army. 'His majesty asked, "By what authority they came?" Joyce answered, "By *this*"; and shewed them his pistol'.[4] The army had staged a significant coup.

From the army's seizure of the King in early June 1647, their demands to Parliament altered. Alienated by concessions already given to 'reformadoes' and the City of London (which still possessed its trained bands), suggesting a possible armed revolt against them, the army now began to urge a constitutional settlement which would include their own claims for fair treatment. This politicization of the army may have been linked to the evolution of the Leveller movement, whose leader, John Lilburne, had been a lieutenant-colonel. Cromwell and other senior officers still averred that settlements should be made by Parliament, but they were forced to reconsider by the 'Declaration of the Army', dated 15 June, drawn up by the Council of the Army (which included 'other ranks' as well as officers) and which claimed that it was they, not Parliament, which truly represented the people, as they were not a mercenary body but one called forth for the defence of liberty.

Whilst the King was in the army's custody, he continued to negotiate with anyone prepared to listen. From the army he accepted a document drawn up by Ireton, 'The Heads of the Proposals', as a basis for negotiation, and he was approached by the Scots (notably the Duke of Hamilton and the Earl of Lauderdale) who offered to support him in return for acceptance of their religious demands. To the army he spoke of toleration, and to the Scots of the suppression of the sectaries. Then he escaped from the army's custody at Hampton Court and fled to the Isle of Wight where, unable to escape to France, he agreed to the Scottish proposals, to the establishment of a Presbyterian system for three years, to suppress the Independents and other sects, and to consent to an assembly of divines to be convened to make 'a permanent religious settlement; in return, by this 'Engagement', the Scots promised to restore him to his throne. Before this pact was sealed, however, the army had begun to pressurize Parliament; on 6 August it

entered London and 11 leaders of the anti-army faction in the Commons fled. The army then retired to Putney, where Cromwell chaired army debates in the face of a growing (but as yet undeclared) republican movement under Leveller influence. Cromwell was still willing to accept the King's restoration if it would return the country to peace, but in the Commons on 20 October he declared that negotiations should only continue if Charles accepted the rigorous terms presented at Newcastle. When it became know that Charles had made an engagement with the Scots Commissioners, however, a vote was carried to stop negotiations and to watch him more closely.

The outbreak of the conflict known as the Second Civil War was founded upon the inability to reach a settlement with the King and the subsequent uncertainty about the future, for although the republican movement was growing and suggestions of impeachment of the King were in the air, the majority still regarded him as the natural (if only symbolic) head of the nation. Secondly, there was growing resentment of the harsher side of Puritanism being enforced in some places, and the continuing dominance of the county committees, originally formed during the war to raise recruits and funds, but which had been given powers to sequester Royalist estates and had become, in the more extreme examples like the administration of Sir Anthony Welden in Kent, virtually local dictatorships. Thus the rising in that county in 1648 was more of a protest against the committees than primarily an expression of loyalty to the King, and the resulting lack of coordination doomed the rising to failure. In the first war it was the King's central direction, wayward though it was at times, which had enabled the Royalists to fight so long; now, the King was powerless and the only central direction was from Fairfax to his ruthlessly efficient New Model. To be strictly accurate, by February 1648 the latter had been replaced officially by a 'Standing Army', incorporating elements other than those of the New Model, notably from the forces of the Northern Association. The new army comprised 14 regiments of horse and 17 of foot, with 30 'loose companies' unaffiliated to any particular regiment.

Medal celebrating the
Earl of Essex (engraving)

8 THE SECOND CIVIL WAR 1648

Perhaps the most succinct account of the Second Civil War (or perhaps of *any* war) was that given by Sir Winston Churchill: 'The story of the Second Civil War is short and simple. King, Lords and Commons, landlords and merchants, the City and the countryside, bishops and presbyters, the Scottish army, the Welsh people, and the English Fleet, all now turned against the New Model Army. The Army beat the lot'.[1]

The first indication of severe disturbance occurred on 9 April when a mob of apprentices in London had to be broken up by cavalry, on Cromwell's orders. Similar civil disorder had occurred the previous Christmas in Canterbury when a popular movement objected to an attempt to prevent the usual seasonal festivities; that, too, had been dispersed by troops but was a pointer towards the mood of even moderate citizens and adumbrated the Kent risings of the following spring.

The first military actions occurred in Wales, where Colonel Poyer, Governor of Pembroke Castle, whose troops were restive over their unpaid wages, declared for the King and roused a revolt over south Wales as he defeated a Parliamentary force near Carmarthen. A decision had been taken in Scotland to raise an 'engager' army, and on 28 April Sir Marmaduke Langdale with Royalists from Scotland captured Berwick-upon-Tweed, and on the following day Carlisle was siezed. Parliament's situation looked serious; Fairfax was faced with the threat of a Scottish invasion, a Welsh rising, disturbances in Kent and Essex and perhaps in the west, against which he had only his Standing Army, as most of

---

PLATE 23

59 Officer of foot, New Model Army
60 Pikeman, New Model Army
61 Musketeer, New Model Army

It appears that the New Model Army wore red uniforms from the beginning: 'The men are Redcoats all, the whole army only are distinguished by several facings of their coats'[1]. These coats are described in the contract books of the New Model, including the various facing colours and 'tape strings' used to fasten the coats; for example,

Two Thousand Coates and Two Thousand Breeches at seventeen shillings a Coat & Breeches. Two Thousand pairs of stockins at Thirteene pence halfe penny a paire. The coates to be of a Red Colour and of Suffolke, Coventry or Gloucestershire Cloth and to be made Three quarters & a nayle long faced with bayse or Cotton with tapestrings according to a pattern delivered into ye said Committee. The Breeches to be of Gray or some other good Coloure & made of Reading Cloth or other Cloth in length Three quarters one eighth well lined and Trimmed sutable to ye patternes presented, the said Cloth both of ye Coates and of ye Breeches to be first shrunke in Cold water. The stockins to be of good Welsh Cotton.[2]

Another example was 4,000 coats and breeches, 'ye tape to bee white, blew, greene, & yellow . . . 100 with orange ribbon, att 16ˢ p pce the Cloth to bee shrunk . . . 1,000 wᵗʰ orange'[3].

Other entries in the contract books include detailed instructions for shirts, shoes of specified sizes, 'Snapsacks large & of good leather' at 8s. a dozen[4], Spanish pikes (15 feet (4.6 metres)) at 4s. each and English pikes (16 feet (4.9 metres)) at 4s. 2d., and musketeers' bandoliers which appear always to have had blue-painted tubes and blue-and-white strings: 'The boxes of the said . . . Bandileers to bee of wood with whole Bottoms, to be turned wᵗʰ in and not Bored, the Heads to be of Wood, and to be layd in oyle (vizt) Three times over, and to be coloured blew wᵗʰ blew and white strings with strong thred twist, and wᵗʰ good belts, att Twenty pence a peece . . .'[5]

The use of these uniforms is confirmed by Cromwell's order, for the army sent to Ireland, of '15,000 cassocks of Venice-red colour shrunk in water', the same number of 'breeches of grey or other good colour' and 10,000 hats and bands[6]; the remaining 5,000 presumably would have been equipped with pikemen's helmets and thus not required hats.

The men illustrated wear what was probably typical New Model uniform, the officer with a partizan as a 'leading staff' and the musketeer with his blue-tubed bandolier. This rather austere character, dutifully reading his Bible, wears the sea-green ribbon of the Levellers tied around his hat.

NOTES
1 *Perfect Passages*, 7 May 1645; see Young, *Edgehill*, p. 25
2 New Model Army Contract Books, 14 February 1645; see *Journal of the Arms and Armour Society* VI (1968) 69
3 *Ibid.* p. 115 (3 April 1645)
4 *Ibid.* p. 100 (22 December 1645)
5 *Ibid.* p. 88 (17 March 1645)
6 Lawson, vol. I, p. 11

PLATE 23

59 Officer of foot, New Model Army   60 Pikeman, New Model Army   61 Musketeer, New Model Army

PLATE 24

62 63 64 Musketeers, New Model Army

PLATE 24

62, 63, 64 Musketeers, New Model Army

The men illustrated wear New Model uniform as described for Plate 23, but two of those armed with firelock muskets have cartridge boxes suspended from a waistbelt instead of a bandolier. These boxes, recommended by Orrery among others, could be worn either inside the coat (which when fastened over the top provided protection from the rain) or outside, and are described in the New Model contract books as 'boxes of stronge plate covered wth black leather 700 of them halfe round & the other 500 double at x[d] a peece'[1]. The firelocks illustrated are of different patterns, one with an old-style butt like that of a matchlock, and one with a carved butt of a relatively modern shape. Both these men wear coats with blue linings and 'tape strings' like Fairfax's Regiment, which it was reported were 'firelocks all' and in common with other New Model foot 'were only distinguished by their facings; Lt. General Fairfax's having blue'[2]. The third musketeer wears green facings and a knitted-wool stocking cap with tassel end, and has the regulation bandolier with blue-painted tubes and blue-and-white strings.

NOTES

1 New Model Army Contract Books, 10 January 1645; see *Journal of the Arms and Armour Society* VI (1968) 90
2 Newspaper report of 30 April 1645; see Lawson, vol. I, p. 11

the town garrisons and local forces had been disbanded. Fairfax despatched Cromwell to reinforce the Parliamentary presence in Wales; Newcastle was held by Sir Arthur Haselrig with two regiments, a further two were already in the west under Sir Hardress Waller, and Gloucester and Oxford were garrisoned. There was a small field army in the north under Major-General John Lambert, an experienced New Model officer from the West Riding who had helped Ireton frame 'The Heads of the Proposals', a capable though ambitious soldier whose unlikely hobbies included growing flowers (learned from Lord Fairfax), painting and needlework.

With these forces to stabilize the situation, Fairfax hoped to crush the unrest in the Home Counties before turning his attention elsewhere. In early May the Scottish Parliament wrote to Westminster demanding that Englishmen take the Presbyterian Covenant, that negotiations with the King be reopened, and that the 'army of sectaries' be disbanded. These demands were rejected. The Scottish army under the Duke of Hamilton was weakened severely by the opposition of Argyll and the clergy, since the invasion of England would involve cooperation with non-Covenant Royalists; most significantly, the Scots' most able commander, David Leslie, declined the appointment of Major-General of Horse.

When Cromwell arrived in Wales he found the rising

already half-crushed, with only the reduction of Pembroke and Chepstow Castles needed to extinguish Royal resistance completely. In Kent, however, the situation was more serious and included a revolt of the crews of ships stationed in the Downs, as well as the seizure of Rochester and Sandwich among other towns. Parliament reappointed the Earl of Warwick as Lord High Admiral (having been deprived of his office by the Self-Denying Ordinance), but even he was unable to regain control of the fleet. But the Royalist risings were not only uncoordinated but also badly led; the Prince of Wales appointed Warwick's brother, the Earl of Holland, as commander-in-chief in England, and he in turn gave local command in the Home Counties to George Goring, Earl of Norwich (father of the dissolute general of horse), a pleasant courtier but totally lacking in military experience, whose one aim was apparently 'to please every man, and comply with every body's humour'[2]. Against this commander and his 11,000 rebels (many of whom more resembled an armed mob than an army) was matched Fairfax and his efficient New Model (or now Standing) Army.

Fairfax arrived outside Maidstone on the evening of 1 June 1646, intending to storm the Royalist-held county capital next day; but as his van became involved in heavy skirmishing, the remainder of the army was drawn in and a furious street fight ensued, all 4,000 of Norwich's decent troops resisting the Parliamentarians. By midnight the barricades were down and Fairfax victorious. As the mopping-up of the Kent insurrection continued, Norwich withdrew towards London but was unable to gain much support. On 4 June the Royalists in Essex rose, their support including part of the trained bands over which Sir Charles Lucas was put in command. On 9 June Lucas' force was joined by Norwich and others from London, including Sir George Lisle and Lord Capel. Their local support was limited, however, the northern county trained bands declaring for Parliament and securing the county magazine at Braintree. Norwich and Lucas withdrew on 12 June to Colchester, Lucas' home where his family popularity might benefit recruiting.

There were other minor risings; Lord Byron, returned from France, siezed Anglesey and prepared the Welsh Royalists to cooperate with the Scottish army when it arrived. In the north, Langdale had surprised and captured Pontefract, compelling Lambert to divide his forces, part to besiege the town and part to intercept Langdale's main body. The revolt in the navy resulted in the Downs fleet sailing for Holland to join the Prince of Wales; they were led by two ex-Parliamentarians, Lord Willoughby of Parham and Admiral Batten, the latter a Presbyterian who disliked the new Independent regime.

Fairfax rushed his 5,000 troops toward Colchester (covering 50 miles (80 kilometres) in two days, a considerable feat) and engaged Lucas' army on 13 June.

'Siege-piece' struck in Colchester, 1648 (engraving)

Lucas withdrew into the town and resisted all Fairfax's attempts to break in, the Parliamentarians suffering severely; with the Scottish danger coming closer, a large part of Parliament's forces were to be tied down besieging Colchester, an advantage, however, upon which the Royalists were unable to capitalize. The Earl of Holland attempted to sieze Reigate with a small Royalist force in early July, but after a sharp fight at Kingston on 7 July with a detachment despatched by Fairfax, the Royalists were scattered and Holland ultimately captured.

Lambert, anticipating a Scottish invasion by the army massing at Dumfries, had to send more troops to contain the Royalists in Northumberland, leaving him (including local levies) with around 2,500 horse and 2,000 foot. Arrayed against him were some 23,000 Scots plus Langdale's English, but commanded by the Duke of Hamilton and his equally incompetent deputy, the Earl of Callander. Baillie commanded the foot and John Middleton the horse, the latter a Parliamentary commander during the First Civil War. Lambert retired before the Scottish invasion and at Otley on 13 August was joined by Cromwell, sent from south Wales now that resistance was ended. Neither side seems to have had any definite plan; as Hamilton intended to march towards London, he held a council of war near Lancaster to decide which route to take, to advance into Yorkshire or continue south through Lancashire. To attempt a junction with Byron's projected rising in Wales, the latter course was selected, though the incompetent Hamilton sacrificed a valuable reinforcement of 3,000 troops brought from Ireland by Sir George Monro by using them only as a reserve, simply because Monro refused to take orders from either Baillie or Callander.

Despite Langdale's warnings that the enemy was near, Hamilton kept his army hopelessly dispersed; thus, his vastly superior numbers could not be concentrated against Cromwell who encountered Langdale's contingent (the Royalist rearguard) outside Preston

on the morning of 17 August. Langdale requested assistance, which Hamilton was prepared to send, but Callander, unwilling to risk his Scottish troops to save the English contingent, persuaded Hamilton to let the Scottish foot go south across the Ribble, leaving Langdale's rearguard to fight alone, though to his credit, Hamilton himself joined Langdale. Langdale's foot resisted stubbornly but after a four-hour fight were overcome, Langdale and his horse moving north to join Monro, and Hamilton rejoining his foot, still moving south. Pressed hard by the Parliamentary forces, the exhausted, half-starved and rain-sodden Scots made a stand at Winwick which cost them dearly, and were compelled to surrender their foot at Warrington, Baillie pleading (unsuccessfully) with his officers to end his disgrace with a pistol ball. The Scottish horse marched towards Chester and north Wales, but were caught and surrendered (including Hamilton) at Uttoxeter. By mid-October Cromwell had moved up into Scotland, where he had little trouble making peace with Argyll (who had opposed the Engagers from the beginning) and Scotland's part in the Second Civil War ended.

Only Colchester remained in arms, still defended stoutly by Norwich, Lucas, Lisle and Capel. Constricted by a regular siege, conditions in Colchester became unbearable, and when news of the defeat at Preston was conveyed to the garrison by means of a note attached to a kite the city surrendered. Sir Charles Lucas and Sir George Lisle, on the excuse of having broken parole, were condemned to death; the idea may have been Ireton's, but the responsibility is Fairfax's, who yielded to the pressure applied by the army. Its practical value (*pour encourager les autres*) seems negligible as the war was already won, and it is hard to justify the act as anything more than vindictiveness. A third Royalist officer earmarked for death, Sir Bernard Gascoigne, was spared on the grounds that as a Florentine mercenary his death might antagonize other Italians. Lucas and Lisle met their end with great fortitude; Lucas was shot first and Lisle stood over his friend's body as the firing party reloaded. Lisle called to them to come closer, to which one replied, 'I'll warrant you, sir, we'll hit you'; with a smile Lisle said, 'Friends, I have been nearer you when you have missed me!'[3]. The Prince of Wales was unable to bring about a naval action with his fleet and the embers of the Second Civil War were extinguished, though Pontefract held out against Lambert until 25 March 1649.

The war had weakened the King's position even further, as fewer Parliamentary and military leaders were prepared to trust him after the 'Engagement'. Although commissioners (mainly members of the old peace party and moderates) were sent to the Isle of Wight to reopen negotiations, Charles recognized the danger and agreed that Parliament should control the armed forces for 20 years, but still refused to accept permanent Presbyterianism for the English church. Colonel Edmund

Ludlow, representing the growing republican movement, complained (with little effect) to Fairfax over the reopening of negotiations, but was received more sympathetically by Henry Ireton. Ireton believed the only way to stop negotiations was to exert influence through the army rather than Parliament, and accordingly composed a 'remonstrance' which he wanted the army to submit to Parliament, demanding constitutional reform and, to ensure the country's safety, that Charles should be put on trial. On 18 November 1648 the army's council of officers accepted the remonstrance. Both Fairfax and Cromwell were carried along by the rest; Fairfax decided with reluctance that the King's deposition was necessary and that the army had to be used to pressurize Parliament, whilst Cromwell would have preferred to have persuaded the House of Commons to discontinue negotiations with the King rather than the drastic measure which was adopted by Ireton and Ludlow. On 6 December the Members arrived to find the Parliament-guard (normally the City trained bands) replaced by regular soldiers, with Colonel Thomas Pride at the entrance to the Parliament House refusing admittance to those Members opposed to the most drastic measures. The so-called 'Pride's Purge' excluded 186 Members

The execution of Charles I (Dutch print)

PLATE 25

65, 66, 67 Gunners, Royalist artillery

It has been stated that the King's artillery train wore blue coats faced with red, the 'traditional' colours of the Royal Artillery. This belief, siezed upon to accord the Royal Artillery uniform with more antiquity than perhaps it warrants, seems based entirely upon a single copy of the frontispiece to Eldred's *Gunner's Glasse* (1642), probably hand-coloured at a later date in the colours then worn by the Royal Artillery. In reality, the crude portrait of Eldred (in his eighty-third year) shows a single-breasted coat with fringe-ended loops of lace on the breast, which may well have been a civilian suit. No other contemporary sources indicate blue artillery uniforms; the earliest reliable descriptions concern striped jackets (1688) and red or crimson coats (1696–1703). In fact, Civil War artillerymen probably wore ordinary civilian clothing or that of the foot, with additional equipment; for example, in March 1643 it was noted that long poleaxes had been delivered to five gunners and twelve matrosses (assistants), and swords to the two wheelwrights, of the train organized for Prince Rupert's siege of Lichfield.

The gunners illustrated include two members of a gun team, one wearing an old 'cabasset' helmet and bearing a rammer, and the other with a knitted woollen cap and carrying a ladle used for transferring powder from the 'budge-barrel' or 'bouget' illustrated into the muzzle of the cannon. Powder-barrels were lined with fabric or leather, enabling the top to be drawn together, and banded with rope rather than iron, to reduce the danger of accidental explosion caused by the striking of sparks. The gunner in the foreground carries a 'linstock' or 'linkstock', in effect a pike or pole which carried a length of match, usually held by metal jaws as illustrated. The burning match could be used to ignite the charge of a cannon directly, by being inserted into the touchhole of the barrel, or be stuck in the ground behind a battery or body of musketeers to provide a light for matches carried by each gun captain or individual musketeer whose match had been extinguished.

and arrested 45 of the most vociferous critics of the plan to depose the King; these included such staunch Parliamentary soldiers as Colonel Massey, Sir William Waller and Generals Browne and Copley. With this exclusion from Parliament of the leading Presbyterians, whose aloofness had prevented compromise with either King or army in war or peace, the King's last hopes disappeared.

The purged House of Commons decided that the negotiations with the King were 'highly dishonourable and destructive of the peace of the kingdom' and established a committee to bring the King to justice. On 1 January 1649 an ordinance was passed establishing a court to try him; on 27 January he was condemned to death as a tyrant and traitor responsible for the bloodshed of his own people. On 30 January, physically brave to the last, King Charles I was beheaded at Whitehall.

PLATE 25

65 66 67 Gunners, Royalist artillery

9 THE THIRD CIVIL WAR 1649–51

The new king, Charles II, had three possible courses open to him: he could attempt to regain his throne with foreign assistance, by an invasion from Ireland, or from Scotland. The first was never feasible; the declining influence and later death of his brother-in-law, William II, Stadholder of the United Netherlands, neutralized his most likely ally, and whilst lending moral support France was preoccupied by her own troubles. Spain, fearing the naval strength of the English, was the first to recognize the Commonwealth Government, the remnants of the House of Commons which had invested sovereign rights in itself.

Invasion from Ireland or Scotland were reasonable possibilities, but unless they actually began could expect little assistance from English Royalists, crushed harder as a result of the Second Civil War and closely scrutinized by the county committees; and in March Lords Holland, Hamilton and Capel were all executed. A fortnight before Charles I's death, however, temporary peace had been brought to Ireland when the Marquis of Ormonde, the King's Lord-Lieutenant, had concluded a treaty at Kilkenny between the Royalist and Confederate Irish factions, by which the Confederates agreed to supply Ormonde with 15,000 men in return for the independence of the Irish Parliament and freedom of religion to Roman Catholics. But Charles II tarried too long in going to Ireland to provide a figurehead to unify the two camps, and by the time he was ready to land it was too late. On 30 March 1649 Cromwell accepted the appointment as Parliament's Lord-Lieutenant and Captain-General in Ireland and took an English army to crush Royal resistance. His army was not prepared without difficulty, for once again objections were raised regarding service in Ireland, causing disaffection and mutiny which was only quelled by Fairfax in May. Even before Cromwell's arrival Ormonde had been defeated at Rathmines (2 August 1649) and Cromwell proceeded to crush the Irish with vigour and barbarity, most notably in the slaughter of the garrison at Drogheda. By May 1650 Cromwell was back in London, leaving an army of occupation in Ireland commanded by his son-in-law Henry Ireton, his Lieutenant-General in the previous campaign.

Scotland was a more fertile ground for Charles' hopes, and on 5 February 1649 a proclamation was issued acknowledging his succession as Charles II and lamenting the 'wicked and trayterous murther wee doe from our soules abominate, and all parties and consenters thereunto'; on 22 February Montrose was appointed the King's Captain-General in Scotland with instructions to raise a loyal army. Rather than accept the severe terms put to him by a Scottish delegation which visited him in Holland in 1649, however, Charles prevaricated in the hopes of success in Ireland. When there was no longer an alternative, he entered into new negotiations with the Scottish Commissioners at Breda. The ruling Scottish Committee of Estates proposed terms which even Argyll considered too strict, but Charles was encouraged by William II to agree, and on 1 May 1650 signed the Treaty of Breda. By this he undertook to impose Presbyterianism upon England, to outlaw Roman Catholicism, to acknowledge the Scottish Parliament and renounce the arrangements with Montrose and Ormonde, in return for an invitation to be crowned in Scotland and to have the Engagers' rights restored to them. Probably neither side intended to abide by these agreements; Charles must have been unenthusiastic about the religious strictures, and the Scots wished only to use him as a figurehead to help further their own ends.

Before the treaty was signed the last acts of a great and gallant general had been played out in Scotland. Montrose, in his last heroic bid in the Royal cause, landed at Kirkwall in the Orkneys on 23 March 1650. With him were some 500 Danish and German mercenaries, 1,000 local recruits, a troop of 50 horse, old Royalists and mercenaries, and the practiced turncoat Urry, once more a Royalist. Montrose's small force – of negligible military value for the Orcadians were totally untrained – awaited the expected Royalist rising among the clans. It never came, and Montrose was crushed by the local forces from Inverness at Carbisdale on 27 April, the Orcadians fleeing without striking a blow. The mercenaries and horse put up a good fight but were overwhelmed. Montrose and Urry were executed in Edinburgh in the following month. Montrose's last words concerned his King and country; his late master, who 'lived a saint and died a martyr', and his present sovereign, in whom 'never any people ... might be more happy in a king'[1]. His dying declaration, 'May Almighty God have mercy on this afflicted country', might well have applied to the whole of the island, for when the king for whom Montrose had died entered Aberdeen en route to his proclamation as king in Edinburgh, having repudiated the principles for which his general had died, he passed through the city gate over which still hung a dismembered arm of the great Marquis.

Ironically, the Third Civil War was not initiated by the Scots but by the Council of State in London which decided that an expedition to Scotland was required to forestall any Scottish offensive. Had they not invaded Scotland, it is unlikely that Argyll and the ruling Covenanters would have initiated conflict at this stage, though there was still resentment at the execution by the English of a Scottish king. There were difficulties in launching an invasion of Scotland as new regiments had to be formed and a commander appointed, Fairfax having declined partly on the grounds that militarily it made better sense to await a Scottish invasion and defeat it in England, and partly that, although he would fight to the death to defend England, he could not invade a country with whom there still existed a Solemn League and Covenant. Ignoring the differences between the Engagers and Covenanters, the Council of State appointed Cromwell commander of the expedition, with Lambert second-in-command and Monck Major-General of Foot. Fairfax, whose wife was a Presbyterian Royalist, had become progressively alienated from the new régime (he had declined to take an oath to the Commonwealth or support the trial of Charles I) and was probably glad to be out of a position of responsibility.

Cromwell's army of eight regiments of horse and nine of foot, totalling probably in excess of 15,000, advanced north via York, Newcastle and Durham, arrived in Berwick on 19 July, and crossed the border three days later. Cromwell manoeuvred until within a mile (1.6 kilometres) of Edinburgh, but on 6 August withdrew to Dunbar, the safest port at which supplies could be landed. Four days previously Charles II had arrived at Leith hoping to get the support of the Scottish army, nominally under the Earl of Leven but actually commanded by Sir David Leslie. To prevent Charles from gaining too much support, the Scots Committee of Estates appointed Commissioners for Purging who dismissed some 80 experienced officers and 3,000 soldiers whose loyalty to the Covenant was considered to be in some doubt, an act which contributed to the eventual Scottish defeat. Charles himself was guilty of saying anything required, whether he believed it or not, to ensure that he would regain his throne; his declarations to the Scots were probably the exact opposite of his true opinions.

The manoeuvres of the next three weeks between Musselburgh and Dunbar achieved little except to weaken the morale and stamina of Cromwell's force, the inclement weather causing considerable illness. By 1 September, outmanoeuvred by Leslie, Cromwell had retired again to Dunbar. With Leslie in a strong position on the Lammermuir Hills, threatening Cromwell's land communications with England, the English army was in some discomfort, as Cromwell noted when writing for

George Monck, Duke of Albemarle

reinforcements to Haselrig in Newcastle: 'We are upon an Engagement very difficult. The enemy hath blocked up our way ... through which we cannot get without almost a miracle ... we know not how to come that way without great difficulty; and our lying here daily consumeth our men, who fall sick beyond imagination'[2]. Then the ministers of the Scottish Kirk intervened, quite unintentionally, on Cromwell's behalf.

The interfering ministers persuaded Leslie to move down from his position and scatter the enemy, as the God of the Covenant would ensure victory. On seeing this, the English council of war decided not to embark their foot and leave the horse to cut their way free, as some wished, but instead to follow Lambert's plan to attack the Scottish army before it could concentrate fully. The manoeuvre was audacious, involving movement by night over difficult terrain, until in the early morning of 3 September Lambert launched a massive attack with his horse against the Scots, who were somewhat demoralized by a night spent in the fields without cover and in inclement weather. Lambert's horse smashed into the Scots, Monck's foot seconded them and Cromwell's flank attack shattered the army completely. The routed Scottish horse rode through and disorganized their own foot, most of whom were resisting grimly, encouraged by their Ministers who 'preached and prayed, and assured them of the victory, till the English were upon them; and some of their preachers were knocked in the head whilst they were promising the victory'[3]. About an hour after the battle began, the entire Scottish army was in flight; estimates of casualties ranged from 3,000 to 6,000, and 10,000 prisoners, whilst Cromwell claimed to have lost 20 to 40 men. It was one of the most complete victories of the Civil Wars, though the campaign could have had a very different outcome had Leslie abided by his own military instincts.

Cromwell's Great Seal for Scotland, showing cuirassier armour of senior officer

Leslie kept some 4,000 men in reasonable order, preventing Cromwell from mopping up completely; Edinburgh was occupied (though the Castle held out until 19 December) and few manoeuvres of significance occurred in the first half of 1651. Charles II was able to press on with his intention of uniting his supporters in England and Scotland, which the defeat of the Covenanters at Dunbar enabled him to do. He was crowned King at Scone on 1 January 1651 and began to revive Royalism in Scotland, though not until June was the Act of Classes (which forbade former Engagers from serving in the Scots army) repealed by the Scottish Parliament. At the same time, preparations were made secretly in England for a concerted Royalist rising to cooperate with the projected Scottish invasion, assisted by the growing Royalism of many English Presbyterians who began to question the current régime. Charles I's offer to accept the Presbyterian Church made whilst he was

PLATE 26

68 Officer, Parliamentary artillery
69 Firelock guard, New Model Army artillery
70 Waggoner, Parliamentary artillery

The officer illustrated (perhaps an expert hired from the continent) carries two items which distinguish him as an officer of artillery: a large flask of priming powder, used to fill the touchhole of a cannon barrel, and a 'gunner's quadrant', an invaluable mathematical instrument without which accurate aiming of an artillery piece would have been impossible.

Escorts for artillery trains appear often to have been drawn from the army's foot, but an important factor in their selection was that they should be armed with firelock muskets, the lighted match of the matchlock proving too hazardous for use around large quantities of gunpowder. For example, it is noted that Lieutenant-General James Wemyss' artillery train of Waller's army in the Cheriton campaign was guarded by two companies of bluecoats armed with firelocks, probably drawn from a regiment of bluecoat foot. In the Royal army, it is noted that Percy's Regiment provided white-coated firelock guards for their artillery train. However, two companies of 'Firelocks' were formed specially to guard the New Model's train, dressed in orange-tawny coats as illustrated; the soldier also carries a knapsack and a frontal cartridge-box.

Drivers for the artillery train were usually hired (or even impressed) civilians, who wore their ordinary clothes; the man illustrated has the smock worn by many agricultural workers and waggoners.

in the Isle of Wight, and the inherent loyalty towards the King of leading Presbyterians, weighed in favour of a Presbyterian acceptance of the monarchy, as did the execution for treason by Parliament of a Presbyterian minister, Christopher Love, previously one of the monarchy's most vehement critics.

Charles II was at last accepted in Scotland and appointed nominal commander-in-chief of the Scottish forces; the Marquis of Argyll retired gloomily to his castle at Inverary. The second Duke of Hamilton was appointed Lieutenant-General and David Leslie Major-General, and it was the latter, entrenched around Stirling, who initiated the 1651 campaign. Cromwell had been ill in the earlier part of the year, and in June 1651, with an army gradually increased by Royalists and Engagers, Leslie made as if to give battle to tempt the English into an indiscretion. Cromwell attempted to make Leslie's position untenable by interrupting his supplies from Fife; Lambert won a minor victory at Inverkeithing (20 July) and by investing Perth (which capitulated on 2 August) Cromwell succeeded in cutting Leslie's lines of communication. The Scots had two options, to stand and fight or march into England to sever Cromwell's communications, and Charles decided upon the latter. Hamilton concurred, but the experienced Leslie was apparently unenthusiastic. Charles,

PLATE 26

68 Officer, Parliamentary artillery   69 Firelock guard, New Model Army artillery   70 Waggoner, Parliamentary artillery

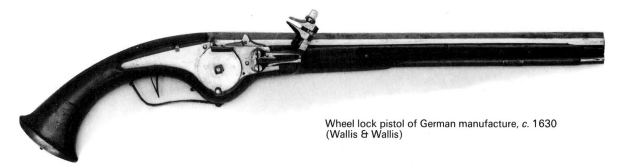

Wheel lock pistol of German manufacture, *c.* 1630
(Wallis & Wallis)

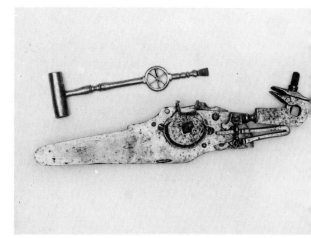

Detached wheel lock mechanism and spanner
(Wallis & Wallis)

however, was confident of the support of English Royalists and thus decided to march through Carlisle, Warrington and Manchester, Royalism being thought still especially strong in Lancashire. It was a grave miscalculation. Most Englishmen, irrespective of religious or political beliefs, still regarded the Scots as their traditional enemy, and the reluctance of the English Royalists to try their hand again was aggravated by a pronouncement issued by the Committee of Ministers, which accompanied the Covenant army, to the effect that both King and army fully subscribed to the Covenant and that no recruits would be accepted who did not concur. The King made a desperate attempt to stop this fatal interference by the ministers by instructing the commander of his vanguard, Edward Massey (who had so energetically defended Gloucester against Charles I but, as a Presbyterian, had fallen foul of the existing regime), to stop the publication of this statement. He was too late, and the English Royalists never rose en masse to support the King's Scottish army. Those who did, like the Earl of Derby who tried to raise Lancashire, were crushed quickly.

As the advance into England progressed, Leslie became increasingly morose and dispirited, confessing to the King that he knew the army, and 'however well soever it looked, would not fight'[4]. In an unfriendly country and including probably considerable numbers of inexperienced levies, the Scottish army, Leslie knew, would not prove half so formidable as when defending their own country. Cromwell despatched Lambert with his horse to pursue the King and engage as soon as possible, whilst he followed with the foot, leaving Monck in command at Perth. In addition to the troops pursuing from Scotland, other regiments and militia had been mobilized in England and were attempting to effect a juncture so as to confront the Scots with as large a force as possible. By the time the King's army reached Worcester on 22 August it was in poor shape, numbering perhaps as few as 13,000 tired, footsore and weary men, with a dispirited leader in Leslie. Charles was greeted warmly by the Mayor of Worcester, but although he received some protestations of support from

some of the Midlands Royalists (including such a hitherto staunch Parliamentary commander as Colonel John Birch), few offered material help, no doubt recognizing the hopelessness of the position of the King's army.

Cromwell, with some 28,000 men of much higher calibre than those of the King, invested the city and attacked on 3 September 1651, the anniversary of the battle of Dunbar. The date was well chosen, and the outcome the same. Cromwell attacked in three columns, across Powick Bridge and the two bridges of boats thrown across the rivers Severn and Teme; the Scots had deployed to the east of the city, sufficiently near for the King to observe the action from the tower of Worcester Cathedral. The Royal command was disrupted by Leslie's antipathy towards General John Middleton, and by an injury to Massey, their most vigorous commander, and the troops were dispirited. Middleton's command bravely resisted Cromwell's attack until Middleton was wounded and the Duke of Hamilton lost a leg to a roundshot (from which he died nine days later), but elsewhere the Royalist army disintegrated. Charles II led a counterattack from Worcester, and when that was beaten gathered a body of horse in the city streets and asked them to join him in one last charge. When he found that only his own servants were following he joined the mob of fugitives.

Worcester was, according to Cromwell, 'a crowning mercy'[5] and ended nine years of civil conflict; and ended it, ironically, only a short distance from the site of the first major skirmish which Prince Rupert had won at Powick Bridge. After his escape from Worcester, the King eluded capture for 45 days until he was able to slip away to France. During this period of 'hairbreadth 'scapes' he met and was aided by innumerable ordinary people whose ancient loyalty was eventually to support his restoration to the throne in 1660. In those few weeks the King would learn more about his subjects, rich and poor, than in all the rest of his privileged existence.

The consequences of the Civil Wars were profound; if the first conflict could be accorded the style of revolution, then so must the conflict within Parliament between those who wished to retain the King as a constitutional monarch and those determined upon his deposition. Cromwell, who became Lord Protector of the Commonwealth, was not the dictator sometimes portrayed but had to accept advice from his Council of State. Though strong he was also tolerant, permitting Anglicans and Roman Catholics to worship privately in London; he permitted Jews to return to England and did not interfere with other sects providing they did not infringe the law. After his death, however, his son Richard proved an ineffectual Protector and the restoration of the monarchy was seen as the most likely road to continued peace. The Civil Wars destroyed forever the feudal powers of the Crown and the King's right to levy taxes without the consent of Parliament which, as it emerged victorious, became the cornerstone of the British constitution. And the supremely professional army and navy of the Commonwealth set the pattern for British military supremacy in the following centuries.

But however profound the political, religious and constitutional effects of the Civil Wars, they exerted even greater influence upon the lives of many ordinary citizens. It is difficult, through lack of statistics, to assess these accurately, for whilst many areas were untouched by the conflict others came near to ruin, exemplified by Derbyshire after the plundering by Newcastle's army in May 1643, 'leaving no place unransacked, but ruining in inhuman and barbarous manner, neither sparing friend or foe'[6]. A different effect upon a rural community can be judged by the case of the parishes of Myddle, Marton and Newton (Shropshire), from which 20 men joined one army or another; no less than 13 of these were killed.

Of the Civil War commanders, some lost their property and died in exile, like Goring (in Spain, 1657); others died in obscurity and varying degrees of comfort, such as Lord Leven who, taken at Dunbar, spent some

PLATE 27

71 Engineer in siege armour
72 Miner
73 Seaman

The engineer wears a set of 'siege armour', enormously-heavy breast- and backplates, thigh guards and a 'death's-head' burgonet, so called from the helmet's resemblance to a skull. Such armour afforded the maximum protection possible for engineers working within musket-shot of the enemy, and as late as 1754 three sets of Civil War siege armour were sent to the army in America for 'the Engineers, who in that Woody Country may be obliged to reconoiter within Musket Shot'[1]. The miner is equipped for digging tunnels and saps, with a leather apron at the rear and knee pads; he carries a short pick and has a hatchet and (in the background) a wooden sledge used for dragging excavated earth from a tunnel.

The sailor illustrated is wearing a military buff-coat for service on land. Sailors participated effectively in the war on land, for example in the defence of Plymouth and Melcombe, and an attack by a landing party of some 200 seamen was a vital factor in the Parliamentary victory of Colby Moor (1645) which resulted in the fall of all the Royalist strongholds in Pembrokeshire. Regulation uniform for seamen was not established until 1857, but preferred styles had been in use for centuries. The first mention of 'slop' clothing (garments made to specifications set by the Navy Commissioners for sale to seamen aboard ship) occurs in 1623, but detailed descriptions date only from 1663, when Monmouth and 'red' caps, blue and white shirts, 'blew neck cloaths', 'canvas suites' and 'blew suites' are mentioned[2]; 'ruggs', coats of a heavy wool or 'rugge', were recommended for night watches as early as Sir Richard Hawkins. The sailor illustrated wears a 'thrum cap', 'thrum' being a woollen material with long nap resembling fur, probably the cap pictured by the Venetian Cesare Vecelli in *Habiti Antichi et Moderni* (1598) upon which the cap illustrated is based. By the date of Wycherley's comedy *The Plain Dealer* (1677) it would appear that red breeches were as characteristic of sailors as soldiers, but it is not known whether this applied to the Civil War, or whether the striped or checked shirts and trousers were as popular as at the end of the century. The coat illustrated has a 'mariner's cuff' with a buttoned seam which could be unfastened to allow the sleeves to be rolled up for work. Hawkins had advocated armour for use in action, but it was issued to ships in such limited quantities that no general use can have been envisaged. Officers probably dressed as those of the army, with breast- and backplates over a buff-coat; the embroidered red 'court dress' confirmed by 1604 seems to have lapsed before the Civil War.

NOTES

1 Blackmore, H.L. *British Military Firearms 1650–1850* (London, 1961) p. 67
2 Jarrett, D. *British Naval Dress* (London, 1960) p. 18

PLATE 27

71 Engineer   72 Miner   73 Seaman

PLATE 28

74 Ensign, Master of Yester's Regt.

75 Musketeer, Scottish foot

PLATE 28

74 Ensign with colour, Master of Yester's Regt.
75 Musketeer, Scottish foot

With clothing generally provided centrally, rather than by individual colonels, a degree of uniformity probably existed in the Scottish army. Most common was clothing of 'hodden grey' colour, a term describing various shades of grey-brown. The use of such common 'country cloth' by the Scottish army seems to have persisted for some years, for as late as 1684 the Privy Council asked merchants and manufacturers to supply 'sufficient cloathes at reasonable rates and of such dye as shall be thought fit to distinguish sojers from other skulking and vagrant persons'[1]. The grey would not be universal, however; some corps are believed to have worn red uniforms made from English cloth, and one, the 'Minister's Regiment' was said to be dressed in black, second-hand clerical clothing. Oblique non-contemporary references to the use of the Stuart colours (red and yellow) for military dress suggest that they may have been worn in the mid seventeenth century, but the first which can be dated with certainty concerns James II, who 'did his utmost to ensure uniformity in the clothing of the army, adopting the family colours'[2]. It has been said that the Scots militia wore blue, but such references may postdate the Civil War, such as the ballad of Bothwell Bridge (1679):[3]

> The Lowdien Mallisha they
> Came with their coates of blew,
> Five hundred men from London came
> Clad in a reddish hue.

One almost universal item was the flat, blue cloth bonnet worn by the Scottish army, including officers. The ensign illustrated wears a gorget over a sleeved buff-coat and carries a slightly-curved hunting sword. The colour of the Master of Yester's Regiment is based upon the national saltaire of St Andrew, with the legend 'Couenant/for Religion/King/and Kingdomes', and a family crest in the centre. John Hay, Master of Yester, commanded the Linlithgow and Tweed-dale Regiment at Marston Moor and the East Lothian Regiment at Preston, where a number of captured colours all bore his own crest, as illustrated.

NOTES
1 Lawson, vol. I, pp. 57–8
2 *Ibid.*, p. 58, quoting Ross, A. *Old Scottish Regimental Colours*
3 See Cripps, W.J. *The Royal North Gloucester* (London, 1875) p. 42

time in captivity but died at an advanced age in his own home in 1661. Others survived to see the Restoration, some (like Monck) playing a major part in its execution and others, like Sir Thomas Fairfax (second baron after his father's death in 1648) and the Earl of Manchester, welcoming the King's return. Some of their old comrades did not; for example, Lambert was held in custody for over 30 years until his death, and Edmund Ludlow, Parliamentary general and regicide (i.e. a signatory to the death warrant of Charles I), died in Switzerland after a 30-year exile. Three of the regicides were kidnapped in Holland in 1662 whilst visiting Delft on business from their retreat at Hanau. Miles Corbet, John Barkstead and Colonel John Okey, the latter the commander of the New Model dragoons, were siezed by Sir George Downing, an agent for Charles II, yet previously Cromwell's scoutmaster-general and even the chaplain to Okey's own regiment. The old dragoon and his two companions were hanged, drawn and quartered at Tyburn. Other old Roundheads and Cavaliers survived to see (and even participate in, to some degree), the 'Glorious Revolution' of 1688, though none of the leading figures, political or military, survived so long as William Hiseland, the last Edgehill survivor, who died in Chelsea Hospital in 1731.

Personal testaments and petitions for relief often show the effects of the Civil Wars in their most tragic light. For every soldier killed in battle or dead of disease, at least one other soldier was broken in health or a family deprived of support. Not all were wounded physically; a case which cannot have been unique was that of Thomas Goad, a chaplain at Marston Moor, who was so unhinged by the carnage of that battle that he lived for the next 16 years in a state of distraction. Applications for pensions reveal the plight of the real victims of the Civil Wars, like Sergeant William Stoakes who fought for the King from Edgehill to Naseby and whose 'many dangerous hurts' left him with a wife and five children to support, but 'Having lost the use of his lymbes is not in any waye able to work for their mayntenance'[7]; he was granted 40s. per annum by Charles II. A similar pension was awarded in 1661 to Corporal Robert Davyes, whose 3½ years' service cost him all his possessions and whose 17 wounds '& ye great losse of bloud ... hath almost lost the sight of his eyes & allmost the use of both Armes whereby he is made unable to worke or use any bodily exercise for & towards the gayning of a livelihood & maynteynance of himselfe wife & fouer children'[8]. Corporal Rowland Humfrey petitioned that in supporting the King he had been short and stabbed in the leg, wounded three times in the arm 'whereby he hath allmost lost the ues of it', suffered a sword cut to the head and finally 'a great blow with a muskett in the mouth wch beate out allmost all his teeth before', so as to render him 'almost unfitt for any bodily Labor & so unable to worke to gayne a Livelihood for himselfe & wife & two children ...'[9]. He received the grand sum of 60s. per annum in return for his loss of livelihood, health and strength, paid some 17 years after the date of his last injury.

Hobbes wrote that 'a Civil War never ends by Treaty without the Sacrifice of those who were on both Sides the sharpest'[10]. Tragically, as proved by the extant records concerning ordinary citizens, the 'sharpest' adherents of either side were not the only ones to be sacrificed upon the fires of the Civil Wars.

10 UNIFORMS

One of the most deeply rooted misconceptions concerning the Civil War is that military uniforms did not exist until the creation of the New Model Army, and that they were the first to wear the traditional British red coat. In actual fact, it had long been the custom for companies or regiments to be clothed in a uniform manner, though as colouring was at the discretion of the commander or proprietor there was little standardization. As early as 1539 the London militia wore uniform white coats; in 1569 the Gloucester levies wore 'blue capps wth yalowe sylke rybands, and ... slopps of blewe clothe gardede with yallowe, and yallowe nether stockins'[1]; and in 1587 the Doncaster Trained Band wore uniform steel caps, fustian doublets, grey woollen 'Friezeland' coats and light blue coarse cloth stockings[2], for example.

Monck advised officers that, 'You must be careful before you march with your Army into the Field to see your Soldiers well Cloathed, well Armed, and well Disciplined; and that you be stored with Shooes and Stockings for the March'[3]; though officers were usually advised against trimming their men's uniforms with their own livery colours:

... a desire you had to put your colours upon your coats for the better knowing of your men ... in mine opinion would much wrong the coat. The differences that Captains use in wars is in the arming of his pikes for the pikemen, which is to be of his colours, and likewise the fringe of his headpiece of the shot [musketeers]. The daubing of a coat with lace of sundry colours, as some do use them, I do neither take to be soldierlike nor profitable for the coat. If a Captain miscarry, he that cometh in his room, his colours being contrary, tears off the former and puts in his own, and by this means often times tears coat and all ...[4]

Provision of clothing was undertaken by the central command or at regimental or unit level. For example, on 6 March 1642 Thomas Bushell undertook to procure 'for the King's Souldiers Cassocks, Breeches, Stockings & Capps at reasonable rates'[5], presumably the 'suites, stockings, shoes and mounteroes' for the 'liefe Guard and three regiments more' noted three months later[6]. In January 1643 tailors in the Oxford area were ordered to produce 5,000 coats, so that in July 'all the common soldiers then at Oxford were newe apparelled, some all in red, coates, breeches & mounteres; & some all in blewe'[7]. Such contracts given to local tailors are ex-

William Barriffe, showing the use of gorget with buff-coat. Note the laces at the front of the coat (portrait from Barriffe's *Military Discipline*)

emplified by an appeal made to Charles II by the Company of Drapers of Worcester, for £453 for red cloth, before the settlement of which 'the army was defeated and then miserably plundered'[8]. Parliamentary uniform provision was similar; for example, on 6 August 1642 the Committee of Lords and Commons for the Safety of the Kingdom ordered that soldiers should receive coats, shoes, shirts and caps to the value of 17s. each man, but the lack of a centralized purchasing system always caused problems. Within the Eastern Association, the Cambridge Committee had great difficulty in getting Essex to equip its levies correctly, and eventually had to buy coats themselves, hoping (in vain) that the county would reimburse them. Conscripts clothed at the expense of their parish were frequently ill-clad; in August 1643, for example, Essex conscripts were described as 'worse tattered soldiers' than ever before seen, and in the following year Silas Titus took command of his new Hertfordshire company but found them 'extreamlie ill provided for ... without shooes, stockings, coates ... they wanted nothing but all'[9].

'Uniform' usually consisted of a coat and sometimes matching breeches, though frequently the latter might be of a different colour or even provided by the individual. Coats were probably mostly of the short-skirted variety, as described by the contract books of the New Model (noted below), though frequent mention is made of the 'cassock', which may describe the ordinary, skirted coat (as distinct from a doublet) or a longer coat as shown in Plate 13. The cassock is noted as early as 1599, worn by troops in Ireland, 'of Kentish broad cloth, lined with cotton, and trimmed, with buttons and loops', or 'of broad cloth with bays, and trimmed with silk lace' for officers[10]; this was probably the greatcoat-like garment used in winter, which originally could be transformed into a cloak with open, hanging sleeves,

Pikeman's corselet and helmet (engraving from Grose's *Antient Armour*)

PLATE 29

76 Lancer, Scottish army
77 Pikeman, Scottish army

The Scottish cavalry, due to the small size and poor quality of their horses, was usually regarded as greatly inferior to that of the English, a somewhat unfair judgement as they performed well on occasion, as at Preston when lancers of the Scottish rearguard killed the commander of the English pursuit, Colonel Thornhaugh. The Scots were the only ones to use lances to any degree, the weapon being largely redundant even on the continent. The lancer illustrated wears a leather jerkin and an old-fashioned burgonet, the 'steill bonnett' beloved of the reivers of the Borders during the previous century. In addition to a lance he is armed with a broadsword and carries baggage and fodder on his saddle; the wooden canteen is privately acquired.

'Hodden grey' appears to have been worn by the Scottish dragoons even after red had been adopted by the remainder of the army; when in 1684 the Privy Council passed an act to allow the importation of English red cloth, General Dayell objected to that colour being worn by dragoons, and an extra act was required to permit the import of grey cloth. When the 'Royal Scots Dragoons' were raised in 1678 they wore grey coats, not adopting red until about 1684–7, the title 'Scots Greys' perhaps referring originally to the colour of their uniforms, not (as later) to their horses.

The pikeman here wears the 'hodden grey' uniform shown in Plate 28, with the addition of an old-fashioned cabasset helmet with its backward-pointing 'pear-stalk' at the top. He carries a leather satchel instead of the sack shown in Plate 28, and has a long knife in his girdle, a common weapon in the Scottish army. His blue bonnet is tucked behind his belt, though it may have been possible to wear it under the helmet.

which Turner termed 'frocks' and recommended should have a hood, 'to keep them from rain, snow and cold'[11] Another overcoat was the 'rocket', presumably a secular version of the ecclesiastical 'rochet', with skirts so long that Colonel Edward Apsley of Sussex was captured in 1643 when some Royalists 'caught hold of my rocket coat, and threw it over my head'[12].

Uniform colouring was governed by the availability of material, the colonel's preference or his livery; for example, Essex's Regiment wore his own 'orange-tawny' colour and in at least two cases around this period, black 'facings' were adopted as a sign of mourning: Richard Cromwell issued red coats 'guarded with black' for his father's funeral[13], and in 1667 Lord Chesterfield clothed his regiment in red coats lined black, 'because I was at that time in mourning for my mother'[14]. It is uncertain exactly how 'facing colours' were displayed during the Civil War, but such references probably indicate the lining visible when the sleeve was turned back off the wrist, though in the case of the New Model, facing colours were apparently also

PLATE 29

76 Lancer, Scottish army

77 Pikeman, Scottish army

'Morion' helmet; a design predating the Civil War by more than a century, but still in use

displayed in the 'tape strings' which fastened the coats instead of buttons. Until the New Model, records of facing colours are sparse, though the Eastern Association certainly used them; in October 1643 Manchester ordered green coats lined with red for his own regiment, and in 1645 the Committee of Both Kingdoms ordered the county of Essex to send their recruits 'commodiously provided, as hath formerly been practised, with 1000 red coats lined with blue'[15]. The colour of a regiment's uniform often gave it a sobriquet; thus in 1642 when disturbances between regiments in Oxford developed into faction fights, the units involved were described as Lord Saye's Oxfordshire Bluecoats and their opponents as Russet-coats. Thus it was usual for regiments to be known by their coat colour, be it the Gloucester Bluecoats (Stamford's Regiment) or Newcastle's renowned Whitecoats.

Red uniforms were popular long before the New Model; an Elizabethan example is the instruction to William Chalderton, Bishop of Chester, to provide 1,000 men 'furnished of redd clokes, without sleeves, and of the length to the knee'[16], and a letter of 1638 suggests that by that date, red breeches had become the mark of a soldier: 'It would be good if Yr. Lordship's men had red breeches to their buff coats, because otherwise being country fellows they will not be so neatly habited as the other Lord's men'[17]. Colour mattered more than style; an example of how colonels endeavoured to keep their troops uniformly clad is found in a letter of 1644 from Sir T. Dallison to Prince Rupert reporting that 'I have had 113 coats and caps for foot soldiers in the house of my Lord Powis, an 100 of which are blue which will well serve your Highness' Regiment of Foot'[18], the remainder being green serving for 'Col. Tylyer's' (Tillier's) and regiments from Ireland which, like Broughton's, it has been suggested may have worn

green as a national colour, though there is no evidence to support this. As may be imagined, similarly coloured uniforms on both sides led to great confusion!

Listed below are those regiments for which uniform colours are known, though due to changes of command and the practice of naming a regiment after its colonel, the same regiments are sometimes listed more than once. For example, the Yellowcoats of Sir Charles Vavasour became Sir Matthew Appleyard's Regiment after Vavasour's death; and Prince Rupert's Bluecoats was a Somerset regiment, raised by Colonel Sir Thomas Lunsford who was captured at Edgehill, and when his brother Colonel Henry Lunsford was fatally wounded at the storm of Bristol (26 July 1643) the regiment became Prince Rupert's, being commanded by Colonel John Russell until it was destroyed at Naseby.

Royalist foot

Queen's Lifeguard	red
King's Lifeguard	red
Prince Rupert's Firelocks	red
Sir Allan Apsley	red
Col. Edward Hopton	red
Prince Charles (C.O. Sir Michael Woodhouse)	blue
Lord Hopton	blue
Prince Rupert	blue
Thomas Lunsford	blue
Henry Lunsford	blue
Charles Gerard	blue
Sir William Pennyman	blue (or red?)
Sir Stephen Hawkins	white
Lord Percy	white
Marquis of Newcastle	white*
Sir Ralph Dutton	white
Col. Thomas Pinchbeck	grey
Col. Sir Henry Bard	grey
Sir Gilbert Talbot	yellow
Sir Charles Vavasour	yellow
Sir Matthew Appleyard	yellow
Sir John Paulet	yellow
Earl of Northampton	green
Col. Robert Broughton	green
Col. Henry Tillier	green
Sir Thomas Blackwall	black

*though Newcastle's seven divisions of northern foot are usually described as Whitecoats, probably some wore grey.

Parliamentary foot

Lord Robartes	red
Col. Denzil Holles	red
Sir Thomas Fairfax	red lined blue
Edward Montague	red lined white
Norfolk Regt.	red
Essex Regts.	red lined blue

Lord Halifax	red lined blue
Earl of Stamford	blue
Col. Henry Cholmley	blue
Sir William Constable	blue
Lord Saye & Sele	blue
Sir Arthur Haselrig	blue
Lord Mandeville (later Earl of Manchester)	blue
Sir William Springate	white (?)
Sir John Gell	grey
Simon Rugeley	grey
Sir John Merrick	grey
Col. Thomas Ballard	grey
Major William Ryves (company)	grey
Earl of Manchester	green lined red
Samuel Jones	green
Col. Byng	green
John Hampden	green*
Col. Thomas Grantham	russet
Earl of Essex	orange
Lord Brooke	purple

*Bund is in error in stating that Hampden's wore grey[19].

Details of the uniform of horse are scarcer, perhaps because the buff-coat and defensive armour precluded the necessity for recognizable uniform; nevertheless, among existing references are notes that the Prince of Wales' Regiment chose red as their main colour, that in May 1644 a quartermaster probably from the Earl of Denbigh's Regiment was issued with $8\frac{1}{2}$ yards (7.8 metres) of grey cloth, in which colour Denbigh (previously Lord Feilding) may have dressed his men as early as Edgehill, that Captain John Moor of Northampton's Horse in 1645 captured some red cloth and reported that he intended to clothe his troop in it, that Lord Hastings dressed his three troops in blue coats underlaid with leather, and that Sir Thomas Dallison (commanding Prince Rupert's) mentioned that he had 300 or 400 yards (275 to 365 metres) of red cloth to make into cloaks. Godwin's *Civil War in Hampshire 1642–45* (1904) mentions that Sir Michael Livesey's Kentish Parliamentary regiment wore red coats with blue facings, but as facings was a later term the reference is perhaps questionable. Much cavalry uniform involved small units, perhaps even less than troops; for example, before Edgehill Francis Russell of Essex's Lifeguard was observed with 12 armed servants, all wearing red cloaks; one Royalist troop accoutred, it was said, by the Earl of Newcastle, rode 'fifty great horses of a darke Bay, handsomely set out with ash-colour'd ribbins, every man gentiely accoutred'[20], and a further example is provided by the troop raised in 1639 by the poet and gambler Sir John Suckling, 'a Troope of 100 very handsome young proper men, whom he clad in white doubletts and scarlet breeches, and scarlett Coates, hatts

and feathers, well horsed and armed. They say 'twas one of the finest sights in those days'[21]. A similar 'personal' unit was the bodyguard of halbardiers dressed in long red cassocks formed by Sir Arthur Aston, Governor of Oxford, following an attempt on his life.

Hats were not always of the broad-brimmed, 'cavalier' style beloved of later generations of artists, but also existed in other guises, with narrower brims and taller crowns. Two varieties of cap were used extensively, the 'Monmouth' and the 'montero'. The former (also mentioned in lists of seamen's slop clothing) was apparently a knitted woollen cap, shaped either like a ski-cap or like a fisherman's 'stocking' cap; Richard Symonds' *Diary* notes of Bewdley in 1644 that 'The only manufacture of this towne is making of capps called Monmouth capps. Knitted by poore people for 2d. apiece, ordinary ones sold for 2s., 3s., 4s. First they are knitt, then they mill them, then block them, then they worke them with tasells, then they sheere them'. In 1642 Parliament paid 23s. a dozen for 'Monmouth caps' for troops serving in Ulster, but when Colonel Richard Bagot bought caps for the 300 foot he raised in April 1643 to garrison Lichfield Close for the King, he paid only 6d. each.

The montero is enigmatic, as the term (originally

Pikeman's breast- and backplates with riveted 'skirts' attached, bearing armourers' marks of reign of James I and Commonwealth (Wallis & Wallis)

Spanish) simply means a cap as worn by horsemen, and its use was probably so common that no-one bothered to describe it. Probably it was similar to the peaked, cloth cap used in France from around 1625, reputedly copied from troops of the Duke of Buckingham, hence its French name of 'boukinkan'. It became so popular as to be adopted by the *Gardes du Roi*, and is shown in an engraving of 1642 upon which the drummer shown on the window of Farndon Church is based. Whether this *was* the montero is uncertain, as surviving descriptions are unclear: Thomas Ellwood wrote of 'a large montero cap of black velvet, the skirt of which was turned up in folds'[22], whilst Sterne's *Tristram Shandy* notes one of 'scarlet, of a superfine Spanish cloth, dyed in grain, and mounted all round with fur, except about four inches in front, which was faced with a light blue, slightly embroidered'. At Naseby a Royalist officer was described 'somewhat in habit like our general, in a red montero as the General had'[23], and in 1645 an attorney was hanged as a spy by Sir Richard Grenville, being 'disguised' by a montero, perhaps implying that it was the recognized mark of a soldier, though as Grenville bore a grudge against the man it may have been merely a convenient excuse. Certainly, it seems that caps were regarded as much an item of uniform as coats, and may even have been in matching colours.

'Linen' consisted of the loose shirt and its appendages, with elaborate lace cuffs (for officers), though very often it was of a more practical style for use in the field. The white linen collar or 'falling band' was usually loose and tied on with strings, though knotted neckcloths seem to have been popular, both to prevent the armour or buff-coat from chafing the skin and as added protection; the lives of at least two members of the 1637 expedition against the Pequod Indians in America were saved by the knots of their neckerchiefs deflecting blows. Stockings were frequently worn two pairs at a time, the inner pair (often of finer material) being drawn up and the outer or 'rowling' pair, which originally protected the inner, rolled down or drawn only partway up the calf, thus creating a deliberately casual appearance which may have originated with the German *landsknechts*. Shoes had buckles or laces, sometimes tied with a bunch of ribbon.

Officers' uniforms were provided individually and thus based on civilian styles, though some uniformity in colouring may have been attempted. Some of these uniforms were very fine, including prodigious quantities of lace; despite an earlier exhortation to the Hertfordshire trained bands to 'forbeare their fyne coort-lyke sutes during the tyme of musters'[24], many officers affected elaborate dress, such as Sir Richard Grenville who received from Parliament 'a great sum of money for the making his equipage, in which he always affected more than ordinary lustre'[25], or Colonel Jordan Prideaux, killed at Marston Moor, who was said to wear a diamond buckle in his hat. Prince Rupert, the archetype cavalier,

PLATE 30

78, 79, 80 Highlanders

The Highland troops wore their ordinary clothes, of which a number of descriptions, but few pictures, survive from the mid seventeenth century, though a well-known print by Koler shows mercenaries of the Thirty Years War wearing Highland 'military' dress. The principal garment was the *Breacan-an fheilidh* or 'belted plaid', a long strip of plaid cloth which could be wound around the waist, held in place by a belt and with one end pulled up over one shoulder, or used as a shawl or cloak, as shown by Koler. The legs were either left bare or covered with stockings of plaid or other cloth, or with one-piece trousers-and-stockings, forerunners of the Scottish *truibhs* (trews), worn either instead of, or underneath, the *Breacan-an fheilidh*. A linen shirt was usually worn, the traditional 'saffron' type probably still in use, and a leather jerkin. At Kilsyth the day was so hot that Montrose ordered his Highlanders to lay aside their plaids and fight in their shirts, knotting the long tails beneath their legs. Footwear consisted of mocassin-type shoes, though many went barefoot, and the common headdress was a blue cloth bonnet worn square upon the head. As clan tartans had not evolved, the patterns of plaid worn by Highlanders were dependent upon personal taste, though certain areas are believed to have had more or less distinctive setts; the colouring of most was probably subdued, and many were probably of simple checks. A legend explaining the traditional white spats of later Highland regiments is probably apocryphal, but records how the Highlanders wrapped the torn remnants of their shirts around their feet during the march through the snow to Inverlochy.

Highland weaponry was traditional and prolific; a roll taken by the Earl of Atholl of four parishes in 1638 records 523 men who between them possessed 112 guns, 11 pistols, 149 bows, 9 poleaxes, 2 halberds, 3 claymores, 448 swords, 125 targes, 8 headpieces, 2 'steel bonnets', a pair of plate sleeves, 11 breastplates and one jack (mail coat); only 21 men were returned as unarmed. The two-handed *claidheamh-mhor* or 'great sword' was largely redundant by this period, the broadsword being the commonest weapon, though the traditional type with decorated basket hilt probably had not evolved fully; some had curved blades resembling a hanger. Unlike the European 'rondel', the Highland shield or targe was flat, made of wood covered with leather and often decorated with brass studs, and had a central boss into which a nine-inch (23-centimetre) spike could be screwed, turning it into a weapon of offence. Simple dirks would be worn at the waist; the predominant staff weapon was the lochaber axe, characterized by a cleaver-like blade and a hook welded to the upper staff socket. The longbow remained a potent weapon in Scotland (probably retained because of shortages of firearms), with arrows carried in a quiver slung over the shoulder.

Highland dress was probably restricted to those unable to afford conventional military clothing, which chieftains and officers might be expected to have worn, though Montrose is mentioned as wearing Highland dress on one occasion, almost certainly with trews to enable him to ride in comfort.

PLATE 30

78 79 80 Highlanders

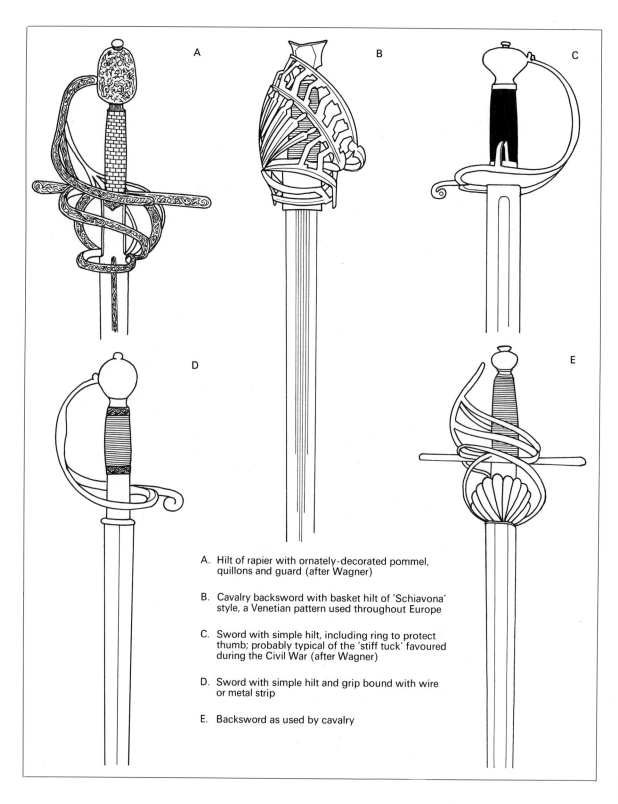

A. Hilt of rapier with ornately-decorated pommel, quillons and guard (after Wagner)

B. Cavalry backsword with basket hilt of 'Schiavona' style, a Venetian pattern used throughout Europe

C. Sword with simple hilt, including ring to protect thumb; probably typical of the 'stiff tuck' favoured during the Civil War (after Wagner)

D. Sword with simple hilt and grip bound with wire or metal strip

E. Backsword as used by cavalry

was noted in a London newsletter of 1645 dressed as befitting his reputation, 'clad in scarlet, very richly laid in silver lace, mounted upon a very gallant black Barbary horse'[26], but such references are as deceptive as the portraits which show officers wearing magnificently-decorated armour. Such ornamentation could only lead to their being singled out by the enemy, to prevent which, for example, Rupert at Brentford 'took off his scarlet coat which was very rich and gave it to his man and buckled on his arms and put a grey coat over it so that he might not be discovered'[27]. Colonel George Lisle at Second Newbury led his men wearing a white shirt and was mistaken by the Parliamentarians for a white witch running up and down the King's army! Adherents to the more austere religious sects usually favoured more sombre clothing, but even this is something of a misconception; for example, Colonel Thomas Harrison, who commanded the King's escort on the way to his trial, was described as wearing a velvet montero, a buff-coat and a crimson silk waist-sash, richly fringed (which at one time would have indicated Royalist

Musketeer armed with caliver and costumed in style pre-dating the Civil War (engraving by N.C. Goodnight after de Gheyn)

sympathy), and in 1650 he wore a scarlet cloak and coat so covered with gold and silver lace that the fabric was barely visible!

The rigours of campaign and shortage of matériel resulted in many Civil War armies going barefoot and almost in rags. Contemporary sources note many examples, such as Sir Samuel Luke's statement that, 'There were 2 in my company that had but one pair of breeches between them so that when one was up, the other must of necessity be in his bed'[28], and a typical *cri de coeur* is found in a letter from Bartholomew Vermuyden, commander of the Norfolk horse, pleading for settlement of his men's arrears of pay, for 'to see our troops goe barefoot and naked this winter wether, and thire horses unshodd for want of your assistance makes me write thus earnestly'[29]. Some troops even began their service in a state of wretchedness, such as those sent by the Essex committee to the Earl of Manchester in September 1643, with 'noe armes, noe clothes, noe coulors, noe drums ... in so naked a posture, that to imploye them were to murther them'[30].

With no universal uniform, recognition in the field was ever a problem; two aids to recognition were adopted, the 'field sign' and the 'field word'. The former, a visible proclamation of the wearer's allegiance, varied from coloured sashes to scraps of paper stuck in the hat. Such practices were not new; for example, Robert Cary, Earl of Monmouth, recalled an assault during the English campaigning in Flanders under the Earl of Essex in the previous century: 'One night there were scaling ladders prepared ... We were all commanded to wear shirts above the armour (I lost many shirts that I lent that night) ...'[31]

Coloured sashes were restricted largely to officers and horse, for, 'Every horseman must weare a skarf of the

PLATE 31

Colours

Top left: Colonel, Tower Hamlets Regt. (Parliamentary).

Top right: 1st captain, Lifeguard of Foot (Royalist). Those of other companies bore different Royal badges.

Centre left: 1st captain, City of Oxford Regt. (Royalist). Lieutenant-colonel's colour bore reversed 'C' cypher below a scroll bearing *FORTIS ET VERITAS*; major's had a pile wavy descending from the St George canton; 2nd captain two lions, 3rd three, etc.

Centre right: 1st captain, Lamplugh's Regt. (Royalist). The only known colours of Newcastle's Whitecoats. This demonstrates how it was not usual for coat colours and flag colours to be the same, though many regiments had similar colouring, for example Brooke's or Hampden's.

Bottom left: 4th captain, Stradling's Regt. (Royalist). Captured at Edgehill.

Bottom right: 2nd captain, Green Regt. of London trained bands (Parliamentary).

PLATE 31

PLATE 32

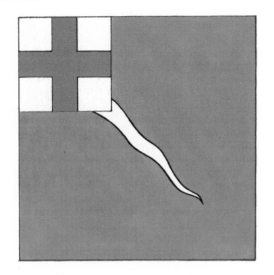

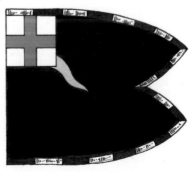

PLATE 32

Colours and standards

Top left: Major, Orange Auxiliaries, London trained bands (Parliamentary). Showing the pile wavy descending from the St George canton.

Top right: Scottish colour of an unidentified regiment, taken at Dunbar. Illustrates interesting features including the use of the St Andrew's saltaire in other colouring than the national white-on-blue, the Covenant motto (spellings varied!) and the use of both heraldic marks of cadency (in this case a golden martlet) and company numeral, indicating the ownership of the 4th captain of the regiment. Prior to 1650, when the Covenant motto was standardized to include loyalty to the King, it was often rendered as 'Religion, Covenant and Country' or 'Covenant for Religion, Crown and Country', etc.

Centre, top left: Standard of Captain Owen Cambridge, Twistleton's Horse (Parliamentary). Example of the common arm-and-cloud motif, typical motto, and in regimental colouring, white with black and yellow design.

Centre, top right: Unidentified Royalist standard captured at Marston Moor. Illustrates the use of symbolic 'cartoons'; presumably refers to the sword cutting the Gordian knot of politics.

Centre, bottom: Standard of Sir Arthur Haselrig (Parliamentary), carried presumably by his troop of horse at Edgehill. The green colouring was retained by his later regiment, on the standards of which the arm-and-cloud motif was displayed.

Bottom left: Standard of Sir William Waller (Parliamentary), representing the personal flags carried by many generals.

Bottom right: Major's guidon, unidentified Royalist dragoon regiment, captured at Marston Moor; illustrates the swallow-tailed guidon of dragoons. Distinguishing marks were like those of foot; Waller's dragoon regiment, for example, had yellow guidons bearing black roundels, one for the major, two for 1st captain, etc. Colonels' guidons were usually plain; distinguishing symbols were as varied as bibles (on black, Sir Samuel Luke's Regiment) or black crescent-moons on white (unidentified Royalist regiment).

Princes colour whom he serveth, and not put if off ... and upon occasions of battell they shall be sure by that means not to offend each other'[32]. Apparently red scarves were the traditional English colour, perhaps taken from the colouring of the national flag; for example, *Hakluytus Posthumus or Purchas His Pilgrims* notes that the English in Java celebrated the Queen's coronation in 1606 by making 'scarves of white and red taffeta, being our country's colours'[33], and red sashes (and red-and-white feathers) were still in use at the coronation of Charles II[34]. Red or 'rose' sashes were used by the Royalist forces in the Civil War, an extant example reputedly worn by the King at Edgehill being eight feet nine inches (2.7 metres) long, embroidered in silver, and now a purplish hue, perhaps having altered in colour over the years. It is often assumed that the

Parliamentary forces in general wore the orange-tawny sashes of the Earl of Essex's army, but this may not have been universal and perhaps applied only to the forces under Essex's actual command. Certainly confusion occurred and other colours of sash were used; for example, at Edgehill Sir Faithfull Fortescue's troop of Parliamentary horse changed sides *en bloc*, shooting their pistols into the ground to signify their change of allegiance, but some were slain by the Royalists for delaying to remove their orange-tawny sashes. Ludlow claimed that Sir John Smith recaptured the Banner Royal at Edgehill by disguising himself with an orange-tawny scarf, whilst at Chalgrove 'the reason why we killed no more was partly because diverse of the Rebells had red scarfes like ours and by following them were Mr Howard and Captain Gardner unawares ingaged and taken ... of the King's party, were some 10 or 12 slain and some of them through mistake being for want of scarfes or their not having the word readily'[36]. Continued use of the red sash by Parliamentarians is proven by the diary of a Royalist defender of Pontefract Castle who recorded the death of a Roundhead wearing 'a gallant shuyt of apparell with a great redd skarfe', the same account noting a Captain Mason at Second Newbury wearing a 'black scarfe about his middle'[36], probably signifying individual mourning. Deliberate deception was practiced, such as that of Colonel Henry Gage whose relief of Basing House in September 1644 was due in part to his troops being disguised by orange sashes and hat ribbons.

Hat ribbons were used to identify ordinary soldiers who would not wear sashes, though their use was not universal. Early in the war the Venetian ambassador reported to the Doge that the Royalists were identified by 'rose-coloured bands on their hats'[37]; when equipment was ordered for the army to go to Ireland, 10,000 hats and bands were included, presumably for the musketeers. Whether cockades as such were worn is unknown, but a painting by Dobson of Prince Rupert with Colonels William Murray and John Russell shows hat-cockades of pink, black and grey (or silver), the fact that Russell is shown dipping his cockade into a glass of wine giving rise to the story that the picture represents an attempt to persuade him not to change sides[38], though a more likely explanation is that it shows Russell receiving his commission as lieutenant-colonel of the Prince's regiment. As Murray was then probably on Rupert's staff, the coloured cockade may have been associated with the Prince's personal service[39]. Hat ribbons were used for other reasons than purely military; Levellers, for example, were distinguished by their sea-green favours.

Field signs were adopted for a particular occasion to distinguish one army from another; for example, a white paper band or handkerchief in the hat was a popular Parliamentary sign, perhaps inspired by the London trained bands who in January 1642 proclaimed their

French engraving of 1632 showing drummer of *Gardes Françaises* wearing a *boukinkan*, not only an English style of headdress but sufficiently familiar in England for figure to be copied, almost exactly, on Farndon window

on Tower Hill supporters of the French ambassador 'marched in great companyes along the street, with every man a white handkerchief tyed about his arme'[40]; the same distinction was employed by Gage's relievers of Basing House in 1644 (a handkerchief tied above the right elbow). Sprigs of foliage were a popular field sign, used (for example) by Parliament at First Newbury, where the 'whole army wore green boughs in their hats, to distinguish us from our enemies, which they perceiving, one Regiment of their Horse had got green boughs and rode up to our regiments crying, 'Friends, friends'; but we let fly at them ...'[41]; the London trained bands, in fact, retained their green boughs until they returned home, though five days earlier the Parliamentarians had worn white handkerchiefs in their hats instead. At Pontefract the Parliamentary foot were recorded 'with Roasemary in theire hattes'[42], whilst at Naseby the Royalists 'had beane stalkes in their hats, we nothing: some of ours on their owne accord had white Linnen, or paper in their hats'[43]. At Marston Moor Parliamentarians wore white handkerchiefs or paper, the Royalists no bands or scarves; at Bristol (July 1643) Rupert ordered his troops to wear green colours, 'either bows or such like'[44] (or 'boughs'?), and to be without band or handkerchief around the neck. Naturally this system was the cause of great confusion; for example, at Marston Moor, Fairfax was able to ride through the enemy by taking the white handkerchief from his hat, whilst at Cheriton both sides adopted the same field sign and pass word (something white in the hat and 'God with us'), and in June 1648 both sides in a skirmish at Bangor wore neither sash nor field sign and used a similar cry, the Royalists 'Resolution' and Parliament 'Religion'.

The 'field word' or pass word was adopted to prevent such confusion, but its use was quite impractical once combat was joined as each side could discover the other's password simply by listening to the enemy's shouts. Random examples are noted below:

	Royalist	Parliamentary
Cheriton	(both orginally	'God with us')
	'God and the	'Jesus help us'
	Cause'	or 'Jesus bless us'
Naseby	'Queen Mary'	'God is our strength'
Thurland Castle, Furness, 1643	'In with Queen Mary'	'God with us'
Colchester	–	'God's our help'
Alton	'Charles'	'Truth and Victory'
Basing House (final assault)	–	'For God and Parliament'
Cropredy Bridge	'Hand and Sword'	'Victory without Quarter'

adherence to Parliament by fastening copies of the Protestation issued by the Commons upon their pikes and hats or tucked into the breasts of their coats. Such favours were not overtly military, as in the 1661 riot

11 COLOURS AND STANDARDS

COLOURS

Each company of foot carried a flag or colour, and each troop of horse had a standard, which served as a recognizable rallying point in action and embodied the honour and reputation of the unit. Loss of a colour was the gravest dishonour and its capture the greatest prize; thus bitter combats raged around them, and traditionally disasters were measured in terms of 'as when a standard-bearer fainteth' (Isaiah x, 18). The term 'colours' originated in the sixteenth century: 'We Englishmen do call them of late Colours, by reason of the variety of colours they be made of ...'[1]. Estimates of the size of a force might be given as 'about fifty colours of foot', i.e. 50 companies. The bearer of a flag (ensign of foot or cornet of horse) filled 'a place of repute and honour, doth not suite every Yeoman, Taylor, or Fidler ... or the like Mechanick fellowes'[2], and, 'In occationes of fightings withe his enemy, he is to sheaw himself dreadfull and terrible, with his sworde in his righte hande, and his Colours in his left ...'[3].

Colours were usually $6\frac{1}{2}$ feet (2 metres) square, with design often dependent upon the colonel's whim, but certain rules were usually followed. Ward's *Animadversions of Warre* (1639) notes that the colonel 'ought to have all the Colours of his Regiment to be alike, both in colour and fashion to avoide confusion so that the souldiers may discerne their owne Regiment from the other Troopes; likewise, every particular Captaine of his Regiment may have some small distinction in their Colours; as their Armes, or some Embleme, or the like, so that one Company may be discerned from another'[4]. Among guides for colour design was Markham's *Souldiers Accidence* which listed the virtues of each colour: yellow 'betokeneth honour, or height of spirit'; white 'signifieth innocencie, or purity of conscience, truth and upright integrity'; black 'wisdome and sobriety'; blue 'faith, constancy, or truth in affection'; red 'justice, or noble worthy anger, in defence of religion or the oppressed'; green 'good hope, or the accomplishment of holy and honourable actions'; purple 'fortitude with discretion, or a most true discharge of any trust reposed'; tunnis or tawny 'merit or desert, and a foe to ingratitude'; ermine 'religion or holiness'; 'From these colours and their mixtures are derived many bastard and dishonourable colours, as carnation, orange tawny, popengie, &c. which signifie craft, pride, and wantonness'[5].

Most colours followed general rules of design which allowed them to indicate not only the regiment but also the officer commanding the particular company. Normally, all bore a St George's cross in the upper canton nearest the staff, not larger than one-sixth of the whole, save the colours of regimental colonels which were usually 'of pure and clean colour'[6] without decorations. The lieutenant-colonel's colour had the St George canton alone, and those of the major and company captains a number of devices, either heraldic badges or 'piles wavy' (tongues of flame issuing from the St George canton), the number of devices depending upon the officer's seniority; the major might have one device, the first captain two, the second captain three, etc., though the arrangement varied. Colouring and devices were usually chosen by the colonel, often based upon his own arms, such as the cinquefoil of Sir Edward Stradling, or even a pun upon his name, as for Talbot's Regiment. Examples are listed below:

Parliamentary foot
London trained bands
Red Regt.: red colours, distinguishing features white piles wavy
White Regt.: white colours, 1–5 red diamonds
Yellow Regt.: yellow colours, black stars
Blue Regt.: blue colours, white roundels
Green Regt.: green colours, white caltraps placed diagonally
Orange Regt.: orange colours, white trefoils
Westminster Liberty Regt.: yellow colours, major's with pile wavy, captains' badges blue roundels
Tower Hamlets Regt.: red colours, with motto *IEHOVA PROVIDE BIT* within silver branches, sprigs of leaves in corners; St George canton for all except colonel's colour; major's and captains' colours distinguished by white roundels in a line along the top edge

London auxiliaries
As for the trained band regiments, except that most used piles wavy to indicate majors and captains, the Green, White, Yellow and Blue Auxiliaries having these of gold, red, blue and gold respectively. The Red and Orange Auxiliaries used white roundels in a diagonal row, the Orange having a pile wavy for the major.

Lord Saye & Sele's Regt. (later Meldrum's): blue colours, gold rampant lions as distinctive badges
Lord Brooke's Regt.: purple colours, white stars
Hampden's Regt.: green colours, colonel's with motto *Nulla Vestigia Retrorsum*
Charles Fairfax's Regt.: blue colours, colonel's with motto *Fideliter Faeliciter* in a circle; major's with white pile wavy, captains' with white stars

Royalist foot

Life Guard of Foot: St George's cross occupying two-fifths of colour nearest pole; remainder red bearing Royal badges as company devices, e.g. crown over gold leopard (colonel), crown over gold rampant griffin (lieutenant-colonel's), crowned portcullis (major), captains' with gold roses
Gerard's Regt.: colours divided diagonally into triangles, top and bottom blue, others yellow (1st captain); others with triangles subdivided in alternate colours
Talbot's Regt.: white colours, distinctive badges black talbots (dogs), one for major, two for 1st captain, etc.
Dyve's Regt.: yellow colours, red roundels
Pennyman's Regt.: green colours, gold piles wavy
Stradling's Regt.: blue colours, white cinquefoils
Lamplugh's Regt.: yellow colours, black crosses
Lord Hopton's Regt.: red colours, white stars
Sir Bernard Astley's Regt. (ex-Marquis of Hertford's): green colours, hawk-lures as distinctive badges
Apsley's Regt.: as Gerard's, but black and white
Duke of York's Regt.: as Gerard's, but black and red

Scottish foot

Most colours were based upon the St Andrew's saltaire. Of those captured at Preston and Dunbar and recorded in *A perfect registry of all the collours taken from the Scots* ...[7], 150 out of 197 bear the saltaire, many in the national colouring of white on blue, or as an upper canton; 15 have white on black whilst others have red, green and yellow fields. In the 1639 war it was reported that all colours bore the motto 'For Christ's Croun and Covenant', and in 1650 the Scottish Parliament ordered that upon 'haill culloris and standards there be "Covenant for Religion King and Kingdomes"', which occurs often on the Preston and Dunbar colours, either in the triangles of the field or on a plain-coloured flag with the St Andrew's saltaire in the upper canton nearest the pole. Most colours bore the armorial devices of their colonel or owner, with a greater use of numerals to

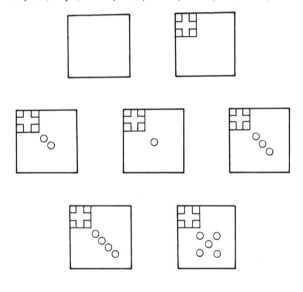

Rank-marking on colours, as exemplified by regiment of foot (Blue Regt. of London trained bands).
Left to right: (top) colonel, lieutenant-colonel, (middle) 1st captain, major, 2nd captain, (bottom) 3rd captain, 4th captain

Alternative system of indicating rank upon colours by means of alternatively-coloured segments, as for example Charles Gerard's Regt. illustrated in Plate 14.
Left to right: 1st captain, 2nd captain, 3rd captain

indicate the company than in English regiments. Some bore the saltaire on a parti-coloured field, such as Stewart of Garscube's colour carried at Worcester which had a field of quartered blue and pink. Others bore political symbols, such as the black colours of Montrose's foot bearing a representation of the severed head of Charles I with the motto *Deo et Victricibus Armus*. Charles II's 'Lyfe Guard of Foote' which fought at Dunbar had blue colours, the colonel's bearing the Scottish Royal Arms and the others a Scottish device on one side and 'Covenant for Religion, King and King-domes' on the other.

STANDARDS

Standards of horse were much smaller; an extant pair preserved at Bromsberrow Church are only two feet (0.6 metres) square. The standards of regimented troops usually had some related design or colouring, but the earlier independent troops carried standards with the widest possible array of designs, based upon the arms of the captain, or political, religious or even risqué symbols and cartoons; unlike foot colours, most were fringed. Many examples are recorded, though a number of the known designs are unidentified. Random examples are noted below:

Guidons of regiment of dragoons which 'did belong to Waller', September 1643 (illustration from contemporary manuscript; National Army Museum, London)

Parliamentary horse

Sergeant-Major Horatio Carey: armoured arms issuing from a cloud (a common design), holding a bow and arrow, the arrowhead touching a winged heart; scroll above bore 'CHARLES THVS PEACE FLYES TO THE'

Capt. Nathaniel Fiennes: warrior in antique costume holding a lance; scroll above read *VTRAQVE PALLADE*

Capt. West of Cambridge: red standard bearing a skull crowned with laurel

Twistleton's Regt.: an example of a regiment with similarly-coloured standards for each troop, but each bearing the captain's own device. All standards white with black-and-white fringe; devices were: Col. Twistleton, plain white; Major James Berry, gold scroll bearing *SI DEVS NOBIS/CVM QVIS/CONTRA NOS*; Capt. Pearte, gold diagonal scroll reading *PRO PACE PUGNO*; Capt. Cambridge, the popular arm-and-cloud motif as in Plate 32; Capt. Nelthorp, a black warhorse with full furniture; Capt. Haines, a scroll bearing *AD ARMA/VOLANS*

Royalist horse

Often used more overtly political and insulting designs than the Parliamentarians, including for example:

Earl of Caernarvon: two standards; (1) six dogs baiting a lion, one larger dog with a scroll issuing from his mouth, inscribed 'KIMBOLTON', and scrolls from the others bearing 'PYM, PYM'; from lion's mouth, *TANDEM*

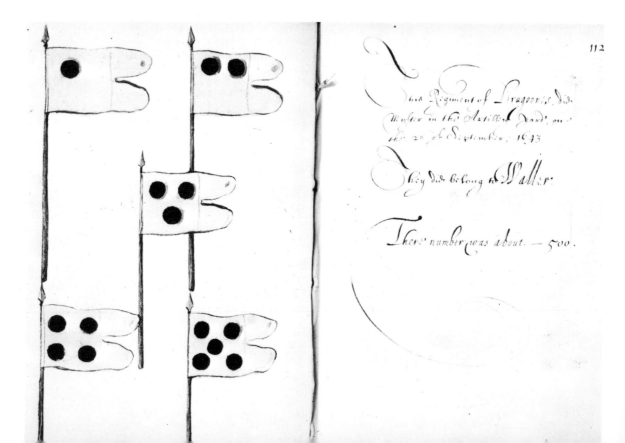

ABUTERIS PATIENTA NOSTRA?; (2) five hands reaching for a crown (representing the King and the 'Five Members'), with an armoured hand issuing from a cloud to defend the crown, with motto *REDDITE CAESARI*. Yellow standard similar to (1) captured at Marston Moor but not identified, though cannot have belonged to Caernarvon's old regiment.

Capt. Lumby (captured at Cirencester): white with gold motto *PRO REGE ET/NOTIS LEGIBUS/ ANGLIAE*

Lt. Col. Caryll Molyneux: repeats the scurrilous story of Essex being a cuckold, showing a reindeer's head (Essex's badge) supported by five hands (the 'Five Members') with motto *AD QUID EXALTATIS CORNU* ('To what dost thou exalt thine horne')

Others: some Royalist troop commanders seem to have borne their entire arms upon their standards, but amongst the recorded but unidentified examples are some of the most blatantly propagandist, bearing mottos such as *TERRIBILIS UT ACIES ORDINATA* (black standard with yellow fringe, sword issuing from a cloud, 'Terrible as a battleline drawn up'); *AUT MORS, AUT VITA DECORA* and a skull ('Death or an honourable life'); *PRO REGE ET REGNO* and white cross on red ('For King and Kingdom'); *MALEM MORI QUAM TARDARE* ('I will die rather than turn aside') on red standard; *VIVE LE ROY* on white standard ('Long live the King'); Lt. Col. Sir Henry Constable bore a cross with *IN HOC SIGNO VINCES* (the motto of Constantine the Great); the Marquis of Winchester bore *DONEC PAX REDEAT TERRIS* ('Until peace returns to the earth'); Sir Edward Widdrington, *DEO ET CAESARI*. The standards of the Queen's Horse reflected the French origin of the Queen and some of its personnel: dark blue fields scattered with fleurs-de-lys, all troop standards bearing a crown in addition.

Scottish horse

Standards of similar character, but more sober and with greater use of heraldic devices; Scott's Horse at Dunbar carried a banner five feet three inches (1.6 metres) long by four feet four inches (1.3 metres) deep, with the white saltaire on blue; others bore versions of the Covenant motto, whilst Montrose's Horse carried black standards bearing three pairs of clasped hands holding swords, with the motto *QUOS PIETAS VIRTUS ET HONOR FECIT AMICOS*.

OTHER FLAGS

In addition to unit colours and standards, senior officers possessed personal standards often different from those borne by their own troop. The King's royal standard (or Banner Royal), so nearly captured at Edgehill, bore the full Royal Arms (first and fourth quarters, quartered arms of England and France, second quarter Scotland, third Ireland), the Scottish version having the Scottish lion in the first and fourth quarters and quartered England and France in the second; and at Edgehill, the King had 'a scarlet cornet larger than the ordinary carryd before him'[8]. At Worcester Charles II used the red rampant lion on gold as befitted the 'King of Scotland'. Prince Rupert's standard captured at Marston Moor bore 'the Ensignes of the Palatine, neere five yards long and broad, with a red crosse in the middle'[9], which due to its size must have marked the Prince's headquarters as it cannot have been borne before him. Leven's arms included 'supporters' bearing standards which may have been his own, red with the St Andrew's canton; Essex's red standard bore the motto *VIRTUTIS/ COMES/INVIDIA*. Sir Thomas Fairfax's was of plain green damask with green 'figuring' interwoven (as a colonel of horse's); Lord Fairfax's white standard bore a crown supported on a vertical sword, impaling a Papal mitre, with the motto *VIVA EL REY/Y MUERRA IL MAL/GOVIERNO* ('Long live the King and death to bad government'). Major-General Philip Skippon had a red standard bearing an arm and a sword issuing from a cloud over a Bible, with the motto *ORA ET PUGNA IUVET ET IUVALET IEHOVA*; the Earl of Manchester's was of green figured damask bearing the powerful motto 'Truth and Peace' diagonally.

Colours were expensive to buy; in December 1644, for example, the New Model's contract books included: '... ffor ye buying Drums Cullers Halberts & partizans for ye furnishing of Collonell Aldrich his Regimt. vizt ffor VIII new Ensignes made of blew florence sarsnett wth Distinctions of gould culler Laurells wth tassels to y^em ... at ye rate of xlv^s a peece ... XVIII^li'[10]. A regiment or troop which lost its colours or standard was normally not allowed to carry another until their disgrace had been wiped out by their capture of an enemy flag; thus, the Prince of Wales' troop which lost its cornet (standard) at Hopton Heath (19 March 1643) had its honour restored when Major Thomas Daniel captured a Roundhead banner at Chalgrove Field (18 June 1643). Colours were a great aid to identification (the White Regiment of London trained bands was visible 1½ miles (2.4 kilometres) away at Cheriton, but as both sides used identical styles of colours, confusion could arise; for example, at Southam (23 August 1642) Major William Legge, and Lieutenant-Colonel Sir Francis Butler at Nantwich (25 January 1644) were both captured by mistaking Parliamentary colours as their own! The number of colours captured was usually regarded as a way of gauging the size of a victory. Colours were normally provided with elaborate cords and tassels, and even with ribbons wrapped around the pole, but other ornaments included those mentioned by Colonel Arthur Goodwin, Hampden's fellow Buckinghamshire M.P., when writing of Hampden's death: '... I pray let me beg of you a broad black ribbon to hang about my standard ...'[11]

APPENDIX: MEDALS

As different from the many commemorative medals and medallions concerning Civil War personages, medals for valour or military service were not prolific. In the Royal army there existed a silver 'Forlorn Hope' medal, instigated apparently by Thomas Bushell, Warden of the Mint, who was commended for his invention, 'for our better knowinge and rewarding the Forlorne Hope with Badges of Silver at your own charge when the soldiers were ready to run away'[1]. These medals were described in a Royal warrant of 18 May 1643: 'Badges of silver, containing our Royal image, and that of our dearest son, Prince Charles, to be delivered to wear on the breast'[2]; it was further decreed to be an offence to wear a medal which had not been earned, or for selling one which had! An extant medal, perhaps of this type, is oval with a loop for suspension, bearing on the obverse a bust of the King and the inscription *Carolus D.G. Mag. Br. Fra. et H. Rex*, and on the reverse a shield within a crowned garter and *Florebunt* above[3].

Sir John Smith and Sir Robert Walsh (or Welsh) were both awarded medals for their part in recovering the Banner Royal at Edgehill: Smith 'had afterwards a large Medal of Gold given him, with the King's Picture on one Side, and the Banner on the other, which he always wore to his dying Day, in a large green watered Ribband, cross his Shoulders'; and Walsh, 'an *Irishman*; who also pretended that he was instrumental in regaining the Standard, did also in the same Manner wear a green Ribband with a Medal; but whether it was given him by Order, or how he came by it, I do not know ...'[4]

The first campaign medal for both officers and other ranks was that voted by Parliament for service at Dunbar, struck in gold for officers and silver for others (bronze examples also exist); the House of Commons was depicted on the reverse and Cromwell on the obverse, with the legend 'Word at Dunbar THE LORD OF HOSTS'. Parliament also issued gold and silver medals bearing *MERVISTI* ('thou hast deserved'), awarded after an act of 1649 decreed that 10 per cent of all prize money resulting from naval actions should be used to reward officers and mariners who had performed 'Extraordinary Service' at sea.

NOTES

Preface

1 See Clarendon, Edward Hyde, Earl of, *History of the Rebellion and Civil Wars in England*, ed. Macray, W.D., (Oxford, 1888), V, 336
2 Hutchinson, Mrs L., *Life of Colonel Hutchinson*, ed. Firth, C.H., (London, 1885), vol. I, p. 170

1. The Road to Civil War

1 Ashton, R. *The English Civil War* (London, 1979)
2 *The Souldiers Catechisme* (London, 1644) (reprinted Cresset Press, n.d.) pp. 3–4
3 Clarendon XI, 239
4 *Ibid.*, 241

2. The Armies

1 See Morrill, J.S. *The Revolt of the Provinces: Conservatives and Radicals in the English Civil War, 1630–50* (London, 1976)
2 *Souldiers Catechisme* pp. 15–16
3 Sir Robert Poyntz to Marquis of Ormonde, 1 June 1643; see Sherwood, R.E. *Civil Strife in the Midlands 1642–51* (Chichester, 1974) p. 8
4 Hutchinson
5 Waller, Sir W. *The Vindication of the Character and Conduct of Sir William Waller* (London, 1793) pp. 12–13
6 Warwick, Sir P. *Memoires of the Reign of King Charles I* (London, 1702) p. 253
7 Trenchard, J. *A Short History of Standing Armies in England* (London, 1698) p. 1
8 The term 'militia' was not in universal use at this time; in 1640 Whitelock in a speech in the Commons described it as a new word.
9 *Cymon and Iphigenia*
10 Ward, R. *Animadversions of Warre* (London, 1639)
11 Corbet, J. *A true and impartiall History of the Militarie Government of the Citie of Gloucester* (London, 1647) p. 11; see Sherwood, p. 15
12 Roberts, J. *Great Yarmouth Exercise* (1638), quoted in Castle, M.A. *History of the Yarmouth Battery* (Norwich, 1927) pp. 13–14
13 Quoted in Ashton, p. 256
14 Windeatt, T.W. 'Notes on the Totnes Trained Bands and Volunteers' in *Transactions of the Devonshire Association* (Plymouth, 1900) vol. 32, pp. 93–105
15 *The Kings Majesties Instructions unto the Earle of Northampton . . .* (London, 1642) pp. 1–2
16 See Holmes, C. *The Eastern Association in the English Civil War* (Cambridge, 1974) p. 166
17 Capt. Robert Clarke on 14 July 1644, in *Transactions of the Royal Historical Society*, (London, 1898) vol. XII, pp. 76–9; see Young, P. *Marston Moor 1644* (Kineton, 1970) p. 251
18 Sir Thomas Nightingale, quoted in Holmes, p. 170
19 Quoted *ibid.*, p. 170
20 Aubrey, J. *Brief Lives* ed. Dick, O.L. (London, 1978) p. 265
21 See his own account in Yates, G.C. 'Colonel Rosworm and the Siege of Manchester' in Axon, E. (ed.) *Bygone Lancashire* (London and Manchester, 1892) pp. 189–201
22 Bund, J.W. Willis *The Civil War in Worcestershire 1642–1646, and the Scotch Invasion of 1651* (1905; reprinted Gloucester, 1979) p. 69
23 Wharton, Sergt. Nehemiah 'Letters' (10 August 1642) ed. Ellis, Sir H. *Archaeologia* XXV (1853)
24 Colonel Walter Slingsby, quoted in Adair, J. *Cheriton 1644* (Kineton, 1973) p. 131

3. Organization, Equipment and Tactics

1 Turner, Sir J. *Pallas Armata: Military Essayes of the . . . Art of War* (London, 1683) p. 178
2 i.e. cuirasses, or corselet
3 Markham, G. *The Souldiers Accidence* (London, 1625); see Grose, F. *Military Antiquities, respecting a History of the English Army, with A Treatise on Ancient Armour and Weapons* (London, 1801) vol. I, p. 132
4 Quoted in Grose, vol. II, p. 335
5 Goold Walker, G. *The Honourable Artillery Company 1537–1926* (London, 1926) pp. 47, 67
6 Turner, p. 169
7 *Ibid.*
8 Monck, General G. (1st Duke of Albemarle) *Observations upon Military and Political Affairs* (London, 1671) pp. 26–7
9 *Ibid.*
10 Markham, *Souldiers Accidence*, see Grose, vol. I, p. 132
11 Quoted in Grose, vol. II, p. 335
12 Turner, p. 176
13 Davies, E. *The Art of War, And Englands Traynings, Plainely Demonstrating the dutie of a private Souldier . . .* (London, 1619); see Grose, vol. II, pp. 126–7
14 *The Military Art of Trayning* (London, 1622); see Grose, vol. II, pp. 264–5
15 See *Le Maniement d'Armes de Nassau avec Rondelles, picques, epees & targes* (Adam van Breen, 1618); Grose, vol. II, p. 308
16 Goold Walker, p. 47
17 e.g. Williams, Sir R. *A Briefe discourse of Warre* (London, 1590)
18 *London Gazette*, 5–9 January 1681
19 Achesone, J. *The Military Garden* (Edinburgh, 1629) p. 8
20 Davies, G. *The Parliamentary Army under the Earl of Essex 1642–45*, (E.H.R., 1934) p. 35; see also Young, Brig. P. *Edgehill* (Kineton, 1967) p. 14
21 Wharton; see Young, *Edgehill*, p. 15
22 Venn, Capt. T. *Military Observation or Tacticks Put into Practice* (London, 1672) p. 34
23 See Grose, vol. I, p. 156, quoting Edmund York
24 Davies, E.; see Grose, vol. II, pp. 121ff
25 *Military Orders and Articles Established by His Majesty* (Oxford, 1643); see *Journal, Arms and Armour Society* September (1968) 53
26 Markham; see Blackmore, H.L. *British Military Firearms* (London, 1961) pp. 18–19
27 Turner, p. 176
28 Clarendon, VI, 276
29 Monck, p. 103
30 Turner, p. 237
31 Gwyn, Capt. J. *Military Memoirs* ed. Scott, Sir W. (Edinburgh, 1822); reprinted in Atkyns, R. & Gwyn, J. *The English Civil War* ed. Young, P. & Tucker, N. (London, 1967) p. 54
32 See Grose, vol. I, p. 159–60
33 *Ibid.*
34 Monck, p. 103
35 Davies, E.; see Grose, vol. II, pp. 121ff

36 *Ibid.*
37 Quoted Young, *Edgehill*, p. 178
38 Ward; see Grose, vol. I, p. 250
39 Davies, E.; see Grose, vol. II, pp. 126–7
40 Monck, pp. 25–6
41 Turner, p. 175
42 See Ffoulkes, C. & Hopkinson, E.C. 'Swords in the British Army' *Journal of the Society for Army Historical Research* XI, 241
43 Bariffe, W. *Military Discipline: Or, The Yong Artillery Man* (1635); see Grose, vol. II, pp. 339–40
44 Turner, p. 175
45 Bariffe; see Grose, vol. II, pp. 339–40
46 Turner, pp. 169–70
47 Windeatt, pp. 93–105
48 Earl of Essex, 1597, quoted in Boynton, L. *The Elizabethan Militia 1558–1638* (Newton Abbot, 1971) p. 195
49 Capt. Dawtrey, 1588, quoted in Boynton, p. 159
50 Quoted in Sherwood, p. 35
51 Quoted in Cripps, W.J. *The Royal North Gloucester* (London, 1875) p. 9
52 Quoted in Grose, vol. II, p. 330
53 *Ibid.*, p. 325
54 Clarendon, VI, 73
55 *Ibid.*
56 *Ibid.*
57 Bulstrode, Sir R. *Memories and Reflections* (London, 1721); see Young, *Edgehill*, p. 272
58 Thomas Fox to Lord Denbigh, March 1644; see Bund, p. 120
59 *Publicola's Postscript to the People of England* (London, 1803)
60 Monck
61 Turner
62 Quoted in Young, *Edgehill*, p. 228
63 Clarendon, VI, 73
64 Turner, p. 169
65 Cruso, J. *Militarie Instructions for the Cavall'rie* (Cambridge, 1632) p. 30; see also Bingham, J. 'The Exercise of the English in the service of the high and mighty Lords . . . of the united Provinces in the Low Countries' in Bingham, J. *The Tactiks of Aelian* (London, 1616) pp. 153–9
66 Grose, vol. II, p. 335
67 Symonds, R. 'The Diary of Richard Symonds' ed. Long, C.E. *Camden Society* 74 (1859) 231 (see also Young, Brig. P. *Civil War England* (London, 1981) pp. 21–2 for biography of Symonds)
68 Clarendon, VI, 1
69 See Grose, vol. I, pp. 108ff
70 Ludlow, E. *Memoirs of Edmund Ludlow* ed. Firth, C.H. (Oxford, 1894); Ludlow's account of Edgehill is reproduced in Young, *Edgehill*, pp. 311–16
71 Verney, P. *The Standard Bearer* (London, 1964) p. 139
72 Markham, *Soldiers Accidence*; see Grose, vol. I, p. 108
73 Atkyns, R. *The Vindication of Richard Atkyns*, (1669); reprinted in Atkyns, R. & Gwyn J. *The English Civil War* ed. Young, P. & Tucker. N. (London, 1967), pp. 24–5
74 Monck, p. 25
75 Cruso, p. 30
76 Turner, p. 171
77 Cruso, pp. 30–1
78 Thomas-Stanford, C. *Sussex in the Great Civil War and Interregnum, 1642–1660* (1910) pp. 76–7
79 Turner, p. 173
80 *Correspondence of the Scots Commissioners in London 1644–46* ed. Meikle, H.W. (Edinburgh, 1917) p. 30
81 *Journal of the Society for Army Historical Research* LIX, quoting B.M. Thomason E449
82 Atkyns, p. 7
83 Quoted Young, *Edgehill*, p. 172
84 Cruso, p. 34
85 Gilbey, Sir W. *The Great Horse* (London, 1899) p. 42; see Tylden, Maj. G. *Horses and Saddlery* (London, 1965) pp. 4–7
86 Quoted Young, *Marston Moor*, p. 129
87 Extract from diary of Stafford Safety Committee, quoted in Sleigh *History of Leek* (small edn.) p. 99
88 Atkyns, p. 8
89 Col. Francis Thornhagh in *Perfect Occurrences*, 9 October 1645; quoted Young, *Civil War England*, p. 32
90 Turner, p. 236
91 Cruso, p. 31
92 Goold-Walker, pp. 24–5
93 Turner, p. 193
94 'Discourse of the Warr in Lancashire' *Chetham Society* vol. 62, old series, quoted in Bagley, J.J. & Lewis, A.S. *Lancashire at War* (Clapham, 1977) p. 24
95 Quoted Bagley & Lewis, pp. 53–4
96 Gough, R. *History of Myddle* ed. Hey. D. (London, 1981) p. 272
97 Secretary Roe 'Military Memoir of Colonel John Birch' *Camden Society* vol. VII, new series, (1873), quoted in Heath-Agnew, E. *Roundhead to Royalist* (Hereford, 1977) p. 43
98 Quoted Grose, vol. I, p. 228
99 Quoted *ibid.*, p. 229
100 *Diary of Henry Townshend of Elmley Lovett* ed. Bund, J.W. Willis (Worcester, 1916) vol. II, p. 123; quoted Sherwood, p. 66
101 Quoted Grose, vol. I, p. 254
102 *Mercurius Aulicus* p. 1055, quoted Toynbee, M. & Young, Brig. P. *Cropredy Bridge, 1644* (Kineton, 1970) p. 87
103 Quoted Young, Brig. P. & Emberton, W. *The Cavalier Army* (London, 1974) p. 128
104 'Discourse of the Warr in Lancashire', quoted Bagley & Lewis, p. 39
105 Atkyns, p. 11
106 *Mercurius Aulicus*, p. 1011, quoted Toynbee & Young, p. 42
107 Ludlow, p. 18
108 Clarendon; note found after VIII, 75

4. The First Civil War 1642–3

1 Clarendon, VI, 402
2 *An Exact and True Relation of the Dangerous and Bloody Fight . . .* (London, 1642) p. 3; see Rogers, Col. H.C.B. *Battles and Generals of the Civil Wars 1642–51* (London, 1968) p. 308
3 Clarendon, VI, 1
4 Clarendon, VIII, 29
5 James II *Life of James II* ed. Clarke, T.S. (London, 1816); see Young, *Edgehill*, p. 278
6 Clarendon, VI, 137
7 Gardiner, S.R. *History of the Great Civil War* (1903) vol. I, p. 56
8 Clarendon, VI, 244
9 Clarendon, VI, 280

10 Garrard, W. *The Arte of Warre* (London, 1591) pp. 4–5
11 See Adair, J. 'The Death of John Hampden' *History Today* XXIX (1979) 656–63
12 Clarendon, VII, 101
13 Coate, M. *Cornwall in the Great Civil War* (1963) p. 77
14 Atkyns, p. 18
15 *Ibid.*, p. 19
16 Clarendon, VII, 132
17 *Ibid.*, 133
18 Cromwell to Committee of Eastern Association, 31 July 1643 in Rushworth, J. *Historical Collections 1618–49* (London, 1659–1701) V, 278; quoted in and see *Oliver Cromwell's Letters and Speeches* ed. Carlyle, J. (London, n.d.) p. 109
19 Clarendon, VII, 195
20 *Ibid.*, 211
21 Clarendon, IV, 198
22 See Henry, D. 'The Death of Lord Falkland' *History Today* XXI (1971) pp. 842–7
23 Quoted Rogers, p. 107
24 Clarendon, VII, 214
25 *Ibid.*, 215
26 Clarendon, III, 30
27 Clarendon, XII, 142
28 Clarendon, VIII, 32

5. The First Civil War 1644

1 Quoted Young, *Marston Moor*, p. 78
2 Clarendon, VI, 406
3 *Ibid.*
4 Quoted Young, *Marston Moor*, pp. 86–7
5 Rupert's 'Diary'; quoted Young, *Marston Moor*, p. 213
6 Clarendon; note found after VIII, 75
7 *Ibid.*
8 Holles, Lord D. *Memoirs* (London, 1699) p. 16
9 Cromwell to Walton, 5 July 1644; see *Oliver Cromwell's Letters and Speeches*, pp. 122–3
10 Rupert's 'Diary'; quoted Young, *Marston Moor*, p. 214

6. New Model: The First Civil War 1645

1 Quoted in Kishlansky, M.A. *The Rise of the New Model Army* (Cambridge, 1979) p. 28
2 *Souldiers Catechisme*, pp. 3–4
3 See Kishlansky, p. 106
4 Waller, p. 7
5 Quoted in Ashley, M. *The English Civil War* (London, 1974) p. 115
6 *A New Tricke to Take Townes* (London, 1645); quoted in Heath-Agnew, p. 225
7 Rushworth VI, 4; see *Oliver Cromwell's Letters and Speeches*, pp. 128–9
8 *Mercurius Aulicus*, No. 35, pp. 1139–40
9 Holmes, p. 285 and note 103
10 Abbott, W.C. *The Writings and Speeches of Oliver Cromwell* (Cambridge, Mass., 1937–47) vol. I, pp. 261–2
11 Quoted Sherwood, p. 198; see Tibbutt, H.G. 'The Letterbooks of Sir Samuel Luke' *Bedfordshire Historical Records Society* 42 (1963)
12 *Souldiers Catechisme*, p. 24

13 *Ibid.*, p. 25
14 Turner, p. 223
15 *Souldiers Catechisme*, pp. 11–12
16 *Ibid.*, p. 16
17 *Ibid.*, pp. 19–20
18 See Emberton, W. *Love Loyalty* (Basingstoke, 1972) pp. 88–9
19 *A Worthy Speech spoken by his excellence the E: of Essex in the head of his armie before his arrivall at Worcester . . .* (1642), quoted Grose, vol. I, pp. 352–4
20 *Souldiers Catechisme*, p. 12
21 Quoted in *Journal of the Society for Army Historical Research*, LIX (1981) 152
22 Sir Thomas Fairfax; quoted *ibid.*
23 Letter to the Mayor and Corporation of Sandwich, November 1642, quoted in Melling, E. *Kent and the Civil War* (Maidstone, 1960) p. 17
24 Reprinted in *London Chronicle*, 30 December 1775
25 Quoted in *Journal of the Society for Army Historical Research*, LIX (1981) 149
26 Baines, E. *History of the County Palatine and Duchy of Lancaster* ed. Harland, J. (London, 1868) vol. I, p. 217
27 Tucker, N. *Conway and its Story* (Denbigh, 1960) p. 80
28 Sherwood, p. 174
29 Andriette, E.A. *Devon and Exeter in the Civil War* (Newton Abbot, 1971) p. 63
30 Quoted in Hastings, M. *Montrose: The King's Champion* (London, 1977) p. 229
31 Clarendon, IX, 34
32 Walker, Sir E. *Historical Discourses upon Severall Occasions* (London, 1705) p. 129; see Sherwood, p. 196
33 Clarendon, IX, 39
34 Clarendon, IX, 40
35 Quoted Ashley, p. 125
36 Clarendon, IX, 135

7. Between the First and Second Civil Wars 1646–7

1 Quoted Rogers, p. 267
2 Clarendon, X, 81
3 See Ashley, p. 139
4 Clarendon, X, 90

8. The Second Civil War 1648

1 Churchill, Sir W. *History of the English Speaking Peoples* (London, 1956) vol. II, pp. 218–19
2 Clarendon, XI, 55
3 Clarendon, XI, 107

9. The Third Civil War 1649–51

1 See Hastings, p. 356
2 Cromwell to Haselrig, 2 September 1650; *Oliver Cromwell's Letters and Speeches*, pp. 377–8
3 Clarendon, XIII, 22
4 Clarendon, XIII, 62
5 Cromwell to William Lenthall, Speaker of Parliament, 4 September 1651; *Oliver Cromwell's Letters and Speeches*, p. 459

6 Quoted in Sherwood, p. 164
7 Quoted in Young, *Edgehill*, p. 221
8 Quoted *ibid.*, p. 229
9 *Ibid.*
10 *Behemoth*, quoted Ashton, p. 187

10. Uniforms

1 Cripps, p. 20
2 Sheardown, W. *The First West York Regiment of Yeomanry Cavalry* (Doncaster, 1871–2) p. 52
3 Monck, p. 77
4 John Malet to Capt. George Trevelyan, 30 August 1643; *Trevelyan Papers*, (Camden Society, 1872), vol. III, p. 242
5 Quoted Young, *Edgehill*, p. 188
6 *Ibid.*, p. 190
7 Wood, A. *Life & Times of Anthony Wood* ed. Clark, A. (Oxford, 1891) vol. I, p. 103
8 Quoted Carman, W.Y. *British Military Uniforms from Contemporary Pictures*, (London, 1957), p. 23
9 See Holmes, p. 167
10 Quoted Grose, vol. I, pp. 327–8
11 Turner, pp. 296–7
12 Thomas-Stanford, pp. 76–7
13 Lawson, C.C.P. *History of the Uniforms of the British Army* (London, 1940) vol. I, p. 11
14 *Ibid.*, p. 16
15 Quoted Young, *Edgehill*, pp. 24–5
16 Quoted Grose, vol. I, pp. 326–7
17 Quoted Lawson, vol. I, p. 9
18 Quoted Carman, p. 23
19 Bund, J.W. Willis *The Civil War in Worcestershire 1642–1646 and the Scotch Invasion of 1651* (1905; reprinted Gloucester, 1979) p. 21
20 Quoted Young, *Edgehill* p. 28
21 Aubrey, p. 450
22 Quoted Young, *Edgehill*, p. 25
23 *Ibid.* p. 25
24 Quoted Boynton, p. 27
25 Clarendon, VIII, 138
26 Quoted *History Today* XXI (1971) 685
27 Warburton, E. *Memoirs of Prince Rupert and the Cavaliers* (London, 1849) vol. II, p. 62
28 Sir Samuel Luke to Earl of Essex, 2 February 1645; see Rogers, p. 193
29 Quoted Holmes, p. 98
30 *Ibid.*, p. 100
31 Laver, J. *British Military Uniforms* (London, 1948) p. 7
32 Cruso, p. 27
33 Quoted Carman, p. 25

34 Walker, Sir E. *Circumstantial Account of the Preparations for the Coronation of His Majesty King Charles II*; see Lawson, vol. I, p. 85
35 *Beating of the Rebels*; see Carman, p. 25
36 See Carman, p. 25
37 *Ibid.* p. 24
38 *The Grenadier Guards – A Tercentenary Exhibition* (London, 1956) p. 6
39 See *Journal of the Society for Army Historical Research* XXXIV, 182–3
40 Gough, p. 98
41 Sergt. Henry Foster, quoted Goold Walker, pp. 56–7
42 See Carman, p. 26
43 *Ibid.*
44 See Lawson, vol. I, p. 11

11. Colours and Standards

1 Barret, R. *The Theorike and Practike of Modern Warres* (London, 1598); see Edwards, Maj. T.J. *Standards, Guidons and Colours of the Commonwealth Forces* (Aldershot, 1953) p. 7
2 Ward, *Animadversions of Warre*; see Edwards, p. 101
3 Barry, G. *A Discourse of Military Discipline* (Brussels, 1634); see Edwards, p. 99
4 Ward, *Animadversions of Warre*; see Edwards, pp. 14–15
5 See Grose, vol. II, pp. 140–41
6 Venn, T. *Military Observations or Tacticks put into Practice* (London, 1672); see Young, *Edgehill*, p. 35
7 See McMillan, W. & Stewart, J.A. *Story of the Scottish Flag* (Glasgow, 1925) pp. 37–45
8 James II, quoted in Young, *Edgehill*, p. 108
9 Stewart, A. *A Full Relation of the Victory at Marstam-Moor*; quoted Young, *Marston Moor*, p. 33
10 See *Journal of the Arms and Armour Society* VI (1968) 75
11 See Adair, J. 'The Death of John Hampden' *History Today* XXIX (1979) 656

Appendix

1 Quoted Young, *Edgehill*, p. 190
2 See Gordon, Maj. L.L. *British Battles and Medals* (Aldershot, 1962) p. 2, where the warrant is quoted in full.
3 See Benson, G. *An Account of the City of York* (York, 1925) pp. 37–8; and Wenham, P. *The Great and Close Siege of York, 1644* (Kineton, 1970) pp. 115–16
4 Bulstrode, Sir R. *Memoirs* (London, 1721); see Young, *Edgehill*, pp. 270–71

GLOSSARY

Some of the military terminology of the mid-seventeenth century is sufficiently obscure to be virtually unintelligible even with a modern dictionary. The following elucidates some of the terms which may be encountered in works of the Civil War period:

Ancient: corruption of 'ensign', junior officer; e.g. ''Tis one Iago, ancient to the general' (*Othello*, II, i)

Boutezselle: trumpet call for 'boots and saddle' (French)

Brigadeer: corporal of horse (orig. French)

Bringer up: officer or N.C.O. at the rear of a unit or file

Captain of arms (or gentleman of arms): N.C.O. responsible for keeping the weapons of a company or troop in good order

Clerk (or Scrivener): N.C.O. keeping company rolls and acting as paymaster

Coat and Conduct: 'coat and conduct' money was the sum paid to a recruit for uniform, accoutrements and journey to his post

Commanded: a 'commanded' party was one selected for a particular task or post

Corps de guard: guard party or guardroom (orig. French)

Curat: set of breast- and backplate, i.e. 'cuirass' (orig. French)

Dian: drum call of reveille (orig. French)

Enfants Perdus: French term for 'Forlorn Hope' (q.v.), sometimes used in England

Forlorn Hope: advance guard; *not* specifically a storming party as the term later came to indicate

Free quarter: payment of meals or lodging by ticket; euphemism for theft

Gatloup: 'running the gatloup' meant running the gauntlet as punishment

Granado: mortar shell

Lancespesata (or lancepresado): continental term encountered occasionally in England signifying a 'broken lance', originally a gentleman of a troop of horse who had lost his mount and become attached to a company of foot until rehorsed; additional N.C.O.

Lunarie: formation of arraying troops in half-moon shape

Last: unit of weight equalling 4,000 lbs. (1,814 kg)

Passelunt: allowance of match for the use of sentinels

Passevolant: an 'invisible man' on a company's muster roll, for whom pay was drawn and appropriated by the captain or other officers; in Sweden this practice was legalized but limited to 10 passevolants per company in the hope that it would prevent further corruption

Patroville: as 'round' (q.v.); also a party doing 'rounds'

Perspective glass: telescope

Picqueer: to skirmish

Pot-piece: variety of mortar

Punchoon: barrel or cask (Scottish)

Rammerwand: musket ramrod

Refusing: tactical disposition of protecting a flank by stationing a unit at the rear of the flank

Round: one who visits sentinels (sentries) during the time of the sentry's duty

Running-trench: approach trench

Sconce: earthwork fortification, usually to house a battery, and usually detached from the main defences of a place

Shot: musketeers

Sow: siege tower as used in the Middle Ages, for assaulting a fortress wall; not in common usage but did exist during the Civil War, one having so uncommon an appearance that it 'sorely frighted our men at Froom' (see Grose, vol. I, pp. 385–6)

Span: to 'span' a wheel lock firearm was to cock it; hence 'spanner' for a wheel lock key.

Square murtherer: variety of mortar

Swine-feather (or Swedish feather): short double-ended pike intended to provide a defence for musketeers, being planted to form a portable palisade

Tertia: brigade

Thill, thiller: cart shafts

Tortle: variety of mortar

Travaille: reveille (orig. French)

Tuck: straight-bladed sword

Zap: sap (from Italian *zappa*, a mattock)

Note: terminology of artillery and small arms is covered in the main text.

SELECT BIBLIOGRAPHY

Publication details of some of the vast literature on the Civil Wars are given in the form of notes to the text. The following select bibliography includes a number of standard histories, representative biographies and certain of the contemporary works which are generally accessible in the form of recent reprints. Bibliographies including comments upon the reliability or bias of various sources may be found in such works as Ashley, Roots, Woolrych, etc., listed below. Certain of those listed (Wagner, Lawson, Carman and various costume histories, etc.) and some of the drill books and contemporary manuals do not bear directly upon the events of the Civil Wars but cover the military theory, equipment and costume of the seventeenth century in a more general manner.

ACHESONE, J. *The Military Garden* (Edinburgh, 1629) (reprinted Amsterdam and Norwood, New Jersey, 1974, in the series of reprints *The English Experience*, a useful series of facsimiles including such important works as Davies' *Art of War* (1619), Kellie's *Pallas Armata* (1627), Markham's *Souldiers Exercise* (1639), etc. Other contemporary pamphlets, *The Kings Majesties Instructions* (1642), *His Majesties Instructions* (1642), *His Majesties Speech . . . at Oxford* (1643), etc., have been reprinted recently by The Toucan Press, St Peter Port, Guernsey)

ADAIR, J. *Cheriton, 1644* (Kineton, 1973)

ADAIR, J. *Roundhead General: A Military Biography of Sir William Waller* (London, 1969)

ASHLEY, M. *The English Civil War* (London, 1974) (includes concise bibliography with pertinent comments)

ASHTON, R. *The English Civil War* (London, 1978)

ASQUITH, S. *New Model Army 1645–60* (London, 1981)

ATKYNS, R. & GWYN, J. *The English Civil War* ed. Young, P. & Tucker, N. (London, 1967) (reprints Atkyns' *Vindication* and Gwyn's *Military Memoirs*)

BURNE, A.H. & YOUNG, P. *The Great Civil War 1642–46* (London, 1959)

CARLYLE, T. (ed.) *Oliver Cromwell's Letters and Speeches* (London, n.d.)

CARMAN, W.Y. *British Military Uniforms from Contemporary Pictures* (London, 1957)

CLARENDON, Edward Hyde, Earl of; *History of the Rebellion and Civil Wars in England* ed. Macray, W.D. (Oxford, 1888) (this edition is most complete; latest reprint 1969. Classic history but biased towards the Royalists and to some degree against the military in general)

COCKLE, M.J.D. *Bibliography of Military Books up to 1642* (London, 1900) (reprinted London, 1978. Valuable work cataloguing all drill books and military treatises available at the beginning of the Civil War)

CRUSO, J. *Militarie Instructions for the Cavallrie*

(Cambridge, 1632) (reprinted Kineton, 1972, with important commentary by P. Young)

CUNNINGTON, C.W. *Handbook of English Costume in the 17th Century* (London, 1955)

EMBERTON, W. *Love Loyalty: The Close and Perilous Siege of Basing House 1643–45* (Basingstoke, 1972)

FIRTH, C.H. *Cromwell's Army* 3rd edn. (London, 1921)

FIRTH, C.H. & DAVIES, G. *The Regimental History of Cromwell's Army* (Oxford, 1940)

FRASER, A. *Cromwell, Our Chief of Men* (London, 1973)

GARDINER, S.R. *History of the Great Civil War 1642–49* (London, 1886–91) (1903 edition has corrections; remains one of the principal standard histories)

GREEN, R.M. *Costume and Fashion in Colour* (Poole, 1975)

GROSE, G. *Military Antiquities respecting a History of the English Army, with A Treatise on Ancient Armour and Weapons* combined edn. (London, 1801)

HASTINGS, M. *Montrose: The King's Champion* (London, 1977)

HEATH-AGNEW, E. *Roundhead to Royalist* (Hereford, 1977) (biography of John Birch)

HILL, C. *God's Englishman: Oliver Cromwell and the English Revolution* (London, 1970)

HOLMES, C. *The Eastern Association in the English Civil War* (Cambridge, 1974)

KISHLANSKY, M.A. *The Rise of the New Model Army* (Cambridge, 1979) (important reassessment)

LAWSON, C.C.P. *History of the Uniforms of the British Army* Vol. I (London, 1940)

MORRAH, P. *Prince Rupert of the Rhine* (London, 1976)

POTTER, R. & EMBLETON, G.A. *The English Civil War 1642–51* (London, 1973)

ROGERS, Col. H.C.B. *Battles and Generals of the Civil Wars 1642–51* (London, 1968)

ROOTS, I. *The Great Rebellion* (London, 1966) (includes important bibliography, with comments)

RUSHWORTH, J. *Historial Collections 1618–49* (London, 1659–1701)

SHERWOOD, R.E. *Civil Strife in the Midlands* (Chichester, 1974)

SPRIGGE, J. *Anglia Rediviva: England's Recovery* (1647)

TOYNBEE, M. & YOUNG, Brig. P. *Cropredy Bridge, 1644* (Kineton, 1970)

TURNER, J. *Pallas Armata: Military Essays ...* (London, 1683) (reprinted New York, 1968)

TUCKER, J. & WINSTOCK, L.S. (ed.) *The English Civil War: A Military Handbook* (London, 1972)

WAGNER, E. *European Weapons and Warfare 1618–48* (Prague, 1979) (English translation, London, 1979)

WAUGH, N. *The Cut of Men's Clothes, 1600–1900* (London, 1964)

WEDGWOOD, C.V. *The King's Peace* (London, 1955)

WEDGWOOD, C.V. *The King's War* (London, 1958)

WEDGWOOD, C.V. *The Trial of Charles I* (London, 1964)

WENHAM, P. *The Great and Close Siege of York, 1644* (Kineton, 1970)

WINSTOCK, L. *Songs and Marches of the Roundheads and Cavaliers* (London, 1971)

WOOLRYCH, A. *Battles of the English Civil War* (London, 1961)

'W.T.' *The Compleat Gunner* (London, 1672) (reprinted Wakefield, 1971; not so contemporary as Eldred's *Gunner's Glasse*, but more accessible due to the modern reprint)

YOUNG, Brig. P. *Civil War England* (London, 1981)

YOUNG, Brig. P. *Edgehill, 1642* (Kineton, 1967)

YOUNG, Brig. P. *Marston Moor 1644* (Kineton, 1970)

YOUNG, Brig. P. *The English Civil War Armies* (London, 1973)

YOUNG, Brig. P. & EMBERTON, W. *Sieges of the Great Civil War* (London, 1978)

YOUNG, Brig. P. & EMBERTON, W. *The Cavalier Army* (London, 1974)

INDEX

References in *italic* refer to black-and-white illustrations and those in bold refer to plate numbers. In some cases, regiments are listed below under the name of their commander.